SAVING
and
SECULAR FAITH

SAVING and SECULAR FAITH

An Invitation to Systematic Theology

B. A. GERRISH

Fortress Press / Minneapolis

SAVING AND SECULAR FAITH
An Invitation to Systematic Theology

Cover design: Joe Bonyata
Author's photo: Action Photo

Library of Congress Cataloging-in-Publication Data
Gerrish, B. A. (Brian Albert)
Saving and secular faith : an invitation to systematic theology / B. A. Gerrish.
p. cm.
Includes bibliographical references and index.
ISBN: 0-8006-2850-0 (alk. paper)
1. Faith—History of doctrines. I. Title.
BT771.2.G45 1999
234'.23—dc21 99-39381
CIP

The paper used in this publication meets the minimum requirements for American National Standard for Information Sciences—Permanence of Paper for Printed Library Materials, ANSI Z329.48–1984.

Manufactured in the U.S.A. AF 1-2850
03 02 01 00 99 1 2 3 4 5 6 7 8 9 10

CONTENTS

For Heather

Love never ends

There is something common to every kind of faith, by virtue of which we put them all together as kin, and something peculiar in each, by virtue of which we separate it from the rest.

Friedrich Schleiermacher

The righteous live by their faith.

Habakkuk 2:4

PREFACE

My first thoughts on the subject of faith were recorded a long time ago, when I wrote a student thesis on Martin Luther's conception of *justifying* or *saving* faith. On leafing through the pages of the thesis again, I was struck by the young author's confident tone, which the passage of time has since eroded. I still believe I was right enough in my reading of Luther, but I now think differently about the place his conception of faith holds, or should hold, in the theological enterprise. In the six chapters of this book I have put some second thoughts together, which come from a variety of perspectives.

A special contribution of Protestantism to the common task of Christian theology may well be the tenacity with which it has pursued the cardinal question: What does it mean to live by faith? But I can now see that the sharp opposition I once discovered between Luther and Thomas Aquinas, and so between Protestant and Roman Catholic conceptions of faith, was overdone. Although differences will always remain within the Christian family, and we are entitled to defend our own preferences, many differences turn out to be variations within a single, recognizable type rather than mutually exclusive alternatives. It will become clear that in my second thoughts on saving faith I have learned most from John Calvin but have no need to drive a theological wedge between Calvin and Luther, or even between Calvin and Thomas. It is a biblical and Christian concept of faith that I wish to start from (in chapter 1), not a sectarian or partisan concept. And I should make it clear that I will be using the qualifier "saving" in a descriptive, not a normative, sense: not to foreclose the question of salvation outside the church but simply to refer to Christian faith as church theologians, both Catholic and Protestant, have commonly described it.

Even if one can propose, at the outset, something like a broadly Christian, nonpartisan concept of faith, that is still to draw the boundaries too tightly. Wilfred Cantwell Smith has urged us to look for faith in all the major religions, not in Christianity alone, and to discover in it a much greater harmony among them than our obsession with distinctive beliefs permits us to notice. Besides, "faith" is not an exclusively religious word at all. It has played an important role in the work of some of our most interesting philosophers and psychologists. My theme, accordingly, is not only saving faith, but what I propose to call *secular* faith as well, stretching the usual connotations of the word to cover both nonreligious faith and religious faith outside the church. Luther's famous translation of 2 Thess. 3:2 states that "faith is not everybody's thing." But if we let ourselves be guided by the philosophical and psychological literature, we must surely ask: Is it only the justified (the "righteous") who live by faith, as the prophet says? Or is there a sense in which all of us do, even those who will tell you that they have no taste for religion? And if we find persuasive reasons for suggesting that faith is in fact a characteristically human mode of existing (chapter 2), then we shall have to ask further whether we are within our rational rights in having faith (chapter 3), how we actually come by the faith we confess (chapter 4), and how saving and secular faith are related to each other (chapters 5–6).

These are the questions I set out to explore, recognizing that they are enormous questions. I cannot hope to do much more than open them up for reflection and discussion. But I try to do so in the form, if not of a linear argument, then at least a cumulative case, however incomplete it may seem to be. Roughly speaking, as will (I hope) be clear, the progression in the first four chapters is historical, psychological, philosophical, and sociological—in that order. In the last two chapters, I assume more directly the standpoint of the Christian theologian. But, taken together, my explorations are theological from beginning to end. It would be presumptuous to imply that I move with equal competence through all the departments I trespass upon in order to reach my goal. In particular, I am not *doing* psychology or sociology in the second and fourth chapters, but *borrowing* from them—trying to see the phenomenon of faith through the eyes of experts in disciplines other than mine. And I will be misunderstood if any one of the perspectives adopted is taken by itself, in isolation, as though it gave the whole picture. It might then be mistakenly inferred that what I assert about, say, the social function of confessions of faith tacitly denies their claim to state the truth. The point, rather, is that in theology the systematic drive, as I understand it, not only seeks order and comprehensiveness in the treatment of Christian doctrines but also searches for their connections with other ways of thinking and speaking that do not (as such) share the dogmatic theologian's standpoint.

All six chapters were occasioned by lectures to audiences made up mainly of theologians, students of theology, and ministers. A lecturer must often sacrifice detail to keep the path to be followed in plain view. But, on reflection, I agreed with friends who urged me not to turn the lectures into a heavy book, which might be more securely argued but would certainly be less generally accessible. Consequently, I may have left myself open, here and there, to the charge of oversimplifying, and I have not paused much to engage alternative approaches or to ward off likely criticisms. I think I know which of my friends will skip impatiently over the first chapter, marveling at my old-fashioned conviction that theology begins with exegetical and historical study; and I know which of them will wish to admonish me that the phenomenon of faith is *not* a suitable object of theological inquiry, which begins and ends with hearing the word of God. I will try to give satisfaction to the critics on both sides—and other possible critics, too—another day. In the present chapters, I am content to chart my own course and to hope that it may be found worth discussing in written form, as it apparently was when presented orally.

The earliest versions of chapters 1–3 and 5 were presented as the Currie Lectures at Austin Presbyterian Theological Seminary (3–5 February 1992). My remarks at Austin on the virtue of doubting and the distinction between faith and belief became, along with a revised version of chapter 1 and a new study on creeds and confessions of faith (chapter 4), my three Earl Lectures at the Pacific School of Religion in Berkeley (26–28 January 1993). Chapter 6 first appeared as the last of my four Sprunt Lectures at Union Theological Seminary in Virginia (24–26 January 1994) with revisions of the Berkeley lectures. Essentially the same four lectures were presented again as the Reid Lectures at Westminster College, Cambridge (9–11 May 1995), and the main argument of chapters 2, 3, and 6 was reworked once more for the Schmiechen Lectures at Eden Theological Seminary (8 October 1997). Parts of the concluding chapter were also included in my Paul Wattson Lecture at Toronto (6 November 1997), sponsored by the Franciscan Friars of the Atonement and the Toronto School of Theology. I am grateful to presidents Jack L. Stotts, Eleanor Scott Meyers, T. Hartley Hall IV, and David M. Greenhaw, to Principal M. H. Cressey, and to Father Timothy MacDonald, S.A.—together with their respective colleagues—for their generous hospitality and the lively exchange of ideas these several lectureships evoked. Critical feedback was especially important to me in the early stages of my explorations. Finally, I want to extend my warm thanks to President Thomas W. Gillespie and his colleagues at Princeton Theological Seminary. The six chapters assumed their present number, sequence, and content as the Warfield Lectures at Princeton (11–14 April 1994), except that time constraints required the omission of a few passages that can now be restored. I recall with gratitude a happy week at Princeton, during which the audience sustained the lecturer, in and outside the lecture room, with their friendship, open-mindedness, and conversation.

My thanks are also due to a number of friends and colleagues who gave me their individual comments on all or part of my manuscript. I hope I am not committing any major sins of omission when I mention, in particular, some who took the pains to give me their comments in detail: Mary Stimming, Frank Reynolds, Clark Gilpin, Paul Griffiths, Bruce McCormack, David Tracy, Chris Gamwell, and John Riggs. To some of their questions I have responded in afterthoughts added to the spoken version, and I have no doubt that next time, thanks to them, I will be making parts of my case somewhat differently, even if not differently enough to satisfy them all. For help with my manuscript, I am indebted to Peggy Edwards and Jill Torbett. Without them, the long delay in publication of this book, occasioned by my retirement and move from the Midwest to Virginia, would have been still longer.

Chapter 1

SAVING FAITH

[Faith is] sure and steadfast knowledge of the fatherly goodwill of God toward us.

John Calvin

Let your face shine, that we may be saved.

Psalms 80:3

"Faith" or "belief" may be said, without fear of controversy, to be one of the key words in the language of the Christian community. Its preeminent status goes back to the beginning, when Jesus came into Galilee preaching the gospel of God and saying, "Repent, and believe in the good news" (Mark 1:14). The medieval church set faith alongside of hope and love as one of the three theological virtues; with the coming of the Protestant Reformation, faith may even seem to have usurped the place of love as the greatest of the three. The watchword of the Reformation was *sola fide*, "by faith alone." But the Apostle Paul had written, as Luther's critics reminded him: "And now faith, hope, and love abide, these three; and the greatest of these is love" (1 Cor. 13:13).

Luther's Reformation has been aptly described as "an immense reduction, a concentration on the one article of saving faith in Christ."[1] This agrees well with one of Luther's own utterances: "In my heart there rules this one doctrine, namely, faith in Christ. From it, through it, and to it all my theological thought flows and returns, day and night."[2] But if we venture to find in these words "an immense reduction," we cannot mean a curtailment of the theological enterprise but only a reduction of it to a proper order or arrangement. It is not that Luther refused to think or talk about anything else except faith in Christ; rather, he was determined to think and talk about everything else strictly in relation to faith in Christ, from which he always began and to which he always came back. Neither, of course, was it his intention to revise the Pauline order and assign faith an absolute precedence over love. His point was simply that it is not love that justifies us: *justifying* or *saving* faith is what Luther was contending for. Faith alone justifies; once it has justified, it is active through love (cf. Gal. 5:6).[3]

Still, even if he had no desire to contradict Paul, it certainly seems as if Luther had a quarrel here with the medieval Schoolmen, who held that faith justifies only because it is "formed by love," that is, receives its special character and worth from the love that makes it perfect. And this, Luther says, is in effect to transfer justification from faith to love.[4] Why pretend? Why not call a spade a spade, deny the entire gospel and Paul, and say plainly that it is not faith in Christ but works of love that justify us?[5] But there, Thomas Aquinas would no doubt reply, in Luther's phrase "works of love" lies a misapprehension. The love that makes faith a theological virtue is not a matter of works but of the cleaving of the soul to God, the Highest Good. "Love" in Thomas stood for much of what "faith" meant to Luther, and what Thomas's concept of faith, taken abstractly, seemed to lack was given back to it (so to say) by the insistence that Christian faith receives its distinctive character from the cleaving of the soul to God in love.

"Belief" and "Trust" in the New Testament

The possibility of mutual misunderstanding between the Protestants and the Roman Catholics was latent in the Scriptures themselves, to which both sides made their appeal. One must be careful not to harmonize the linguistic data of the New Testament more than the evidence allows. Can it really be maintained, for instance, that Paul, James, and the unknown author of the Letter to the Hebrews all held a common notion of what it means to have faith—*pistis?* Probably not. But it can be said in general that New Testament *pistis* is a two-sided concept, corresponding to the two-sidedness of the word in classical Greek. For this reason, it may be taken in two rather different ways, depending on where you put the emphasis. In one of its senses, *pistis* corresponds to the English word "belief," and in the other to "trust." The two senses are commonly distinguished as intellectual and moral, respectively, and it may be simpler to illustrate the contrast from the verbal form *pisteuein,* "to believe" or "to have faith."

First, the verb may convey assent or credence: belief in a statement or in the person making the statement. To believe is to accept something as true or to take the person who says it as speaking the truth. "If you believed Moses, you would believe me, for he wrote about me" (John 5:46). The statement made need not be a religious assertion; it need not even be true. "The Jews did not believe that [the man] had been blind and had received his sight . . ." (John 9:18). Here, to believe means to assent to what is reported about an alleged event or empirical fact: the "Jews," as the Evangelist tendentiously calls them, did not believe, assent to, the report about what had happened. Again, we read that God sends delusions on those who are destined to perish, "leading them to believe what is false" (2 Thess. 2:11). This time, there is indeed belief, but the belief is mistaken. More commonly, however, the assent intended is directed to the central affirmations of the Christian gospel, presented as unquestioned religious truths. "But if we have died with Christ, we believe that we will also live with him" (Rom. 6:8). "For since we believe that Jesus died and rose again, even so, through Jesus, God will bring with him those who have died" (1 Thess. 4:14). And so on. In this usage, to believe is intellectual in the sense that it means giving the assent of the intellect to what is proposed as indubitable truth.

Second, the verb *pisteuein* often means "to trust," and this usage is said to be moral in the sense—a slightly odd sense, perhaps—that it denotes a disposition of the will. In the New Testament, the object of trust is commonly introduced, not (as in classical Greek) by a simple dative case, but by a preposition: one trusts in (*eis*: literally "into") or on (*epi*) God or Jesus—an idiom that underscores the reliance, confidence, and commitment the believer exercises toward the object of faith. "Whoever believes in [*eis*] the Son has eternal life" (John 3:36). "Believe on [*epi*] the Lord Jesus, and you will be saved" (Acts 16:31). "Whoever believes in [*ep'*] him will not be put to shame" (1 Pet. 2:6). Sometimes, the RSV and the NRSV translate the idiom *pisteuein epi* ("believe in") quite simply as "trust": "But to one who . . . trusts him who justifies the ungodly, such faith is reckoned as righteousness" (Rom. 4:5).

The two-sidedness of New Testament faith, as both belief and trust, does not need to give rise to any conflict of meaning. On the contrary, it seems plain enough that we do not have saving faith as the New Testament presents it if the second, moral element is slighted; equally plain, that New Testament faith includes assent to the truths conveyed in the Christian message. I am not even persuaded that either element can be said to have precedence. Nevertheless, the argument has sometimes been made that the moral element is in fact primary, and that this attests the fundamentally Hebraic, rather than Hellenic, character of the New Testament.

It is pointed out that, in the Septuagint, *pistis* translates the Hebrew word *emunah*, which suggests steadfastness, or faithfulness, not intellectual belief. But all this proves, I think, is that *emunah* is not really the equivalent of the English word "faith." Although it appears scores of times in English versions of the New Testament, the word "faith" occurs only twice in our English translations of the Old Testament, and in both instances "faith" is incorrect (Deut. 32:20, Hab. 2:4).[6] It does not follow that the Hebrew Scriptures simply have no concept of faith, since the verb for *having* faith (the Hiph'il of *aman*) is used freely, and it exhibits exactly the two-sidedness of the Greek *pisteuein*. The only conclusion we can draw, then, is that whereas Greek uses both the noun (*pistis*) and the verb (*pisteuein*), Hebrew prefers the verb, but in the same double sense of "believing" and "trusting." The thesis that New Testament faith carries a Hebrew, rather than a Greek, meaning no longer wins much support.[7]

An almost exactly opposite thesis was advanced by the Jewish scholar Martin Buber (1878–1965) in his provocative book *Two Types of Faith* (first published in 1945). Whereas a number of Christian theologians have tried to interpret the meaning of Christian faith by the Hebrew *emunah*, playing down the element of intellectual belief, Buber argues that it is precisely the obsession with belief that tends to separate Christianity from Judaism, and he made his case from the New Testament: the real originator of distinctively Christian faith was Paul, not Jesus.[8]

Jesus, according to Buber, belonged on the side of all that is best in Judaism, which is to say, on the side of the very Pharisaism that the Gospels represent Jesus as opposing. In authentic Judaism, observing the Torah (law) is not a matter of scrupulously carrying out rules but rather of surrendering to the will of God. Everything depends on the direction of the heart. The Torah requires actions agreeable to God in order to direct the heart to God, and this direction of the heart is nothing other than *emunah*—one of the only possible types of faith (*Glaubensweisen*).[9]

For Paul, by contrast, faith meant belief about Jesus, and he understood Jesus not as a teacher of *emunah*, but as "Lord," a heavenly being sent by God to save the elect from their bondage to oppressive cosmic powers. Faith (*pistis*) is believing the word about this heavenly being, the "Lord": "If you confess with your lips that Jesus is Lord and believe in your heart that God raised him from the dead, you will be saved" (Rom. 10:9). In the Pauline scheme, the law merely serves to establish our bondage, and so to make way for grace. Salvation is granted to those who have "faith" in the other sense of the word: a *belief that*. Faith of this kind is not personal trust, nurtured by the community; it is acceptance of a truth that requires individual conversion.[10]

Buber's challenging thesis is a healthy antidote to one-sided emphasis on the element of trust in New Testament *pistis*. Not only James and the Letter to the Hebrews treat faith as *belief that* (James 2:19, Heb.

11:6); Paul does, too, as recent biblical scholarship has duly noted. *Pistis* includes acceptance of the *kerygma*, or proclamation about Christ.[11] But it is impossible not to feel that Buber has substituted his own one-sidedness for the other one. The Apostle Paul's faith in Christ was *trust*, a personal commitment (think, for instance, of those remarkable passages in Gal. 2:19-21 and Phil. 3:3-14); and Paul's trust in Christ gave rise to precisely the confidence in God taught by the Jesus of the Gospels. To Paul, the death of Christ for sinners was the proof of God's love (Rom. 5:8) and the ground on which his unshakable confidence in God's love reposed (Rom. 8:38-39). This, certainly, departs from Judaism insofar as Jesus becomes not only the teacher of *emunah* but the mediator of it. And yet the faith mediated is surely the "direction of the heart to God."

In spite of his obvious dislike of Paul, Buber did not wish to make an absolute separation between Judaism and Christianity, or between *emunah* and *pistis*. Each of the two types of faith, as he put it, "has extended its roots into the other camp."[12] And that could hardly have happened if they were logically exclusive types. Buber acknowledged a kind of two-way traffic between them: for while trust leads me to accept what the one I trust says, the acceptance of truth leads in turn to commerce with the one whom it proclaims.[13] Presumably, then, the mutual connection we have proposed between belief and trust is something Buber would, in principle, approve. But we have to ask next whether the connection came unraveled in the conflict between Protestants and Roman Catholics.

"Assent" in Thomas Aquinas

There can be no objection to taking Thomas Aquinas (ca. 1225–74) to represent Roman Catholic faith. It is true that some of his opinions were condemned at Paris shortly after his death. But in the sixteenth century his theology gained a place of honor in the Roman church, partly as a weapon against the Protestant critique of the church's doctrines. Legend has it that at the Council of Trent (1545–63), summoned to deal with the crisis of the Reformation, a copy of his great *Summa theologiae* was laid on the altar beside the Bible. Since the end of the nineteenth century, Thomas has become in truth what one of his nicknames calls him: *doctor communis*, "common teacher" of all the theological schools in the Roman Catholic Church.[14]

Like everything else in the *Summa*, Thomas's discussion of faith is subtle and complex: one section qualifies another, and everything has to be seen as part of a single system.[15] It is not easy, in a paragraph or two, to give a just account of such a carefully constructed discussion. I can venture only a few comments, which no doubt stand in need of more refinement than I can offer here. For our purposes, Thomas's two most important themes are faith as assent and faith as formed by love ("charity"). The second qualifies the first and brings the Thomistic concept of faith much closer to the two-sided concept we have found in the New Testament.

First, as Thomas understands it, faith is *assent*. Everyone who looks into the questions on faith in the *Summa theologiae* is immediately struck by the heavily intellectualist language. Some note this evident characteristic disapprovingly; others commend it as an antidote to the supposed lack of intellectual content in Protestant faith. In any case, the inward act of Thomistic faith is to believe, and to believe is to think with assent. The psychological location of faith is therefore in the intellect: faith is intellectual assent to what is proposed for belief—that is, to "propositions." But it is not "knowledge" in the strictest sense (not "science") because, in believing, the intellect is not compelled to assent by the proposition itself. The truths of faith are not self-evident, nor are they logical inferences from self-evident truth. The intellect must be moved to assent to them by a deliberate choice of the will, and that is why faith acquires merit. There is nothing meritorious about the assent of the intellect to irrefutable proof, but it is certainly meritorious if the will moves the intellect to believe divine truth in the absence of coercive evidence.[16]

In this scheme, faith and strict or scientific knowledge are mutually exclusive concepts. (Calvin, as we will see, defines faith as knowledge, but his definition does not use Thomas's word for strict, scientific knowledge, *scientia*.) To know scientifically, according to Thomas, is to see that something is so, either by immediate sense-perception or by logical inference, and faith is the conviction of things not seen (Heb. 11:1). It does not follow that faith must be uncertain. If you were anxious that some alternative to what is proposed for your belief might be true, you would not have faith but only opinion. Thomistic *faith* is an assent of the intellect that falls on the cognitive scale midway between scientific *knowledge* and mere *opinion*. All three are modes of assent to truths proposed, whereas *doubt* is withholding assent because you cannot make up your mind and choose between the available options. Faith differs from opinion because it is certain; and it differs from knowledge (in the strict sense) because its certainty is not derived from self-evident truth.[17]

The question that immediately arises is: How exactly are the things to be believed proposed to us? Where does their certainty come from? Thomas's argument leads him inexorably to a virtual equation of faith with submission to the infallible authority of the Roman church. To be sure, the certainty of faith rests on the authority of God, who has revealed in Scripture the things that are to be believed. But the main articles of faith are clearly and conveniently summarized in the creeds set forth by the authority of the church, which cannot err; and the supreme pontiff can always summon a council and add to the existing creeds, in order to rule out any new errors that may arise. Between them, the Apostles and Nicene Creeds contain fourteen main articles, and to these explicit assent must be given. Other items need to be believed only implicitly: you must be ready to assent to them once it becomes clear to you that they do in fact belong to the doctrine of faith. And there are those equipped with a fuller knowledge of matters of belief whose office it is to teach the rest of us. To have faith thus means, in practice, to give your assent to the articles of belief defined by the church's creeds and, at the same time, to be ready to accept anything else that may be proposed for your belief by those who exercise the church's teaching office.[18] As Thomas says in a striking assertion: "Although not all who have faith understand fully the things that are proposed to be believed, yet they understand that they ought to believe them, and that they ought nowise to deviate from them."[19] Which brings us to the intimidating questions on heresy.

Faith is not just a series of disconnected acts of assent; it is the habit of mind that produces them. Hence you are not to pick and choose at will among the church's teachings. A heretic who disbelieves even a single article of faith proves thereby that she lacks the habit of faith, and that is the same as to say that she is not willing to submit to the infallible teaching of the church in every item. Thomas excuses anyone who neglects to follow the church's doctrine out of ignorance or honest error. But so heinous is the offense of stubborn heresy that those who have once embraced the faith must be compelled to retain it, by force if necessary. Indeed, heretics are like an infection in the body and must be cut off, not just from the church, but also from the land of the living. The church shows mercy in condemning them only after two warnings, but then she follows the counsel of Jerome: "Cut off the decayed flesh; expel the mangy sheep from the fold. . . ." Even if a repeat offender changes his mind, the church receives his penance and delivers him up to be burned anyway.[20]

Although one would not wish to argue that the concept of faith as assent to authorized propositions necessarily leads to the burning of deviant Christian believers, in Thomas the logical connection is clear. But faith as intellectual assent is not the whole of our Thomistic agenda. Having tracked the theme of intellectual assent through the pertinent questions of the *Summa* to what may or may not be its chilling conclusion, we must now retrace our steps and note something that is easily overlooked along the way. Faith, secondly, is *formed by love*.

Properly speaking, as we have had occasion to note in passing, faith is what Thomas calls a "habit": a disposition to act in one way rather than another. As a *good* habit, faith is classed among the virtues, and as a habit imparted or infused by God, rather than acquired for ourselves, it is a *theological* virtue. Though Thomas sometimes speaks as if faith *were* assent, assenting is more correctly what faith *does*: it is the inward act of faith. (Confession is the corresponding outward act.) Hence, echoing Heb. 11:1, Thomas asserts that faith is a habit of mind that makes the intellect assent to things unseen.[21] And if we ask what it is that "forms" the habit of faith and causes it to issue in lively assent, the answer is: love (*caritas*), by which is meant, as Thomas puts it, "friendship for God." It pertains to love that one should give oneself to God, adhering to God by a union of spirit.[22]

Here, then, we have Thomas's own explanation of the formula *fides caritate formata* ("faith formed by love"), which Luther and his offspring have found so dangerous. The Divine Good at which faith aims is properly the object of love, and that is why only love can "form" faith: it enlivens the act of faith, making it spring from a lively communion with God. Perhaps that still leaves us with some differences between Thomistic and Lutheran faith. But the gap is not so great as the heat of polemic has led us to suppose. For Thomas, the act of faith is not bare assent to propositions but an act inspired by love for God. Of course, an act of assent is sometimes possible without this love, but then it is not saving faith. In properly Christian faith, the will that moves the intellect to assent is acting under the movement of grace, which imparts love for God. Strictly, therefore, it is misleading to speak as though faith had a multitude of objects (or even fourteen objects). Thomas insists that the one and only object of faith is God or "First Truth"; it is simply that the believer *apprehends* the one object through a multitude of propositions.[23] Terence Penelhum puts the matter like this: "In less technical terms, I take St. Thomas to hold that a man who has a living faith is a man who assents inwardly and outwardly to the articles of the faith out of love for God and out of a live trust in him. . . ."[24] This, I think, is right. The most we could say is that, in his preoccupation with assent and heresy, Thomas lets his exposition obscure one side of the two-sided concept of Christian faith. We must ask next whether Martin Luther obscured the other, intellectual side.

"Confidence" in Martin Luther

According to his Roman Catholic critics, Martin Luther (1483–1546) held a purely "fiducial" faith: a faith that is no more than *fiducia*, "confidence." Luther's faith is then identified as the defective faith of Protestants in general. Instead of finding its security in the doctrines and sacraments of the church, Protestant or fiducial faith, it is said, seeks assurance in subjective feeling. Hence the believer is turned in upon him- or herself in a disastrous quest for certainty of grace and forgiveness.[25]

There is little need to delay very long over this misconception of Lutheran faith, but it may well provide us with our point of entry to a more sympathetic interpretation. Luther did indeed stress the so-called fiducial element in faith. He even asserted that we are not justified unless we trust we are justified.[26] But he was trying to counter what seemed to him a one-sidedly intellectual concept of faith. He never denied that faith is assent; he only insisted that it is something more as well. On occasion, he could sound very like Thomas. In a comparison between faith and hope, for instance, he asserted that faith is in the intellect, that it is a kind of knowledge (*notitia*), and that its object is truth.[27] But Luther was troubled by what he called *fides historica*: a merely "historical faith" that consists of nothing more than assent to the truth of the gospel story. In this sense, even the devil has faith and it does not save him.[28]

Not in place of assent, but in addition to it, there must be a trust that stakes everything on the promises of the gospel. In an oft-quoted passage, Luther puts it like this:

> We should note that there are two ways of believing. One way is to believe *about* God, as I do when I believe that what is said of God is true; just as I do when I believe what is said about the Turk, the devil or hell. This faith is knowledge or observation rather than faith. The other way is to believe *in* God, as I do when I not only believe that what is said about Him is true, but put my trust in Him, surrender myself to Him and make bold to deal with Him, believing without doubt that He will be to me and do to me just what is said of Him.[29]

Clearly, Luther is affirming here exactly the two-sided concept of faith that we found in the New Testament. The words *to me* are emphatic: the true believer—or, if you like, the believer in the full sense—does not merely accept what is said of God, but appropriates it for herself. Hence unbelief, for Luther, is not heresy but lack of trust. (Unbelief is also idolatry, putting your trust in the wrong thing or in a god of your own making.) Anyone who does not believe is like the person who must cross the sea, but will not trust the boat and is too nervous to get on board.[30] "Faith," Luther says, "is a living, daring confidence in God's grace, so sure and certain that the believer would stake his life on it a thousand times."[31]

There is, then, not so much an absolute contrast between Thomistic and Lutheran faith as a reversal of priorities. Thomas speaks mostly of assent to propositions about God; Luther, of trust in God. But Thomas thinks of the propositions as the medium in which we have faith in Godself; and Luther never for one moment suggests that we could trust God without believing anything about God. For both, there is no saving faith where there is no cleaving of the soul to God. Thomas finds this indispensable factor in his notion that faith is formed by love. For Luther, it is already given in the notion of faith as trust, believing *in*. One point at which they do seem to differ materially, however, is when the question arises: How is saving faith related to the person and work of Christ? For Thomas, the grace that infuses love for God into the soul flows from the merits of Christ, who is, so to say, the remote cause of grace. Luther's faith, by contrast, thinks of Christ as made present in the gospel story and takes hold upon him as the one in whom he has God's fatherly heart. In the confidence of the believer's heart (*fiducia cordis*) Christ is present.[32] And where Christ is, there God is no longer a remorseless judge.

Lutheran faith, in other words, has to do with the way we perceive the character of God in Christ; it is, quite simply, "right thinking about God (*recte cogitare de Deo*)."[33] We know from Luther's own testimony that his spiritual distress in the Augustinian monastery came from what he later discovered to be a false image of God and Christ. Not only the Father, but the Son too, appeared to his imagination in the guise of an exacting taskmaster or a rigorous judge, so that the very mention of Christ's name was enough to set him quaking with terror. What must be required of him, he thought, was scrupulous performance of his monastic duties. But the more feverish his efforts, the more troubled became his conscience. Even occasional success brought defeat: for if he could sometimes end the day saying, "I have done nothing wrong," he worried that he had fallen into the trap of spiritual pride and self-satisfaction.[34]

I cannot recount the events (or the controversies) surrounding Luther's so-called rediscovery of the gospel.[35] But this much is clear, if we trust Luther's testimony: with the rediscovery came a radical change in his dominant image of God and Christ. As Luther said many years afterward: "The doctrine of the Gospel and of grace . . . says that Christ did not come into the world to break the bruised reed or to quench the dimly burning wick (Isa. 42:3) but to announce the Gospel to the poor, to bind up the brokenhearted, and to proclaim liberty to the captives (Isa.

61:1)."[36] In the gospel, as these words make clear, Luther's faith grasped a Christ whose proper work is the work not of a lawgiver but of a savior. But this Christ, he says, is the mirror in which we see *God* and know God's *will*. God does not want to be known, nor can God be known, otherwise than through Christ; and in Christ, God appears not as an angry taskmaster but as a gracious and kindly father.[37]

Luther's "fiducial faith," if we dare to retain the expression, was by no means devoid of cognitive content. It rested as securely on divine revelation as did Thomas's faith. But for Luther the revelation was given in the gospel story itself, not so much in propositions or articles of faith. In the gospel, Luther heard—and gave his trust to—the God who says: "Whoever takes hold of this Son and of Me or of My promise in Him through faith—to him I am God, to him I am Father. . . ."[38] And this "sure knowledge of God," as Luther called it,[39] is precisely what Calvin, too, understood by faith. Calvin's definition of "faith" in the *Institutes* reads almost like a more placid summary of Luther's lively utterances on faith in his *Lectures on Galatians* (1535). Moreover, Calvin suggests (rightly, I think) that the kind of knowledge we are talking about in Protestant faith is "recognition" (*agnitio*).

"Recognition" in John Calvin

The chapter on faith in the 1559 *Institutes* (book 3, chapter 2), like many of the other chapters, is a patchwork of new materials stitched together with old materials from earlier editions. But it is artfully organized around a formal definition (in section 7). As is his custom, John Calvin (1509–64) does not begin with his definition but works up to it, so that the reader can see immediately, even if only provisionally, why it seems to be an appropriate definition. Once given, the definition is set over against erroneous views of faith (secs. 8–13) and then examined in detail, member by member (secs. 14–40). Finally, an appended segment (secs. 41–43) briefly compares faith with hope and love. Calvin's avowed intention throughout is strictly exegetical: "Our task is simply to explain the nature of faith as it is set forth in the Word of God."[40] And he is fully aware that this poses systematic difficulties because there are different strands of meaning in scriptural usage of the term: "We must understand that the meaning of the word 'faith' is ambiguous."[41] But I think it can safely be said that in the main he follows Paul and only at the end seeks to harmonize Paul's concept of faith with faith in the Letter to the Hebrews, which he did not consider to be Pauline (though he sometimes speaks as if he did).

Partly because Calvin understands his task as exegetical, he does not attempt—or at least does not achieve—anything like the conceptual precision or tidy order of Thomas, whose models were philosophical or dialectical. But there is another, immensely important reason for Calvin's relative lack of conceptual precision. Besides the appeal to Scripture, he constantly listens to actual Christian experience, which sometimes confirms, sometimes subverts, the categories he advocates. This lends his entire discussion a kind of existential realism that appears to be missing from Thomas. I say *appears* to be because it is arguable that the two theologians are describing different experiences: medieval believing, on the one hand, and, on the other, something surprisingly close to modern believing insofar as the threat of doubt is taken seriously. "Surely," Calvin admits, "while we teach that faith ought to be certain and assured, we cannot imagine any certainty that is not tinged with doubt, or any assurance that is not assailed by some anxiety."[42] One may be tempted to protest: How can *assurance* be tinged with *doubt* since the two terms appear to be logically exclusive? But in Calvin conceptual tidiness yields to the experience of uncertainty, whereas in Thomas it eliminates the concept of doubt (except in the odd sense of imperfect understanding).[43]

Calvin's definition of faith has four members or parts: "Now we can agree on the right definition of faith if we say that it is firm and certain knowledge of the divine goodwill toward us, based on the truth of the free promise in Christ, and both revealed to our minds and sealed on our hearts through the Holy Spirit."[44] The essence of Calvin's concept of faith lies in the first two members: Faith is (1) knowledge (2) of God's goodwill. The third member specifies the *grounds* of this knowledge, and the fourth the inward *means* by which it is imparted. Perhaps we could view the third and fourth members as added descriptions, rather than parts of the actual concept, of faith. They serve to inform us that faith, in the sense defined in 1 and 2, (3) rests on the truth of the free promise in Christ and (4) is revealed to the mind and sealed on the heart by the Spirit.

But what kind of knowledge does Calvin have in mind? The answer is already implicit in his designation of the object of faith, which is not a proposition or catalog of propositions about God, but God's goodwill (*benevolentia*: "benevolence"). Knowledge of this sort is bound to be closer to what we would call "personal acquaintance" rather than empirical observation. And in two places Calvin indicates expressly that what he means by "knowledge" (*cognitio*) is actually "recognition" (*agnitio*). In the one place he writes: "The Lord has 'made manifest to his saints' the secret of his will, which had been 'hidden for ages and generations'

[Col. 1:26. . .]. For very good reason, then, faith is frequently called 'recognition'. . . ."[45] Faith, that is to say, is properly called *recognition* because its knowledge is the response to God's disclosing of God's will, and it is quite unlike the *comprehension* we have of things that are readily accessible to sense perception. In the other passage, Calvin points out that Paul (in Rom 10:10) "requires explicit recognition of the divine goodness upon which our righteousness rests."[46] Here his point is one he makes repeatedly against the Roman Catholic notion of implicit faith. A vague, unexamined idea of God is not going to support the practice of godliness ("piety"), in which the entire Christian life consists. Faith's act of recognition in response to God's self-disclosure must be explicit: a plain, forthright acknowledgment of God's goodness. And this agrees with what Calvin elsewhere lays down as the fundamental rule of piety: to be clear about who the God is that you worship.[47]

Calvinist faith, then, like Lutheran faith, is recognition of the goodwill or benevolence of God disclosed in the gospel. Even more emphatically than Luther, Calvin links the divine goodwill with the image of "father," although he points out in his commentaries that God also compares Godself to a mother.[48] The heart of the matter appears clearly in this passage from the *Institutes*:

> Faith does not rest on ignorance but on knowledge—knowledge not simply of God, but of God's will. We attain salvation not because we are ready to embrace as truth whatever the church has prescribed, or because we delegate to the church the duty of inquiring and learning, but rather when we *recognize that God is a father who is well disposed to us* (now reconciliation has been brought about through Christ) and that Christ has been given to us as our righteousness, sanctification, and life. It is by this knowledge, I say, not by surrendering our minds, that we obtain access to the kingdom of God.[49]

In this quotation the content of saving faith is not *reduced* to the recognition of God's fatherly disposition but *includes* it—and, indeed, in first place. Elsewhere, even in the same chapter of the *Institutes*, Calvin virtually *equates* the two, and the preacher in him clinches the theological point with an allusion to Ps. 80:3, which he renders: "Let him show his face, and we will be saved."[50]

Saving faith, as Calvin describes it, is not a bland, sentimental thing, though he does insist that it involves the heart and not the brain only.[51] It proves itself in suffering and obedience. Faith recognizes the fatherly intention of God even amid what Calvin calls "earthly miseries and calamities."[52] This is why it must be "firm." When Calvin says, commenting on Eph. 3:12, that confidence *(fiducia)* is derived from faith *(fides),*[53] this is the faith he has in mind—defined in his catechism quite simply as "steadfast [*stabilem*: 'stable' or 'constant'] knowledge of the fatherly goodwill of God toward us."[54] And if we ask Calvin, as we did Thomas and Luther: What, then, is *unbelief*, the opposite of faith? his answer is: thinking that God is against you, misperceiving God as your enemy. In Christ faith sees God as God is: not as enemy, even when God disciplines the believer and expects obedience, as parents do.[55]

If our skip through the history of Christian theology can be regarded as an actual progress in the elucidation of an idea, then we have arrived at a Christian concept of faith—"saving" faith—that goes like this.[56] Faith includes elements of both belief and trust. However their relationship is understood (and different opinions are clearly possible on the subject), belief and trust are not to be separated from each other. Further, belief in God may be specified as in essence the recognition of God's goodwill. It is from this recognition that trust or confidence arises, and beliefs (plural) are means by which the recognition of God's goodwill is both explicated and nurtured.

But perhaps, in these more subjective times of ours, we would be more likely to speak of faith as a "construction" or "construal" rather than as "recognition." If we do so, however, this must not be taken to imply that faith is fantasy and not, as Christians have always held, a response to revelation. (It may be a delusion, and to that possibility we shall have to return. But no such implication is intended by the use of the words "construction" or "construal.") What Christians do, then, in believing the gospel, is to construe the story of Christ as a surprising, even paradoxical, disclosure of a divine benevolence that resembles parental care. The recognition of God's parental will in Jesus Christ then enables them to turn to the entire range of their experience and to construe it, too, as in every moment the work of a parentlike goodwill, so that even the negative experiences of suffering and adversity now make sense as discipline, not punishment. In short: *Saving faith is both (1) perceiving one's experience under the image of divine benevolence* (fides) *and (2) a consequent living of one's life out of an attitude of confidence or trust* (fiducia). We shall need to turn next to the question whether saving faith, so defined, makes Christians a wholly peculiar people, or whether, in having faith, they are doing in their own way what everyone does all of the time. And to answer that question, we shall have to enlist the help of the historians of religion and the psychologists.

Chapter 2
SECULAR FAITH

Thus knowing is not knowledge as an effect of an unknown external cause, but is knowledge as we so interpret that our meaning is the actual meaning of our environment.

John Oman

God has not left Godself without a witness.

Acts 14:17

A great deal more could be said about the notion of "saving faith" as it has emerged, developed, and been repeatedly modified in Christian history. It would be interesting, for instance, to try out on the biblical texts the experiment we made in passing with Thomas Aquinas, Martin Luther, and John Calvin, and to see if we could define what each of the New Testament sources presents as the absence, or the opposite, of faith. For Thomas, we have seen, the opposite of faith was heresy; for Luther, it was distrust; for Calvin, it was misrepresenting the character of God. Each of them would no doubt wish to say that faith, as a complex notion, can have more than one opposite.[1] Similarly, the richness and complexity of New Testament faith appear as soon as you notice that the absence of faith is fear or anxiety in the Synoptic Gospels, boasting or overscrupulousness in Paul, and blindness in the Fourth Gospel.

In his Sermon on the Mount, Jesus says, "But if God so clothes the grass of the field, which is alive today and tomorrow is thrown into the oven, will he not much more clothe you—you of little faith? Therefore do not worry, saying . . . 'What will we wear?'" (Matt. 6:30-31; cf. Luke 12:28-29). And to the panic-stricken disciples in the sinking boat, he says, "Why are you afraid? Have you still no faith?" (Mark 4:40; cf. Matt. 8:26, Luke 8:25). Faith is opposed to worry or to fear. There is a clear shift of accent when Paul asks: "Then what becomes of boasting? It is excluded. By what law? By that of works? No, but by the law of faith" (Rom. 3:27). Here, in Paul's Letter to the Romans, faith is set over against conceit.

Further on in the same letter, he contrasts a sturdy faith with the timidity of those who are always wondering if it is all right for Christians to eat meat, to drink wine, or not to keep the Sabbath. Concerning the weak in faith, as he calls them, he writes: "But those who have doubts [i.e., scruples] are condemned if they eat, because they do not act from faith; for whatever does not proceed from faith [i.e., from a firm conviction] is sin" (14:23). Finally, John writes that those who do not believe in the Son of God are condemned because "light has come into the world, and people loved darkness rather than light . . ." (John 3:19; cf. 9:39). Their disbelief is blindness.[2]

These are not discrepancies in the concept of faith, but subtle—and fascinating—differences of tone. Perhaps they could all be worked into some tidy scheme. But I cannot pursue them further now. I must make do with the broad distinction between two aspects of New Testament faith: as belief and as trust. The Thomistic concept of faith initially strikes us as problematic because it stresses the first aspect so one-sidedly and seems to make it, in effect, a matter of submission to ecclesiastical authority. Thomistic faith is assent to propositions authorized by the Roman church. The problem is worsened when Thomas attempts to support the church's authority by what can only impress us nowadays as weak arguments—from the fulfillment of prophecy, the occurrence of miracles, and so on.[3] Nevertheless, his constant assumption is that the act of faith, if it is genuine Christian faith, is possible only because love for God has been poured into the believer's heart through the Holy Spirit (cf. Rom. 5:5); and this, surely, corresponds to the other aspect of New Testament faith.

If it cannot be asserted, in the final analysis, that Thomas ignored the second aspect of faith, it is even less true that Martin Luther saw nothing else. Luther did not overlook the intellectual side of faith; rather, he made the important contribution of seeing it, not as assent to propositions but as "right thinking about God"—which is to say, thinking of God under the correct image as father, not as judge. And it fell to Calvin, following up Luther's insight (or so I assume), to specify this cognitive act properly as an act of "recognition." The two-sidedness of New Testament faith is then maintained by speaking of faith as the recognition of God's parental goodwill and the confidence that it generates. Saving faith, in short, is recognition plus confidence.

It is, I think, a mistake (phenomenologically speaking) when in one place Calvin makes such faith contingent on prior acceptance of divine truth, as though one had first to be convinced of the authority of God's word before one could recognize God's parental goodwill.[4] Experience shows that sometimes, at least, the believer is persuaded of the truth of God's word because, in the word, she has first encountered the God of Jesus Christ. Faith occurs as an immediate recognition of God's character and will in the proclamation of the word, not as an inference from the truth of the word. As such, faith makes it possible to view all of one's experience as determined in every moment by a divine purpose that means us well, even if it is sometimes severe. We found Calvin realistic enough to admit that this peculiar knowledge occurs only in the context of existential (not merely theoretical) doubt, which seduces believers into wondering in moments of affliction if God is actually against them. Nevertheless, faith's recognition of God's goodness suffices to make possible a life lived in confidence or trust.

The line I have traced from the New Testament to John Calvin is, I hope, plausible enough. His notion of saving faith as recognition of God's paternal goodwill is firmly grounded in the Apostle Paul's teaching that God the "Father of our Lord Jesus Christ" (Rom. 15:6; 2 Cor. 1:3, 11:31; cf. Eph. 1:3; 1 Pet. 1:3) adopts believers as God's children and makes them joint heirs with Christ (Rom. 8:15-17; Gal. 4:4-7). I do not imagine, however, that everyone will see my trajectory through Christian history as an undoubted progress. And it may be that Thomas, Luther, and Calvin would all be a little suspicious of the concluding remarks I made in the first chapter about faith as a way of construing both the story of Jesus and the believer's own personal story. I hope to provide reassurance as we go along. But I admit that I moved tentatively beyond historical interpretation to a point from which I can now take my next step: from saving to secular faith.

There has been a strong tendency in recent religious thought to extend the use of the word "faith" to other religions and even to nonreligious modes of experience, and it is the notion of "meaning construction" that provides the link with Christian "saving faith." In calling the other kinds of faith *secular*, I am perhaps stretching the old sense of the word—to mean first "nonecclesiastical," or pertaining to the world (*saeculum*) outside the organized church, and secondly "nonreligious," or not sacred at all. I do not mean to imply either that Christian faith belongs in a cloister or that secular faith is in no sense "saving." No such normative judgments are intended at this stage of my argument. Thomas, Luther, and Calvin wanted to tell us how we *ought* to believe. But my own approach thus far has been historical, and it must now be descriptive, at least indirectly: I shall no longer be tracing a concept through Christian history but reporting the conclusions of some present-day researchers who have examined faith simply as it *is*. They have been asking, not what one should believe, but what, as a matter of fact, is going on in the act of believing or having faith. I have in mind chiefly the psychologists. But a convenient bridge to their observations is provided—for reasons that will become clear—by the work of the eminent historian of religions Wilfred Cantwell Smith (b. 1916).

Faith and Religion

A Canadian Presbyterian by upbringing, Smith arrived at the point where he could envision a "world theology" that would embrace not his inherited faith alone but every religion.[5] His program for the future rests in part on distinctions between the terms "religion," "faith," and "belief." In his widely discussed book *Faith and Belief* (1979), Smith argues that the study of religion has been focused, until now, on the *outside* of religious traditions: their visible manifestations in myths, beliefs, symbols, and rituals. But the *inside* of religion, to which we should now turn our attention, is a personal relation to the transcendent, and this in essence is what Smith means by "faith," which is not the same as "belief."[6] More copiously, he describes faith as "an orientation of the personality, to oneself, to one's neighbor, to the universe; a total response; a way of seeing whatever one sees and of handling whatever one handles; a capacity to live at a more than mundane level; to see, to feel, to act in terms of, a transcendent dimension." And he adds: "Belief, on the other hand, is the holding of certain ideas."[7]

The very word "belief," as Smith argues at length in formidable linguistic studies, no longer means what it used to mean: "prizing," "giving allegiance to," "trusting," the reality of the object believed being taken for granted. It has come to suggest instead the entertaining of a proposition that is very likely false. Smith points out that in the *Random House Dictionary* the first illustration of "belief" is the belief that the earth is flat. From this revealing choice the contemporary discussion has coined the expression "Random House belief": that is, belief understood as obstinate addiction to some exploded error or superstition. Given the peculiarities of present-day usage, Smith insists that what we are to study is neither religion nor beliefs, as commonly understood, but the faith that comes to expression in religious traditions. We can look forward to a world theology, he thinks, because faiths do not differ nearly as much as beliefs: God gives us faith, our century our beliefs.[8]

In comparison with our previous guides, Smith can be said to move the discussion from the particular to the general. He is not mainly interested in the beliefs, or even the faiths, of particular historical communities (as were Thomas, Luther, Calvin, and Buber) but rather in faith as a universally human phenomenon that need not take explicit or conventional religious form. Indeed, so interpreted, faith defines the generically human: humans are beings who are open to transcendence and, as such, find meaning in the world and in their own lives, whether they identify themselves with a religious tradition or not. The opposite of faith is then, not disbelief in some proposition or other, but the loss of order, meaning, and purpose—in a word, nihilism.[9]

This, in my opinion, is an important contribution to our inquiry into the nature of faith, though it does, of course, invite the question how "faith," in Smith's sense, is related to "faith" in Calvin's sense. But it is misleading when Smith affirms the novelty of his approach, as he frequently does. In one of his other books, *The Meaning and End of Religion* (1963), he announced: "For a century now serious historical studies have made major advances in uncovering and making known what I am calling the cumulative traditions of mankind's religious life. The next step is to discover and make known the personal faith. . . that those traditions have served."[10] One reviewer thought it unlikely that Rudolf Otto, Gerhardus van der Leeuw, Raffaele Pettazzoni, Jean Daniélou, Louis Massignon, Mircea Eliade, and Ernst Benz somehow managed to overlook the kernel of faith in the religious husks that they studied.[11] He wondered if he must be missing something in Smith's argument since the distinction between faith and belief has been around for a long time: it is found, for instance, in Paul Tillich's popular little book *The Dynamics of Faith*.[12]

In Smith's defense, one may perhaps reply that he is just trying to get attention in the only way authors can—not by being right, but by being contentious. His entire point is that he is attempting to recover something that, while not in itself new, is sometimes buried beneath the semantic confusion of our time. From our own reflections on the biblical data (in the first chapter) a distinction immediately emerged between faith as personal trust and faith as propositional assent. That is not quite Smith's distinction, because biblical faith is context-specific as faith in Yahweh, or faith in Jesus Christ. But the need for *some* distinction between a personal disposition, or engagement, or involvement, and bare intellectual assent is a theological commonplace. Smith simply wants to make sure we don't overlook its importance.

But could it be said that what is novel in Smith's approach is his search for the element of faith in every religion, not in Christianity alone? I think not. What is surprising to me is that in his work of retrieval Smith identifies a potential ally as the one who got theology off on the wrong track. He wants theology to attempt a *generic* understanding of faith, and he charges previous Christian theologians with confining their attention to *Christian* faith, adding (in a note): "This has been explicitly the case since Schleiermacher."[13] In fact, Friedrich Schleiermacher (1768–1834) undertook to do dogmatics on the explicit assumption that Christianity can only be understood as one among several faiths—the assumption that "faith" is a generic concept. Smith is apparently misled by the title of Schleiermacher's great dogmatic work, *The Christian Faith* (1821–22, 1830–31^{2}). In his introduction, Schleiermacher made clear his intention to present Christian faith precisely as one way of having faith (one *Glaubensweise*) among others. And Schleiermacher also argued, in his earlier *Speeches on Religion* (1799), that to understand religion one must get behind the outside manifestations to the inner essence that produced them. I shall need to come back to Schleiermacher later (in chapter 5). Suffice it to say, for now, that I am entirely in sympathy with the quest for a generic concept of faith, but so was Schleiermacher; and I think it was one of his merits to have shown how a generic concept could be brought into relation with specifically Christian faith.[14]

It is, of course, possible to object that Smith, in naming the common substance of all religions "faith," is unconsciously speaking out of his own Christian and Protestant upbringing.[15] But he does, after all, try to give a neutral, not a Christian, account of faith. He refuses to offer a formal definition. The core notion, however, as I have indicated, appears to be that faith is a personal relation to transcendence that enables one to find meaning in one's life. And the real difficulty is not that Smith uses the Christian word "faith," nor even that he declines to give a formal definition of it, but that he leaves us somewhat in the dark about how he understands transcendence. His descriptive phrases yield a range of possible meanings—from whatever goes beyond our normal, mundane existence to eternal and unchanging reality.[16] And I suspect, at least, that the more specific he tried to be, the more faith looked like belief. In other words, the apparent value of the term "faith" for denoting the underlying unity of diverse beliefs holds good only insofar as it denotes no more than a formal or structural parallel between one religion and another. This may not be such a bad road to take, but I am not sure how it could lead us to Smith's world theology. Or would a world theology be precisely a comparative-structural theology?

Be that as it may, the price Smith seems to pay for a world theology is that he cannot talk very comfortably about a normative special revelation, which, as far as I can see, is a fundamental religious (not just

Christian) category. Once again, he might have learned from Schleiermacher, for whom revelation, like faith, is a generic concept but allows for genuine moments of crisis (so to say) in the history of religions. Smith has ridiculed what he calls the "big bang" theory of origins, preferring a theory of "continuous creation," and there is wisdom in his preference insofar as it frees the concept of revelation from mythological divine partiality and intervention. But it says a great deal less than most religionists have usually wanted to claim for the anchorage of their faith in a normative past, and it therefore makes peace among them seem a lot more feasible than it probably is.[17]

In sum, Wilfred Cantwell Smith opens up, or follows, a potentially fruitful line of reflection, but the path is mined with difficulties. I shall come back to some of the difficulties in my final chapter. I want first to explore further the possibility that faith is not a peculiarly Christian concept but a generically religious, indeed universally human, phenomenon, and that it has to do with the discovery of personal meaning in one's existence. Smith arrived at this conclusion from his erudite studies of the world's religions. Others, notably James Fowler (who was at one time a student of Smith's), have argued for a similar conclusion on the basis of empirical research. But before I turn to Fowler's contribution, I will make a few remarks on the interesting work of the late Austrian psychiatrist Viktor Emil Frankl (1905–97). I know I leave myself open to the charge of arbitrary selection among the psychologists, who differ even more among themselves than theologians or economists. But no attempt to give a psychological account of faith and the construction of meaning at the present time could leave out the two contributions I have chosen, and we have to begin somewhere.

The Search for Meaning

Frankl is well known in America from the astonishing public reception of his "best-seller" *Man's Search for Meaning* (Eng. trans., 1959). As he himself remarks in the preface to the 1984 edition: "If hundreds of thousands of people reach out for a book whose very title promises to deal with the question of a meaning to life, it must be a question that burns under their fingernails."[18] In professional circles, Frankl has not quite been elevated to the ranks of the immortals Sigmund Freud (1856–1939) and Alfred Adler (1870–1937), but his approach has often been compared with theirs as establishing a third Viennese school of psychotherapy. He held that the primary motivation of human behavior is neither the will-to-pleasure nor the will-to-power, but the will-to-meaning.

Existential problems—that is, problems arising from the search for meaning in one's existence—are part and parcel of being human. "What's the point?" "Who am I?" "Why are we here?" These, sooner or later, are virtually everyone's questions, especially in moments of crisis. In *Man's Search for Meaning* Frankl maintains that at least *some* psychological disorders (the "noögenic neuroses") can be traced to the frustration of the will-to-meaning. The technique for dealing with disorders of the *nous* or mind he calls "logotherapy," which attempts to make the patient aware of the hidden *logos*, "reason," in his or her existence. Frankl is abridging some fairly complex linguistic data when he says simply that *logos* is a Greek word that denotes "meaning." But the important question is this: How can the *logos* (reason, meaning) in one's life be identified or, when hidden, brought to consciousness through therapy? Frankl points to three distinct ways: (1) by creating a significant work or doing a significant deed, (2) by experiencing something of value or experiencing another person through love, and (3) by the attitude one takes to unavoidable suffering. The presupposition of this therapeutic strategy is that, in the end, a person becomes what he or she chooses to become; within the limits imposed by endowment and environment, each of us makes him- or herself. Guilt then becomes an opportunity for self-improvement; the sense of life's transitoriness becomes an incentive to take responsible action; and so on. Life remains potentially meaningful under any conditions whatever, even the most miserable.[19]

It is always tempting to react to such cheerful theories with skepticism or scorn, and to assume that they must have been dreamed up in the relative comfort of some professor's armchair. Counter-instances, especially of senseless, barren suffering, leap to mind. But one reason that Frankl's theory has attracted wide attention is that it was tested in his own grim encounter with pain and degradation. The original version of his book, first published in 1946, was titled (in German) *A Psychologist Experiences the Concentration Camp*. Frankl survived three years in Auschwitz, Dachau, and two other German concentration camps. He was not used in the camps as a psychiatrist, and only for the last few weeks was he employed as a doctor. He became Number 119,104 and provided slave labor for a construction company, digging and laying tracks for railroad lines. Like his fellow prisoners, he endured squalor, degradation, and sadistic brutality, never knowing when his turn might come for the gallows or the gas chamber. The first part of *Man's Search for Meaning* contains an insider's reflections on how humans react when pushed to the limit. Frankl writes: "We who lived in concentration camps can remember the men who walked through the huts comforting others, giving away their last piece of bread. They may have been few in number, but they offer sufficient proof that everything can be taken from a man but one thing: the last of the human freedoms—to choose one's attitude in any given set of circumstances, to choose one's own way."[20] They did not necessarily survive—these few memorable heroes. Frankl admits: "The best of us did not return."[21] Generally, the survivors were those who abandoned every scruple to save themselves. But then, in Frankl's view, the last human triumph is not staying alive but knowing how to die, like those who did not disappoint the living but entered the gas chamber upright, "with the Lord's Prayer or the *Shema Yisrael* on [their] lips."[22]

The concentration camp is not the only place where the lesson of meaning in suffering is learned. Frankl liked to mention the amazing courage of Jerry Long, a quadriplegic since a diving accident when he was seventeen. He learned to use a mouth-stick to type, and he took college courses by means of a special intercom. Long wrote to Frankl, assuring him: "I view my life as being abundant with meaning and purpose. The attitude that I adopted on that fateful day has become my personal credo for life: I broke my neck, it didn't break me." He reported that he was enrolled in his first psychology course in college, and concluded: "I believe that my handicap will only enhance my ability to help others. I know that without the suffering, the growth that I have achieved would have been impossible."[23]

So, what is the meaning of life according to Frankl? Occasionally, he does speak of "the meaning of one's life as a whole," or of "the final meaning of life," or even (more darkly) of an "ultimate purpose." But on the whole he looks for more limited meanings, relative to particular situations. Such meanings are inescapably personal: to perceive them is simply to become aware of what you can do about a given situation. It follows that the meaning of life differs from person to person, from day to day, even from hour to hour. To ask in the gross, What is the meaning of life? is like asking a chess master, What is the best move in the world? It all depends on how the pieces stand at the moment.[24] Frankl sometimes suggests that the absolutizing of a single value—such as parenthood or one's work—is like idolatry, in which he sees the possibility for a great deal of emotional mischief.[25] In his own reminiscences of the concentration camp, he writes of not one but a number of activities that kept him from giving up: contemplating the precious mental image of his wife; struggling painfully to reconstruct on scraps of paper the book manuscript taken from him in the disinfection chamber; and, in the last few weeks of captivity, sticking to his patients when he could have tried to escape.[26] It has been a long time now since Auschwitz and Dachau, and Frankl accomplished a great deal in his lifetime. If you look him up in *Who's Who in America* (51st ed., 1997), you will find this simple but eloquent testament: "I have seen the meaning of my life in helping others to see in their lives a meaning."

Now it is arguable that some of the meanings Frankl discovered in his own life, or enabled others to discover in theirs, point to more comprehensive realms of significance: the realm of moral commitment, for instance. And there were times when he seemed to identify himself with explicitly religious commitments—not just displaying the psychiatrist's willingness to employ religious belief therapeutically if the patient has it. But, as far as I recall, in *Man's Search for Meaning* he uses the word "faith" only in the phrase "faith in the future." Although he shows a strong sense of what we might call the "inamissibility of the past" (the impossibility of ever losing a course of action once we have chosen it), he insists that humans live by looking to the future. The prisoner who gave up hope, knowing the chances for survival were slim, was always doomed. Faith in the future is essential to our very existence; and in fact we never know what possibilities may open up for us, however hopeless things may look at the moment. A wider use of the word "faith" does not, I think, appear in *Man's Search for Meaning*.[27]

What is important for our inquiry, however, is not Frankl's limited use of the word "faith" but the activity of meaning construction that he describes, since this is exactly what others have called faith. Take, for instance, the following story—a "logodrama," as Frankl terms it. A woman's younger son dies at the age of eleven and she is left alone with her other son, who has been permanently crippled by infantile paralysis. She decides to take both her own life and his, but he prevents her. For him, life is still worth living; and it becomes worth living for her when she learns to reconstrue the pattern of her existence. Her wish to have children has been granted her, and the older boy, though paralyzed and helpless, is still her boy who needs her. She becomes convinced that her life is, after all, full of meaning.[28] In the work of James W. Fowler (b. 1940) the attempt is made to integrate such meaning construction into a broader pattern of individual faith development, only the last stages of which are described as essentially religious.

Stages of Faith

Fowler's most important work so far is titled *Stages of Faith: The Psychology of Human Development and the Quest for Meaning* (1981). It is the development, rather than the concept, of faith that chiefly interests him: he takes up previous work in developmental psychology and shows how it can be extended into the domain of faith. Pioneering studies in cognitive development by the Swiss psychologist Jean Piaget (1896–1980) and in moral development by the American Lawrence Kohlberg (b. 1927) suggested that there are certain more or less clearly marked steps in the emergence of the cognitive and moral capacities. From the results of 359 interviews conducted in the period from 1972 to 1981, Fowler concludes that faith, too, develops in distinguishable stages. They are, of course, formal or structural stages: not the content of faith, but its changing structure is the object of inquiry. And the method pursued is empirical, although this does not exclude a normative claim: that each successive stage marks an advance over the previous one, the form of faith at the last stage being also the most desirable. But linear progress from the first stage to the last is by no means inevitable; even if each stage has its own natural time, arrestment can and does occur. In fact, Fowler judges that most middle-class American churchgoers are stuck around Stage 3, which is typically the stage of adolescence. In many ways, he thinks, religious institutions work best if their members advance no further.[29]

In all, Fowler discovers six stages, preceded by one "pre-stage." It is difficult, perhaps impossible, to summarize them clearly and succinctly. Fowler might not even wish us to. Like Smith, he wants to avoid the kind of analytical precision that overschematizes. But if I may take a shot at a working summary, I think it should go something like this. In the pre-stage of primal or undifferentiated faith, an unreflective trust in the environment takes shape in the infant's relationship with the provider of care. Thereafter we move into the six stages proper.

At Stage 1, uncoordinated images give episodic meaning to the young child's experience in an activity Fowler describes as *intuitive-projective faith*. At Stage 2, the schoolboy or schoolgirl begins to assimilate the stories, symbols, attitudes, and observances of his or her immediate community, and more stable forms of conscious interpretation emerge. On the analogy of a ruler or parent who cares, *mythic-literal faith* constructs a world in which goodness is rewarded, badness punished. At the adolescent Stage 3, experience reaches beyond the family, and reflection begins on the meanings of conflicting attitudes and stories. *Synthetic-conventional faith* generates a personal myth but still takes its sense of personal worth from the approval of others: growing recognition of the relativity of values does not supplant external authority. By contrast, the *individuative-reflective faith* of the young adult, at Stage 4, assumes greater responsibility for his or her own personal beliefs and attitudes. Symbols and myths are examined critically, their meanings converted into concepts: this is the "demythologizing" stage. At Stage 5, however, which is not usually reached before midlife, *conjunctive faith* recognizes that life cannot be fitted into a tidy conceptual scheme. Taking up Paul Ricoeur's expression, Fowler identifies this as the stage of a "second naïveté," in which symbolic power is reunited with conceptual meanings. There is now an acceptance of tension and paradox, but also a striving to unify opposites while admitting that meanings are inescapably relative. Finally, at Stage 6, which is attained only by a few in their maturity, a *universalizing faith* draws the affections beyond every finite center of value or power to the Ultimate, which Christian faith symbolizes as the kingdom of God. For these few saints and sages there is but one human community, universal in extent.

Intriguing though this six- or seven-fold scheme may be, my own chief interest is in the concept of faith that emerges from, or is at work in, Fowler's attempt to show how faith develops. A theory of faith development necessarily entails a concept of faith, and this is what I want to extract from Fowler's writings. It has been argued that faith, as he speaks of it, is "amorphous and unwieldy" and in the end impossible to distinguish from individual development in general.[30] In other words the whole of human behavior is viewed under the rubric of faith, and the concept accordingly loses precise defining characteristics. Fowler himself insists that faith is an extremely complex phenomenon, not to be oversimplified, and he tends to describe it by saying what it does, or implies, or is about, rather than what it is. Even when he says what it is, he piles up so many descriptive phrases that it is easy to lose it from sight again. Still, I do think that a sympathetic eye can spot the main contours of Fowler's concept of faith. Here are some sample utterances:

> *Faith* has to do with the making, maintenance, and transformation of human meaning. It is a mode of knowing and being.[31]
>
> Faith . . . is our way of finding coherence in and giving meaning to the multiple forces and relations that make up our lives.[32]
>
> We might say that faith is our way of discerning and committing ourselves to centers of value and power that exert ordering influence in our lives.[33]

Occasionally, Fowler does venture to incorporate scattered utterances like these into something close to formal definitions. The definitions repay careful reflection, though they tend to be unwieldy and the terms employed in them could themselves use some definition. In his essay "Faith and the Structuring of Meaning," for example, Fowler asserts that faith is:

The process of constitutive-knowing
Underlying a person's composition and maintenance of a comprehensive frame (or frames) of meaning
Generated from the person's attachments or commitments to centers of supraordinate value which have power to unify his or her experience of the world
Thereby endowing the relationships, contexts, and patterns of everyday life, past and future, with significance.[34]

Up to a point, it seems to me, this "composite definition" (as Fowler calls it) is not so very different from Calvin's. Faith is knowing, but not of the sort we acquire when we read off, and assent to, a straightforward proposition, such as "German troops invaded Poland on 1 September 1939." Rather, Calvin's act of recognition and Fowler's "process of constitutive knowing" are *interpretative* activities in which the data of experience are seen one way, not another, and so are organized into a pattern that makes sense. More exactly, the overall pattern takes shape as the whole of one's experience is referred to a focal *center* of meaning—for Calvin, God perceived as parentlike and watching beneficently over the lives of his children.

One difference is that Calvin does not for a moment think of his faith in the Father-God as an instance of a class: only Christians have faith, in Calvin's sense (or so he assumes). For James Fowler, on the other hand, faith is a universally human phenomenon, albeit not always self-conscious or reflective. "In some form," as he puts it, "[faith] is necessary and inevitable for human beings."[35] It need not be Christian; it need not even be religious (as usually understood), although it does most often come to expression through the symbols, rituals, and beliefs of particular religious traditions. We may say, then, that in this view what Christians do when they have faith in the Father of the Lord Jesus Christ is structurally similar to the faith or meaning construction that occurs even among agnostics or atheists, as they too organize their experience into patterns of significance through some focal center (or centers) of value. The only apparent qualification of the universality of faith appears in Fowler's statement that at Stages 5 and 6 it will "take *essentially* religious forms."[36] I interpret this to mean (although I am not sure) that while everyone engages in the meaning construction that is faith, the nonreligious will not be able to carry this activity beyond the fourth stage, because any further advance would require "a representation of the ultimate environment as objectively real and as the final and primal source of all being and value."[37] Oddly, then, in Fowler's theory the atheist does not lack faith but can have only an immature faith. Needless to say, this is not how atheists usually see themselves; they are more likely to announce that they have grown out of faith.

Faith and Inclusive Meaning

Fowler's work has naturally attracted a great deal of attention from those whose job it is not merely to talk about faith but to nurture it as pastors, teachers, and counselors. I am not qualified to comment on faith-development theory as a psychologist, only as a theologian who thinks that faith is worth nurturing. Let me pose, and try to answer, four questions that will enable me to carry forward my own constructive case.

First, why use the word "faith" for the whole range of meaning construction that Fowler's development theory is about? Why is "faith" the appropriate umbrella under which all six stages—and the pre-stage—are covered? Fowler's answer is indicated, I think, in his assertion that "faith" implies trust, and that the other side of faith as trust is faith as commitment or loyalty. In other words (my words, not his), the appropriateness of the word "faith" in Fowler's development theory arises out of what we have distinguished as the second aspect of the New Testament term *pistis*.

Fowler does not begin with the New Testament. Following Josiah Royce (1855–1916) and H. Richard Niebuhr (1894–1962), he discovers at the foundation of every human community—and therefore of all personal identity—a relationship by which the self is bound in mutual trust to an other through a common loyalty to a shared value. The shape of community is triadic or triangular, including as it does self, other, and the object of loyalty; and it is essentially a relationship of trust and commitment—in a word, of faith. I am bound to other U.S. citizens, for example, by our common loyalty to the rights affirmed in the Constitution. I am bound to my colleagues in the university by our commitment to open inquiry and the quest for truth. And so on. "I can think of no lasting human association," Fowler remarks, "that does not exhibit something approximating this fiduciary or covenantal pattern."[38]

Each of us belongs in a number of faith triangles constituted by the family, the workplace, the nation, and so on. But there is one triangle that embraces all the others because in it "the self relates to the canvas of meaning itself," which Fowler sometimes calls our "ultimate environment."[39] Now it seems to me that, to avoid stretching the word "faith" too far, we would do well to reserve it for just this perception, or construction, of those all-inclusive patterns of meaning by which we try to grasp the world and our being-in-the-world as a single whole. Sometimes, Fowler himself seems to do exactly that. "Faith . . . ," he says, "composes 'wholes'. . . . A spread of meaning, a canopy of significance is composed to backdrop or fund more immediate, everyday action."[40] In his overall scheme, however, even the fragmentary, disconnected meanings of Stage 1 are said to be faith constructs, and Fowler would probably caution us that while a more restricted use of the word "faith" might underscore the special character of our total interpretations, it might also cause us to miss their structural continuity with our lesser meanings. I shall return to this point, because I do, in fact, want to reserve the word "faith" for total, comprehensive meanings but without overlooking the continuity of faith, so understood, with more limited meaning constructs.[41] Our constructs of inclusive meaning imply commitment (*pistis* in the second sense) to some regulative value, or source of value, that orders and unifies our total experience—an "ultimate concern," if you like Paul Tillich's familiar term.[42]

Second, even if they can see the point of Fowler's use of the word "faith," should Christian theologians nevertheless insist that meaning making and Christian faith are two utterly different activities between which, in the end, one has to make a choice? This seems to be the position taken by Craig Dykstra and Sharon Parks, who say: "The basic issue here is whether faith is really a human universal or a mode of life that is grounded in a more or less conscious and chosen responsiveness to the activity of God in the world."[43] For my part, I need to be persuaded that these are exclusive alternatives. They at least *could* be two ways of looking at the same phenomenon—the one more characteristic of the psychologist, the other of the theologian.

Dykstra insists (very properly) that Christian faith is a relation to God, that it depends on God's revelation, and that it is therefore the gift of God.[44] Very well. But what if God's revelation imparts the gift of saving faith by causing the Christian to construe the meaning of his or her existence correctly? How else, in fact, *could* the gift of saving faith be imparted, if Calvin has rightly defined it? Calvin, it is true, insists on a mysterious operation of the Holy Spirit when faith is given to the elect. But what the Spirit brings about in them is recognition of the goodwill of God revealed in the gospel—and therefore recognized in the whole of their lives. Saving faith, it seems to me, really does have structural similarities with what I am calling "secular faith": other, nonecclesiastical or even nonreligious meaning constructs that are also inclusive in scope. I cannot pursue this line of thought here as much as I would like. But the direction in which we are now moving is the direction indicated by John Hick, partly under the guidance of John Wood Oman (1860–1939), who has provided me with my first epigraph for the present chapter.[45]

Revelation as the communication of meaning and faith as the construal of meaning are correlative, not contrary, activities. In so saying, I have anticipated the answer to my third question.

Third, it may be asked, does Fowler's "constructivist approach" (as he calls it) fall into hopeless relativism and subjectivism? This certainly appears to be the case in the following description of faith in Fowler's *Stages*. Faith is:

> People's evolved and evolving ways
> of experiencing self, others and world
> (as they construct them)
>
> as related to and affected by the
> ultimate conditions of existence
> (as they construct them)
>
> and of shaping their lives' purposes and meanings,
> trusts and loyalties, in light of the
> character of being, value and power
> determining the ultimate conditions
> of existence (as grasped in their
> operative images—conscious and
> unconscious—of them).[46]

In the first two parts of this intriguing but intricate passage, the repeated phrase "as they construct them" seems to imply that self, others, and world do not *have* meaning but are *assigned* meanings by the creative activity of the mind and the imagination. The last part of the description seems at first to affirm that the "being, value, and power determining the ultimate conditions of existence" actually *have* a certain character. But even this is immediately qualified: the meanings that faith generates are relative to the "images" people have of ultimate conditions, so that here too meaning is, so to say, imagined meaning. And different people are bound to have different individual images and constructs.

Subjectivism and relativism do seem at first glance, then, to be the price we would have to pay for extending the concept of faith as Fowler does. In his language, humans are makers of meaning. He likes the description of the human species as *homo poeta*: "man the meaning-maker, the singular animal," as he puts it, "burdened with the challenge of composing a meaningful world."[47] This, however, need not be the last word on the subject. The poet and the artist seldom create a world wholly out of their own fantasy; as a rule, they portray the only world there is as it impinges on their imagination or as it reveals itself to their prophetic vision. "That's the way I see it!" is one standard retort of the artist to the person who objects, "But it doesn't look like that." To picture human existence under the image of the kingdom of God, for example, need not be a vain fantasy, even if human society looks otherwise to the literal eye; it may be a way of seeing more deeply what is or what ought to be. I do not recall Fowler ever making an express appeal to such an understanding of the artistic enterprise, but I think it fits most of what he says better than an unqualified subjectivism, which would view meanings as pure fictions. To be sure, *some* meanings may be just that—pure fictions. But my point, for now, is that the notion of meaning construction does not necessarily entail that *all* meanings are fictional. It is always logically possible that the meanings we ascribe to our environment are meanings it actually has. And the very fact that the human species is so inescapably constrained to invent meanings may attest the biblical claim that God reaches out unceasingly in revelation: God is never left without a witness.[48]

The fourth and final question that I want to put to Fowler is this: If growth in faith is in general a matter of moving up to the next stage, what sense can be made of the Christian view that (to put it in Luther's terms) the word of God, when it comes, comes in judgment?[49] The gospel is addressed not to the immature but to sinners in need of redemption, so that faith is often, if not always, born in a personal crisis. At the end of one interview reported in *Stages of Faith*, "Miss T." is asked about her understanding of sin.

> MISS T.: Sin!? I don't use the word sin, *ever*.
>
> INTERVIEWER: Why?
>
> MISS T.: I think, on the whole, people are doing the best they can with what light they have.[50]

While reading about faith development, the critical reader may sometimes wonder if Miss T. speaks for Fowler. But is this fair?

Luther and Calvin, no doubt, would be surprised to hear that the emergence and growth of faith have a high degree of predictability—that they follow a genetically programmed timetable. That seems to allow too much to the natural capacities of the fallen will, not enough to the free, creative deed of God that brings new life to the dead. But qualifications immediately spring to mind. The same Calvin who insisted that faith is new life for the dead thought that even baptized infants have a rudimentary faith, which, he admitted, cannot be quite like our faith.[51] He designed his catechism for children, though you might not guess it from the level of theological sophistication it presupposes. He wanted the reformed church to recover the ancient rite of confirmation, in which children approaching adolescence gave account of their faith before the church.[52] He did not believe that children should be admitted to the Lord's Supper until they were capable of the self-examination the sacrament requires. Plainly, in all these ways Calvin's ministry presupposed that faith develops, and that its development is contingent on the growth of the cognitive capacities—that is, on the biological process of maturation.

On the other side, Fowler, though he talks mostly of development, talks sometimes of sin. He has even more to say about conversion, and his book *Stages of Faith* ends with a brief reflection on grace. "Grace," he says, "implies both gift and gift freely given. It also implies a gift bestowed beyond the powers of the recipient to claim or to demand."[53] Once again, it seems, the theological challenge is to hold together two points of view that strike us initially as mutually exclusive. This time, clearly, it is the old, old antithesis of nature and grace that arises before us in a new form.

To conclude: Saving faith cannot, of course, be simply assigned to any one stage in Fowler's developmental scheme. As we have had occasion to notice, he thinks that most middle-class churchgoers in America are caught at Stage 3—or a little higher. And although he uses explicitly Christian language in describing Stage 6, this does not enable us to identify the final stage with Christian faith. As exemplars of universalizing faith, Fowler mentions the Jewish theologian Abraham Heschel (1907–72) and the eclectic Indian sage Mahatma Gandhi (1869–1948) along with the Christians Martin Luther King Jr., Mother Teresa of Calcutta, Dietrich Bonhoeffer, and Thomas Merton.[54] And if there are adherents of other faiths at the sixth stage, not every Christian will be placed there, or will even wish to be. Fowler recognizes that many devout people, including devout Christians, do not take kindly to the suggestion that a mature faith puts in question every claim to an absolute truth within history. Calvinist faith, for instance, though Christian, is not the universalizing faith of Stage 6 in Fowler's scheme: according to Calvin, as we all know, the divine goodwill works effectively only for the salvation of the elect, and the human community is thus split into two.

It appears, then, that Christians belong at more than one stage along Fowler's way—not necessarily by default, sometimes by choice. The coexistence of saving faith and secular faith suggests, however, that we are now in a position to attempt a *generic* concept of faith that will embrace them both. I do not need to assert that what I am calling "generic faith" is strictly universal, much less that it is the essence of all religions or constitutive of human nature. To demonstrate such universal claims empirically would be impossible, and one counter-instance would suffice to defeat them. My limited purpose is to show that Christian faith belongs to a genus and in this way to advance the systematic enterprise, which searches for the connections of Christian thought with other ways of thinking outside the church. An appropriate definition will go, I propose, something like this: *Generic faith is the perception of meaning and purpose in one's life through commitment to an object of ultimate loyalty in which one finds security*. Saving faith, as recognition plus confidence, is a particular instance of generic faith in this sense.[55] So also is secular faith outside the Christian community, whether religious and non-Christian, or not religious at all. And there we must leave our argument for the next chapter, in which we will ask: Can there be any rational justification for the faith we choose to live by?

Chapter 3

THE JUSTIFICATION OF FAITH

The philosopher asks what creed reason requires him to accept. I ask on what terms the creed which is in fact accepted can most reasonably be held.

Arthur James Balfour

In the beginning was the logos.

John 1:1

In the first chapter we worked our way from peak to peak to peak (so to say) in the history of Christian thought, until we arrived at a usable definition of "saving faith." It was borrowed mostly from John Calvin, who held that faith is recognition of the fatherly goodwill of God revealed in the gospel, and that this recognition issues in confidence. We have now tried the experiment, in the second chapter, of moving this distinctively Christian concept of faith into a wider frame of reference. I left the door open to just such a move by suggesting that Calvin's recognition language goes readily into our own current idiom as the language of "construal." Saving faith can then be described as construal of the story of Jesus, and therefore of our own story, as the work of a parentlike God who means us well, and in whom we accordingly place our trust. This, I proposed, gives our theological inquiry a point of convergence with both the history of religions and psychological studies. Colleagues in these other two fields have insisted that faith cannot be reduced to intellectual belief but is rather "a way of seeing whatever one sees" (W. C. Smith), or "our way of finding coherence in and giving meaning to the multiple forces and relations that make up our lives" (James Fowler). What the Christian does when she has faith in Christ is distinctive in content, but in form one instance among many of a generic faith, which is the perception of meaning and purpose in one's life through commitment to an object of ultimate loyalty. It is entirely possible to have such faith without Christ and even without religion, and in this double sense (not

Christian, or not religious) I am calling it "secular" faith. In one form or another, then, faith is a common human phenomenon.

Notice, however, that I have not identified generic faith with any and every kind of meaning construction. What makes it, in the full sense, *faith* is the commitment to an object held to be of ultimate value, which for the Christian is God the Father of the Lord Jesus Christ. In the severe language of the Protestant Reformers, any other object of ultimate loyalty is an idol. Martin Luther writes, in the familiar words of his *Large Catechism* (1529): "As I have often said, the trust and faith of the heart alone make both God and an idol. . . . That to which your heart clings and entrusts itself is, I say, really your God."[1] It follows that if your trust is misdirected, your god is not the true God—whether your idol is wealth, learning, power, prestige, family, pleasure, or anything else. These are the idols Luther himself identifies. I think we can simply subsume both his true God and the idols under the neutral term "ultimate value," by which I mean the last value in the series, or whatever one values more than anything else and not for the sake of other things. It is the commitment to such an ultimate value, even if unspoken and unreflective, that unifies and organizes our experience into patterns of meaning and purpose we can describe as "faiths."

There are, no doubt, both risks and potential gains that result from placing Christian faith in a broader category along with secular faiths. It does not make for clarity if we apply the word "faith" so widely and indiscriminately as to include even our most limited and transitory attempts to construct fragments of meaning. The faith that interests us constructs—or discovers—*comprehensive* meanings, in which we try to embrace as one whole thing our entire being-in-the-world. On the other hand, we cast our conceptual net too narrowly if we speak as though it were only the mention of God and Christ that legitimized use of the word "faith." We cannot rule out in advance the possibility that Christian faith itself may be better understood if set alongside other expressions of comprehensive meaning, whether religious or not. The result may turn out to be not a leveling of Christian faith but a clearer grasp of both its distinctiveness and its universal appeal. For while the gospel is distinctive in proclaiming redemption through Christ, it seems to be addressed to something universal in the depths of humanity that we may well name (with Victor Frankl) the "will-to-meaning." I shall come back to this claim in the fifth chapter, which I have designated "dogmatic" in approach. But I must ask first—in a more apologetic mode—why it is that "faith" is such a bad word in the minds of many educated people, especially perhaps scientists and philosophers, and how we can justify continued use of a word that has become something of a liability.

The Lost Virtue of Believing

The argument now takes us back to what we distinguished as the first aspect of New Testament faith: faith as belief. In the second chapter we looked at writers who insist that faith is not just intellectual belief. But, as their polemical tone betrays, they are in the minority; most theologians and philosophers assume that faith either is or includes belief. The imbalance we detected (and tried to excuse) in Thomas Aquinas is not peculiar to Thomas's church. Other churches, too, have thrown a heavy, one-sided emphasis on belief or assent, including Calvin's church. Take, for instance, the Second Helvetic Confession (1566), perhaps the most influential of the Reformed confessions. Its author, Heinrich Bullinger (1504–75) asks, "What is faith?" and answers: "Christian faith is not an opinion or human conviction, but a most firm assurance and a clear and steadfast assent of the mind, and then a most certain apprehension of the truth of God presented in the Scriptures and in the Apostles' Creed, and thus also of God himself, the greatest good, and especially of God's promise and of Christ who is the fulfillment of all promises."[2] How far removed this lumbering definition is from the direct simplicity of Calvin's catechism, which defines faith as "steadfast knowledge of the fatherly goodwill of God"! In all but the clumsiness of his style, Bullinger is actually closer to Thomas Aquinas than to Calvin. Faith has again become confident assent to a checklist of revealed truths.

Now for Thomas, faith was a virtue and to believe was meritorious. If the truths proposed for our belief by the church could be *seen* to be true, the mind would be *obliged* to yield assent to them, and there would be no merit in assenting. But because revealed truth is neither self-evident nor open to proof, assent to it requires the assistance of an act of will, and this is why believing can qualify as a merit. That it is in fact divine truth that the church proposes to our intellect for its assent can be supported by evidence. But this evidence, too, is noncoercive—except to demons, who have naturally sharp minds and therefore, unlike us, deserve no praise for believing.[3] Faith, in short, is belief; believing is taking something to be true on somebody else's authority; and to believe (in this sense) is good, virtuous, and worthy of merit. So secure did this system of belief seem to be that it afforded the justification for burning heretics. But the system began to crumble in the sixteenth century, and in the eighteenth century it collapsed.

Calvin, we have seen, defined faith differently than Thomas. Nevertheless, Calvin's Geneva preserved the medieval conviction that a heretic is a canker on the body of Christ and must be cut out. When Michael

Servetus (1511–53) came to town, Calvin himself drew up a list of forty charges against him. It was suggested that Servetus should be turned over to the Roman Inquisitors, whom Calvin had already provided with evidence of the accused's guilt. But Servetus begged to be tried in Geneva. His wish (a miscalculation) was granted him, and it was in Reformed Geneva that he was burned for denying the doctrine of the Trinity and repudiating catholic baptism (that is, the baptism of infants). Calvin, it is true, asked the civil authorities to show clemency: he suggested that Servetus should not be burned, but have his head cut off. But Calvin had no problem with the death penalty for heretics. Servetus's last words as he burned to death were: "Jesus, Son of the Eternal God, have pity on me!" And Calvin's colleague, William Farel (1489–1565), pointed out that Servetus put the adjective in the wrong place: he should have said, "Jesus, eternal Son of God," and he would not have had to die. He committed an error of belief.[4]

Calvin's firmness in the trial and execution of Servetus was widely applauded, but not by everyone. The most famous exception was Sebastian Castellio (1515–63), who had his reasons for not liking the Genevan Reformer. When Castellio was rector of the old College of Geneva, Calvin had opposed his admission to the ministry on the grounds of his misinterpretation of the Song of Songs. Castellio judged it to be a "lascivious and obscene poem," in which King Solomon recounted his sexual escapades. Calvin explained that actually the Song of Songs tells us allegorically about Christ's love for the church. Castellio left Geneva, and he was living in Basel as a Greek-language instructor when the Servetus case became public. Soon afterward, he compiled his book *On Heretics: Whether They Should Be Persecuted and How They Are to Be Treated* (1554). It was followed later by a fascinating study titled *On the Art of Doubting and Being Certain, of Not Knowing and Knowing*, which he himself never published.

Alongside the old virtue of believing, there now appears the new virtue of doubting. As Castellio sees it, "there is a time to doubt and a time to believe, a time to be ignorant and a time to know," and it is "the matter of doubting and not knowing" that he judges more in need of his attention. The case for doubting is twofold: epistemological and moral. In the first place, many things are uncertain—even in the Bible—and should be doubted, not made into matters of contention between closed minds. Such are the doctrines of baptism, the Lord's Supper, justification, and predestination. Castellio does not venture an opinion on the doctrine of the Trinity (the chief cause of Servetus's downfall) but reports a hitherto unpublished conversation with the early church father Athanasius (ca. 296–373). As the saint drones on in the words of the Athanasian Creed, an anonymous interlocutor tries to interrupt him with expressions of incredulity. Here is a sample:

> ATHANASIUS. "So the Father is God; the Son is God; and the Holy Ghost is God. And yet they are not three Gods, but one God . . . ."
>
> ANONYMOUS. This is as if you should say, "Abraham is an old man, Isaac is an old man, and Jacob is an old man; yet they are not three old men, but one old man." If I were to believe this, Athanasius, I should have to say farewell to reason . . . .[5]

This, clearly, is as unlike Thomas and Calvin in tone as it is in content, and one can understand why Castellio pretends to be repeating somebody else's anonymous thoughts, for which he, Castellio, cannot be held accountable.

In the second place, our salvation lies in doing our duty, not in busying ourselves with subtle, useless questions. In his book *Concerning Heretics*, Castellio invites Duke Christoph of Württemberg, to whom the book was dedicated, to consider a hypothetical question: How would he judge his subjects if he told them to meet him in white garments and found them arguing instead?

> Suppose further that the controversy was being conducted not merely by words but by blows and swords, and that one group wounded and killed the others who did not agree with them. "He will come on a horse," one would say.
>
> "No, in a chariot," another would retort.
>
> "You lie."
>
> "You're the liar. Take that." He punches him.
>
> "And [you] take that in the belly." The other stabs.
>
> Would you, O Prince, commend such citizens?[6]

The moral is clear. When Christ appears, will he find his servants arrayed in white robes, living in Christian love; or will he find them arguing about the Trinity, predestination, and other insoluble puzzles, and burning or hanging those who hold different opinions on these matters than do those in positions of power?

The principle that doubt is better than contention or persecution, if the issues are uncertain, becomes in the Enlightenment a more general rule: The wise always proportion their belief to the evidence. The scantier the evidence, the more tentative should be their belief. And the evidence that comes to them secondhand from someone else will never be permitted to outweigh what they know perfectly well to be true from the evidence of their own observations. The very notion of "belief" or "faith" becomes suspect precisely because it is being taken in a sense close to that of St. Thomas, whose "act of faith" was tantamount to acquiescence in ecclesiastical authority. John Locke (1632–1704) defined faith as "the Assent to any Proposition, not . . . made out by the Deductions of Reason; but upon the Credit of the Proposer, as coming from GOD, in some extraordinary way of Communication."[7] In other words, faith is accepting a quite stupendous claim because somebody else tells us to. Throughout the eighteenth century, so-called freethinkers tirelessly warned against such claims, coming as they do from clergy whose livelihood depends on them. The clergy entreat us: "Do not argue, but believe." We should be on our guard because they have a vested interest in winning our compliance; and if they succeed, we fall back—by our own foolish choice—into infantile dependence. As the great Immanuel Kant (1724–1804) forcefully proclaimed in his *Answer to the Question, "What Is Enlightenment?"* (1784):

> Enlightenment is man's release from his self-incurred tutelage. Tutelage is man's inability to make use of his understanding without direction from another. Self-incurred is this tutelage when its cause lies not in lack of reason but in lack of resolution and courage to use it without direction from another. . . . It is so easy not to be of age. If I have a book which understands for me, a pastor who has a conscience for me, a physician who decides my diet, and so forth, I need not trouble myself. I need not think, if I can only pay—others will readily undertake the irksome work for me.[8]

In short: in a world come of age, believing is no longer a virtue. It is better to think for yourself.

Now we may be tempted to reply: "But that's not what faith is—other-directed thinking! If Calvin continued the venerable custom of executing the heretic, that was a terrible lapse from his own concept of faith. He opposed the scholastic notion of implicit faith, which acquiesces in the authority of the church, and called instead for an explicit faith, which is express recognition of God's fatherly hand in the course of the world. This recognition can only be, in the nature of the case, *our* recognition, not somebody else's. In their rejection of implicit faith, Calvin and the other Reformers were true forerunners of the Enlightenment and its insistence that men and women come of age must do their thinking for themselves."

Very well. But there remains a difficulty. Even if faith is not resigning to the church one's responsibility to think for oneself, it is still a conviction that cannot be proved. This seems, in fact, to be the plight both of saving faith and of the varieties of secular faith: whether as intellectual belief or as meaning construction, faith does not rest on proof. And this leaves it still open to suspicion even when the matter of external authority is set aside. There is full agreement between Thomas Aquinas and the eighteenth-century Enlightenment on the criterion of strict knowledge or "science": it is knowledge either of what we see immediately to be true, or else of what we can infer from self-evident truth by necessary argument. It follows that the negative defining characteristic of faith is likewise held in common by the schoolman and the freethinker: faith is assent that *lacks* the support of self-evidence or proof. The question is therefore what rational justification, if any, can be offered for clinging to what we cannot show to be true. One possible line of defense is to argue that at least some beliefs, though not demonstrable, are nonetheless inevitable—justified simply because none of us can do without them. I want to take a look at two candidates for the status of "inevitable belief": belief that our world is an orderly environment, and belief that the order is in part moral. To open the discussion, I turn to two German philosophers who are very little known but who present the issues with uncommon clarity: F. H. Jacobi and Friedrich Forberg.[9]

Existential Belief: The World as Order

"Faith" or "belief" (*Glaube*) was the central concept in the thought of Friedrich Henrich Jacobi (1743–1819): his philosophy was named "the philosophy of faith" (*Glaubensphilosophie*). This makes him, as far as I know, a unique figure in the history of ideas. But his contribution has not attracted much attention. His contemporaries were unimpressed by his intellectual abilities, except when he was criticizing other people's opinions. The great genius of the day, Johann Wolfgang von Goethe (1749–1832), remarked condescendingly that metaphysical speculation was Jacobi's bad luck: he was neither born nor educated for it.[10] In a way, that is true. Jacobi was brought up in an intense pietistic environment. (We are told that, as a boy, instead of going out to play with other boys, he liked to stay indoors and discuss the condition of his soul with an elderly maidservant.) His father was a sugar merchant, not an academic. But young Friedrich had little interest in business: from the time of his student days in Geneva, he was obsessed with the difficulty of harmonizing faith and philosophy. If his resolution of the problem was not appreciated, that is in part because he was out of step with the times.

Jacobi's name became linked with Johann Georg Hamann's (1730–88) in the revolt against the Enlightenment. A devout Lutheran, Hamann was convinced that, so far from marking the advent of intellectual freedom, the Enlightenment had imposed a new captivity—a despotism of reason in place of the old despotism of the pope. The attempt to bring every department of life under the sway of reason overlooks the fact that the human person is not an abstract intellect but a complex unity of thinking and feeling. Indeed, the primacy belongs to feeling: "The heart beats before the head thinks." Poetry and myth are therefore just as likely as the intellect to yield insight and understanding, and in the final analysis we can only live by faith. In a letter to Immanuel Kant (27 July 1759), Hamann protested that even the great skeptic David Hume (1711–76) "needs faith when he eats an egg or drinks a glass of water." Hume's philosophy, in other words, demonstrates the limits of reason, which was actually given to teach us our ignorance, as the law was given to reveal to us our sin. What Hume says in jest can therefore be affirmed without embarrassment: reason is not sufficient to convince us of the truth of Christianity, but we assent to it by faith.[11]

The appeal to David Hume fascinated Hamann's friend Jacobi. Ridiculed as an obscurantist and an enemy of reason, Jacobi replied with a book titled *David Hume on Belief, or Idealism and Realism: A Dialogue* (1787), in which he triumphantly enlisted Hume for the cause of faith. He has been accused, he says, of teaching blind belief, which is to say, assent based on mere authority. In fact, he uses the German word *Glaube* in a strictly philosophical sense, to mean a knowing that cannot be proved. And this is exactly how David Hume understands the English word "belief," as, for instance, when he speaks of our belief in the existence of an external world: "Without any reasoning," he says, " . . . we always suppose an external universe, which depends not on our perception."[12] We cannot prove that our sense experience is experience of an actual object out there, but we cannot bring ourselves to doubt it very seriously either. Here, then, is at least one case in which the legitimacy of belief without proof is taken for granted. It is not a matter of blind submission to authority. But it is, in a sense, trust in revelation since we can only say that objects are *revealed* to the senses, not *demonstrated* by reason. If anyone chooses to doubt the evidence of her senses and demands proof, there is nothing we can do for her because no other evidence is possible. Any proof we might construct would have to go back in the end to revelation and faith. "The decided realist," Jacobi concludes, "who without doubting accepts external things on the evidence of his senses, views this certainty as an original conviction and cannot but think that every use of the intellect to acquire knowledge of the external world must be grounded on this fundamental experience."[13]

But Jacobi presses his case further. The conversation moves on to Hume's critique of the concept of causality, and once again we have no other option but to fall back on an indefeasible conviction that we cannot support by argument. The assertion that things are interconnected in a causal network, like the assertion that there is a world outside our minds, is justified by faith. Hume's doubting it merely convinces us that we cannot *prove* the connection of material objects in a causal system; the doubt remains purely theoretical. "If you can let yourself be troubled by such doubt," Jacobi says, "I don't know how to help you. But I think your belief overcomes it just as easily as mine does."[14]

In the pertinent section of the dialogue, the discussion moves strictly within the epistemological limits of British empiricism. Nothing is said about religious belief, but a respectable philosophical use for the term "belief" as an original conviction has been established.[15] Jacobi's ultimate design, however, was, of course, apologetic—to defend his religious faith. The utility of his case for this end became explicit when he published a second edition of his dialogue (1815). The preface grew into a general introduction to Jacobi's entire philosophical output. A few changes had been made in his thinking, or at least in his language, since 1787, but they need not detain us. The important point is that he now argues for an application of the word "belief" (in his sense) to the revelation of what he calls "supersensible things." The justification of cognitive claims in this domain, too, as in the domain of material objects, can only be a matter of faith. Here also, every attempted proof must go back eventually to a conviction without proof—the conviction that we are dealing with reality and truth. "One can only *believe* in virtue, and so in freedom, and so in spirit and God."[16] But this is no more than to say that our knowledge of objects beyond nature is neither more nor less secure than the knowledge that comes from sense perception. Jacobi now uses the word "reason" for the organ by which we are aware of a spiritual world, and he writes in summary: "Man believes his senses necessarily, and he believes his reason necessarily; and there is no certainty higher than the certainty of this belief."[17] In neither domain is any guarantee needed beyond the revelation things give of themselves.

Jacobi clearly takes us a step further in our inquiry into the concept of faith. In a sense, he adds another variety of what we have called "secular faith": faith that is not specifically Christian and need not be religious at all. He points us to an ineradicable strand of belief—of unproved and unprovable conviction—that underlies every department of human existence, not Christianity alone, nor even religion alone. "The element of all human knowledge and activity," as he puts it, "is faith."[18] We can only know by faith, and we can only act at all as human beings in the light of what we thus know. Faith (in Jacobi's sense) is not peculiar to religious people, if we mean by that people who adhere to some institutional variety of religious beliefs, symbols, and practices; it is common to all, whether they realize it or not. It belongs to human existence as such, and for this reason we might name its content *existential belief*. Jacobi is the very model of those religious apologists who want to renounce a theology of proofs without taking a flight into the blind faith of mere fideism. Their defense of religious faith lies in showing that it conforms in structure to the element of belief in all knowing. Hence, even if belief in supersensible realities admittedly has no final defense against radical doubt, at least it is in no worse case than belief in a material world independent of our senses.

Plainly, there are two parts to Jacobi's case, and we may not judge them to be of equal worth. First, he argues that there is a faith of sorts underlying the whole of human existence. Second, he thinks that this renders religious faith less vulnerable. His contribution on the first point seems to me incontrovertible. If we confine ourselves for the moment to belief in the existence and regularity of an external world, the significance of his case is evident; for these are the presuppositions of every scientific experiment and every scientific generalization. We are convinced, without being able to prove it, that there is a world out there to be investigated, and that it behaves so consistently that observations made on Monday yield data our research can use on Tuesday and a discovery made in Cambridge will hold good in Göttingen or Chicago. Objects are not simply there, but are also bound together in a network of law-governed events. Our twofold conviction, though it is in a sense faith, is not blind assent to somebody else's say-so; in all of us, it arises inevitably out of our own actual commerce with the world of sense, and all further commerce with the world of sense depends in turn on preserving the conviction. It simply is not the case that whereas religion rests on faith, science rests on reason or demonstration. But if this need not make you wonder about science, does it reassure you about religion? That brings me to Jacobi's case, part two.

Commerce with the material world is so basic to our survival that only a few seem able to doubt the reality of a world of sense.[19] But does the same hold good for commerce with a supersensible world? Well, it depends in part on what a supersensible world contains. And the difficulty with Jacobi's view is that his supersensible world contains a variety of things, which do not all seem to enjoy the same status. He mentions, for instance, the Kantian triad of God, freedom, and immortality; but also the

Platonic triad of truth, goodness, and beauty. And we must surely ask: If belief is the inescapable conviction of reality, of how many things in the supersensible world are we inescapably convinced? How do we know when to stop, when to close the list? The notion of existential belief cannot be invoked to justify any belief we please. There is a bite in Arthur Schopenhauer's (1788–1860) malicious comment that Jacobi's little weakness was to take all he learned and approved before his fifteenth year for innate ideas of the human mind.[20] Obviously, a detailed critique of Jacobi would have to take up each item on his list of supersensible things in turn. But I must move on. I will come back to the general question whether his notion of an original conviction lends support to his Christian belief in God. Before I do so, I turn to my second candidate for the status of inevitable belief: the belief that the ordered world in which we find ourselves is, at least in part, a moral order. It will then be time to assess the role inevitable beliefs might play in Christian apologetic.

Practical Belief: The World Order as Moral

To broach the theme of belief in a moral order, I could very well stay with Jacobi, who included the recognition of good among his original convictions. The fundamental point I want to make at this stage of my argument is in fact expressed as acutely as one could hope for in Jacobi's aphorism "Out of man's *willing* springs his truest *knowing*."[21] Or, I could equally well turn to Immanuel Kant himself, whose greatness as a philosopher lay partly in his insistence that there are two sources, not just one, from which we gain insight into the world and our own place in it: not empirical observation alone, but also moral awareness. The external world of sense was not the only subject Kant found worthy of his best thinking; he was fascinated, in addition, by the moral law within him. But I turn instead to an admittedly less distinguished thinker, who found himself swept up into the Kantian revolution: Friedrich Karl Forberg (1770–1848).

One unkind historian describes Forberg as a "philosophical author without philosophical talent."[22] He achieved brief notoriety in 1798, when an article he wrote on religion sparked the famous Atheism Controversy. The controversy drew in some of the most eminent German thinkers of the day—Fichte, Schiller, Goethe, and others. Forberg himself was quickly forgotten in the battle of the giants. But he remains interesting to me for the tenacity with which he tried to think through one of the fundamental problems of Kant's philosophy: What is the connection between religion and morals? His answer by no means betrays a lack of philosophical talent.

Forberg had started out as a candidate for the Protestant ministry. But the study of philosophy convinced him that it is hard to believe any longer in the existence of supernatural beings. In the article that launched the debate on atheism, he tried to show that such doubts should leave morality wholly unaffected. For moral commitment is not *believing that* there is a God who presides over the world as its moral governor, but *acting as if* there were. Forberg proposed that we should call this acting-as-if "practical," as distinct from "theoretical," belief, and he insisted that genuine religion is nothing other than practical belief. To be religious is to behave as if a moral kingdom were coming and as if you wanted it to come. But, as purely practical belief, religion is commitment to doing good whether or not there is in fact a kingdom to come or a God who steers the world toward the victory of good. In this way, the old religious symbols are not discarded but reinterpreted as moral incentives that work on the will through the imagination.[23]

Forberg did not actually deny the existence of God; he denied only that the existence of God matters to religion or morals. But he was immediately accused of atheism in an open letter written by an anxious father to his son, who was away at college.[24] The father's main point is that students away from home will not behave unless threatened with retribution in the world to come. Take away their conviction that there really is a Divine Judge, who will one day punish all their wickedness, and their moral collapse will be the inevitable result. The Weimar government agreed, and Forberg received an official letter of censure. His work as superintendent of a high school in Saalfeld became impossible: enrollment declined as word of his unorthodoxy spread. He felt obliged to move on to Coburg (1801), where he became curator of the duke's library and did the one thing for which he is remembered in the English-speaking world. He collected all the erotic passages he could find in classical literature and published the results in an illustrated handbook.[25] I will not attempt to explain why Forberg's manual has been translated into English but his writings on God and religion have not. The translator suggests in his preface that the manual will be found useful by students of the classics, lawyers, psychologists, and medical men. But the anxious father perhaps found there the proof of a connection between atheism and wickedness. History does not say.

Before he gave up philosophy, Forberg defended himself against the charge of atheism in a detailed and fascinating *Apology* (182 pages long), which he published in 1799—the year after the article that earned him official censure. Here he repeats his fundamental point that morality does not depend on theoretical or factual belief in the existence of God or a judgment to come. "One ought because one ought, not because one wants something else, nor because God wants it."[26]

Forberg denies that he is in fact an atheist, but he suggests that an attack of atheism might help us to grasp his important point. "A mild attack of theoretical atheism is accordingly something everyone should actually wish to have at least once in his lifetime, to make an experiment on his own heart: to see whether it wills the good for its own sake, as it should, or solely for the sake of some advantage to be expected—if not in this world, then in another."[27] In Forberg's view, the truly religious disposition shines brightest in the total pessimist who scorns all hope of a golden age—*and yet still* acts resolutely for the common good. For religion is not believing in the good time coming but committing oneself wholeheartedly to an ideal realm of goodness even if one believes it will never come.[28] Thus far, the argument is much the same as in the ill-starred article. But Forberg now has more to say.

The argument has driven him to insist that moral obligation is a wholly unconditioned demand upon us, no matter how the world goes or what the world is like. But he now recognizes that a pure moral disposition, which does its duty for duty's sake alone, is itself—when you come to think about it—a remarkable feature of the world we live in. And we do not have just the rare example of the dutiful pessimist to guide us: each of us can hear the voice of the moral law within. A little surprisingly, Forberg thus *ends* with the factual religious claims he refused to *begin* with: "I teach," he says, "that at a certain point of speculation the moral disposition unavoidably appears as belief in a moral world order, hence also as a belief in a *principle* of the moral world order"—which, of course, is God understood as moral governor.[29] Humans, in short, live in a moral order as their distinctively human element.[30]

Once again, as in our look at F. H. Jacobi, I am convinced that something immensely important is being said here, which must have its place in our quest for a workable concept of faith. It is an astonishing fact of human existence that we all habitually assume, or imply, or assert, there are things we ought to do and things we ought not to do. Of course, it does not follow that we agree on which things are which; and many of our species think they owe little or nothing to anyone outside their own family or tribe. Yet as long as there is (as we say) honor among thieves, there is no denying that one characteristic of our species is to construe the environment not only as order but as a moral order.[31]

But this belief in a moral order, it seems to me, is what we might more properly call *practical* belief: not, that is (as Forberg wants), a belief that does not really believe at all but only acts-as-if; a belief, rather, that is evoked by action and reflection on action. Only on this semantic point am I inclined to quarrel with Forberg. Believing simply is not acting-as-if (in any sense that Webster or Random House would endorse). But there is a kind of belief that arises out of acting, or at least out of willing, and in this sense is practical belief: the belief, namely, that we act in a moral environment and that we are never more firmly in contact with reality than when another human being confronts us as a moral demand. We cannot prove that we ought to respond to moral demands, but it is difficult, even (I suspect) impossible, for us to brush them aside under every circumstance whatever.[32] If so, then we have another instance of faith, not as assent to authority, but as inevitable belief—an original conviction that we can neither prove nor discard.

It would perhaps be possible, in conclusion, to subsume existential belief and practical belief under the concept of faith construction explored in chapter two. Both of them could be seen as instances of comprehensive meaning construction: we construe our world as an ordered environment, and we construe it as a moral environment. In a sense, these inevitable beliefs are as inclusive as saving faith, since they refer to our experience as a whole. But there is an important difference. The two inevitable beliefs are more abstract, capable of being filled out with more than one specific content. Our persuasion that experience discloses an ordered environment is compatible with many alternative accounts of what the order is like; and our persuasion that, as humans, we find ourselves in a network of moral obligations does not by itself specify the nature of moral community. For this reason, I want to keep existential and practical beliefs in a distinct class as presuppositions, rather than instances, of full-blown faith construction. Later (in chapter 5), I will term these inevitable beliefs collectively "elemental faith" and try to draw out more fully their connection with saving, Christian faith. For the present I can wind up the discussion thus far with a third definition, to go with the definitions of saving faith and generic faith: *Existential belief in an ordered environment and practical belief in a moral environment are inevitable beliefs that cannot be either proved or discarded and, as such, are presuppositions of saving and secular faith.*

Naturally, we must now be careful not to fall into the pit we dug for Jacobi, who was too quick to assume that in justifying the concept of an original conviction he had justified belief in God. Much depends on how you define "God." A kind of minimal belief in God is, I think, implicit in existential or practical belief. But Christians want to say a great deal more about God than simply that God is the order we perceive in nature or the moral order we perceive in the company of our fellow human beings. God is the Father of the Lord Jesus Christ, they will say; and there is no reason to suppose that belief in God, so understood, is an original human conviction. Jacobi let his Christian faith run ahead of his argument. The correct conclusion to a discussion of inevitable beliefs is to be found, I think, in the move A. J. Balfour (1848–1930) suggests. Belief in God is not one of the inevitable beliefs we all hold in our ordinary waking moments, even those of us who like to deny them in theory. But belief in God is more supportive of our inevitable beliefs than is the naturalism that many people suppose to be scientific.[33] And there, in part, lies the rational justification for belief in God.

It by no means follows that one believes in God because one can offer this, or any other, justification of believing. That would not only be unwarranted by observation and experience; it would also be a confusion of categories. The acquisition of faith is not the same as the justification of faith—as though one found it at the conclusion of an argument. The two are distinct operations of the mind. If we ask: How, then, do those who have it actually come by their faith in God? the answer must surely take note of the fact that faith seems to be given to them in community—in the company of the faithful. Important insights can be borrowed here from the sociologists. There is a social dimension of faith that, so far, we have touched on only obliquely. From a sociological viewpoint, it is entirely natural that Christian faith in God is expressed in collective creeds or confessions sanctioned by a church. And this brings us to the next item on our agenda: *confession* of faith, which we will need to interpret in the light of the distinction already made between faith and belief—if we are to turn the edge of the sharp antidogmatism of the Enlightenment. Confession is not surrender of the mind to ecclesiastical formulas. As Thomas Aquinas rightly says, it is the outward act of faith.[34] But it has as much to do with the birth and nurture of faith as with its outward expression.

Chapter 4

THE CONFESSION OF FAITH

> Extra ecclesiam nulla salus. *By* salus *we mean here (with due apologies to the theologians who had other things in mind when they coined the phrase) the empirically successful accomplishment of conversion. It is only within the religious community, the ecclesia, that the conversion can be effectively maintained as plausible.*
>
> Peter L. Berger and Thomas Luckmann

> *I am not better than my fathers.*
>
> Elijah (1 Kings 19:4 KJV)

The "golden age" in the history of Christian creeds or confessions of faith was, in some ways, the Reformation era. Just to consider the space the sixteenth century takes up in Philip Schaff's monumental work *The Creeds of Christendom* is to realize what an unprecedented flood of creed-making the Reformation let loose. In scope, as in number, the Lutheran and Reformed confessions extend far beyond the tight limits of the three so-called ecumenical symbols: the Apostles', Nicene, and Athanasian creeds. And the Protestant confessions evoked a detailed Roman Catholic response in the Canons and Decrees of the Council of Trent (published in 1564), which are also usually classed as an extended "creed." Both directly and indirectly, the Reformation swelled the treasury of the creeds of Christendom.

It is ironic, then, that the Reformation at the same time undermined the plausibility of creeds. With Martin Luther and Ulrich Zwingli (1484–1531) begins the long decline into pluralism, which, along with secularization, weakens every claim to ecclesiastical authority; and a creed, by definition, claims authority as an official codification of Christian faith. Secularization reinforces skepticism about the dogmatic content of creeds; pluralism casts doubt over the very concept of a creed. For how can it seriously be imagined that any one of the rival statements of faith happens to coincide with the absolute truth of divine revelation?

The Protestants did not reform the church; they divided it. And one inevitable casualty was belief in the church itself as a divine institution whose leaders spoke with the voice of God. Henceforth one had to ask: *Which* church? Ernst Troeltsch (1865–1923) is only a little unfair when he writes caustically: "Three infallible 'Churches,' unchurching and anathematizing one another, discredited the idea of the Church, for which there is no plural."[1] While inaugurating the confessional age, the Protestants were, in a sense, digging confessionalism's grave. At the very least, the concept of an authoritative creed, like the concept of an authoritative church, had to be revised.

Creeds and Confessional Pluralism

It is true that this consequence of the Reformation was not immediately apparent, and to some people it still isn't. Before pluralism comes to be acknowledged, there is an intermediate stage in which the existence of other Christian bodies is explained by the unfortunate proneness of other people to blindness and error. Hence, although the authority of Rome had been challenged, it was natural enough for the Roman Catholics to rest their assurance of being right on their belonging to the *big* church—with its splendid pedigree going all the way back to St. Peter, the rock on whom Christ chose to build. With no less assurance, Luther thought that in Wittenberg, at least, the gospel was purely proclaimed—and hardly anywhere else.[2] And John Calvin's spiritual progeny could always fall back on their happy awareness of being God's chosen people. "For many are called, but few are chosen" (Matt. 22:14).

It remains possible even today, though with decreasing plausibility, to fence oneself against pluralism by assuming that there *must* be unalloyed truth *somewhere*. A good colleague of mine told me of his pain when his stepdaughter chose to marry a minister in a tiny splinter church. It had broken away from a denomination that already took pride in its absolute orthodoxy. "How many congregations does it have?" I asked (perhaps irrelevantly). "One," he replied. For many years, another friend of mine wandered from church to church seeking in vain a minister who preached pure doctrine. He ended up spending Sunday mornings alone with a large Bible on his lap. Rejecting pluralism, he added to it. And there, the Roman Catholics will say, you have the logical outcome of the Protestant Reformation.

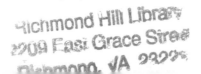

At least since the end of the seventeenth and the beginning of the eighteenth century, the embarrassment of pluralism has worsened. It was then that party loyalty became as important as confessional (or denominational) membership. A Reformed pietist and a Reformed rationalist in Germany, for instance, might have found less in common with each other than each would have found individually with his or her Lutheran counterpart. The total of religious claims then became the number of denominations times the number of parties. And in the New World, with the severance of the old bond between church and state, pluralism evolved into a full-blown market.[3] You are now entirely free to pick both church and party, as you please, from a huge variety of available options.

In the post-Reformation world, new creeds, it seems, must have a necessarily particular stamp: they confess a fragmentary faith even when they try to be catholic. But there is a further problem. In the last two hundred years, especially in North America, the walls between the divided churches have begun to crumble; arguably, they should. The preservation of a confessional tradition now seems to work in North America only where a strong ethnic tie persists, and ethnic ties are eroding. Take my own Presbyterian church, for example. Nearly half of the born Presbyterians in America leave the denomination, and of the remainder fewer and fewer marry "within the faith" (as we used to say).[4] The membership rolls are partially restored by recruits (besides spouses) from other denominations. But the plight of the American Presbyterians is not only that between 1966 and 1987 they lost, on balance, a staggering 1.2 million members, but also that fewer of the remaining 3 million have any reason to be self-consciously Presbyterian.[5] I do not assume that to be a committed Presbyterian (or anything else) you have to be born and raised that way. The point, rather, is that old boundaries have become permeable, and the question must be honestly faced whether it makes sense any more to insist on theological differences that once justified separate existence. Have the old creeds become anachronisms? Is confessionalism—that is, the preservation of a *particular* creedal standpoint—a mistake?

Well, some may reply that it always *was* a mistake. Already in the seventeenth century, there were Protestants who repudiated binding creeds for at least three reasons: that they compete with the unique authority of Scripture; that they violate freedom of conscience; and that they close the mind to new communications of the Holy Spirit. It would be imprudent for Presbyterians, like me, not to hear these criticisms. The Reformed churches have shown a morbid appetite for heresy hunts, and they need to ask themselves whether all the trials and condemnations have ever really been worth it. If not, must the preservation of a distinctive Reformed tradition be rejected as an unworthy, wrongheaded goal, which is bound to keep the fires burning?

Michael Servetus was not the last "hunted heretic" in the Reformed church. In early seventeenth-century Holland, the eminent scholar Hugo Grotius (1583–1645), who was soft on Arminianism, was sentenced to life imprisonment. His resourceful wife arranged his escape in a crate of books. Another Arminian sympathizer, John van Olden Barneveldt (1549–1619) was not so lucky; he was beheaded on a trumped-up charge of treason. In Scotland, at the end of the century (1697), a young student named Thomas Aikenhead was publicly executed for "the crime of blasphemy or railing and cursing against God or the persons of the Holy Trinity."[6] Milder penalties have been exacted in more recent times. In 1831, John McLeod Campbell (1800–72) was deposed by the General Assembly of the Church of Scotland for teaching that Christ died for everyone, not for the elect only. "God," he had said, "loves every child of Adam with a love the measure of which is to be seen in the agony of Christ."[7] What a heresy! The advent of historical-critical methods for studying the Bible led heresy hunters in the American Presbyterian church during the 1890s to drive out three of their brightest luminaries: Charles Augustus Briggs (1841–1913), Henry Preserved Smith (1847–1927), and Arthur Cushman McGiffert (1861–1933). Briggs found a gentler home in the Protestant Episcopal Church; Smith and McGiffert joined the Congregationalists. And so we might go on.

It is a dismal story, both longer and much more complicated than I can relate here. I am not conceding that the Reformed churches have been uniquely intolerant. In sixteenth-century England, Protestants or Catholics, depending on which party was currently in power, were executed by the dozen. In Saxony, Philipp Melanchthon (1497–1560) prepared a document (1536) demanding the death penalty for denial of any article of the Apostles' Creed, and Martin Luther signed. It would be difficult to distribute the blame of intolerance fairly. But that is not the issue. The moral I wish to draw is obvious enough: creeds have been retained in the divided churches as instruments for the persecution, or prosecution, of deviant believers and critics of the prevailing beliefs. The heterodox always think they are going to start a discussion; they are silenced with a creed, and the majority does not often pause to wonder if the Spirit has been quenched. One of John McLeod Campbell's accusers summed it all up perfectly when he said: "I do not think there was ever a simpler proposition submitted to this Assembly. There is the libel [i.e., the formal charge], and there is the [Westminster] Confession of Faith."[8] The forum of theological debate became a court of law, and the confession was the law.[9] By the time the Church of Scotland was ready to take the theological question seriously, the questioner was no longer in the church.

If there is to be a reappropriation of a confessional tradition in a pluralistic age, it will have to be defended against some very plausible criticisms. Anticredalism is a legitimate protest against the reckless use of creeds as tests of orthodoxy.[10] But, we shall insist, they have a better use, which is: to engender and nurture faith. Obviously, the defense will rest on the distinction I have made between "beliefs" and "faith." No absolute separation is intended. But if it is wrong to equate faith with beliefs, it is equally wrong to reduce confessions of faith to *tests* of belief. The abuse of creeds illustrates the perils of mistaking belief for faith; their proper use requires us to hold on firmly to the understanding of faith as the attainment (or gift) of personal identity through the perception of meaning and purpose in one's life.

My case falls into two parts, which explore in turn the ideas of a "confessing church" and a "confessional theology." Borrowing a term from the sociologists, I want to suggest that creeds, positively interpreted, are instruments not of intolerance but of "socialization," and that the task of a confessional theology is strictly subordinate to this same objective. My starting point is the recognition of faith's inescapably social character.

A Confessing Church

It may seem as if the progress of my thoughts in the first chapter was toward a highly individualistic view of faith. I moved from implicit to explicit faith, and it would be easy to interpret the move as a shift to individualism. In Thomas Aquinas and Roman Catholicism, implicit faith is readiness to believe what the church teaches: the Thomistic act of faith, though the act of an individual, is unthinkable apart from the collective life of the community. Calvin's explicit faith, on the other hand, seems at first glance to isolate the individual, throwing the entire burden of the act of faith on him- or herself. Saving faith is confidence in the fatherly goodwill of God, and no one can have it for us. As the Lutheran aphorism has it, each must do their own believing as surely as each must do their own dying.[11]

In fact, Calvin's faith too has a necessarily corporate context, though one might not guess it from his definition of faith. He agrees with Cyprian that to have God for Father is to have the church for your Mother. "There is no other entrance into life unless she conceive us in her womb, give birth to us, feed us at her breasts, and, finally, protect us with her care and guidance until, putting off this mortal flesh, we become like the angels."[12] But let's translate this principle into more prosaic sociological language. For, as John Wesley (1703–91) said, "The Gospel of Christ knows no religion, but *social*."[13]

Faith and Community

Faith, I have argued, construes the events of my daily experience as a meaningful sequence. But it is in community, we must now add, that I first acquire the categories for seeing the pattern. I internalize the mental world of my society or group, and I discover my place in it. Adopting a particular religious outlook is more like learning a language than passing a test; answering the questions put to me at my initiation or appointment to office testifies that the language of the community has in fact shaped the way I see myself. In short, having faith is being "socialized"—learning to think, speak, and act as the group does. The process is not a purely deliberate and rational one: I don't learn the rules only by studying the grammar book, but much more from conversation in the group. On the other hand, learning the language is not like programming a machine; it calls for deliberate affirmation of the community's world of meaning as *my* world of meaning. Faith is born, the craving for meaning is satisfied, as the individual learns to construe his or her existence in the light of the views and values that sustain the community. In this sense, our faith and even what we take to be our knowledge have a sociological side to them, and this is crucial for understanding faith and confessions of faith alike.[14]

It follows that neither a solitary faith nor a mere faith in general, so to say, is conceivable—unless by an act of mental abstraction from the way things actually and empirically are. I can certainly examine my Christian faith as *my* faith, but normally, perhaps invariably, it comes to me in the first place through the medium of a believing community: either directly, if I went to church, or, if I didn't, then indirectly through the beliefs and symbols that the church has engraved on the cultural consciousness around me. Even if, by some extraordinary circumstance, I acquired my faith in solitude, I could not sustain it for long except in communication with others. And because, in the nature of the case, I am a particular individual and can communicate only with particular others, my faith will be a particular faith: if it is Christian faith, it will differ in some respects even from the faith of many other Christians.

What happens, for instance, in the "testimony" meetings that are held in many of our evangelical groups? By relating the story of God's dealings with my soul, I receive the community's acceptance of me and the community's confirmation of my self-understanding. This is the point, a little mischievously expressed, of my epigraph from Berger and Luckmann.[15] There is no salvation outside the church because only within a religious community is our religious experience verified—given the stamp of authenticity. Take the written testimony John Bunyan (1628–88) sent from prison. Today, we pick up *Grace Abounding* (1666) and read it as one man's unique story. And, in a sense, it is. But Bunyan's narrative had its value in its own day because it was both shaped and authenticated by the Puritan group to which Bunyan belonged and because it served, in turn, to shape and authenticate the experience of others. It was but one of hundreds of such narratives; the appearance of a lonely struggle is (from this point of view) illusory. Bunyan construes the events that befall him through the language of English Puritanism, or of one variety of Puritanism. The narrative is not a unique autobiography; it is an exercise in religious socialization both for the author and for his readers.[16]

One may certainly speak of Bunyan's religious experience as an instance of what I am calling "generic faith." But it was a very specific instance, fully understandable only in the setting of English Puritanism. He acquired not faith in general but Puritan faith. Recall one of the most important, but often overlooked, insights of Friedrich Schleiermacher: you can *define* religion in general, but you cannot *be* religious in general. This is why the argument in his pioneering *Speeches on Religion* (1799) must be read all the way through to the final speech, in which he moves from the abstract essence of religion to what it means to be actually religious. He makes the interesting remark that to claim citizenship in the world of religion you have to *settle* in some particular religion. In John Oman's happy translation: you have to "pitch [your] camp" somewhere.[17] And if you cannot be religious in general, neither can you choose to be Christian in general. "Even as Christians," Karl Barth (1886–1968) says, "we all belong *somewhere*, whether or not we realize it or care to realize it."[18] Hence Christian faith, while Christian, is bound to be Roman Catholic or Lutheran or Anglican or Presbyterian or Methodist or Baptist, and so on. In other words, the inescapably social character of faith has to be seen in relation to an inescapably pluralistic society. When religion and society are no longer coextensive, then (from a sociological point of view) to have faith is to construe one's experience through the language of a subsociety's world of meaning. We are both religious and Christian only as we pitch our tent in a particular community of believers.

Creeds and Social Identity

The next step is to move these reflections on the social character of faith into the discussion of creeds or confessions. A confession of faith then appears, quite simply, as an instrument of socialization: it is one of the devices by which the believing community maintains its world of meaning and so both reaffirms its own identity and confers identity on its individual members. The two main threats to the survival and health of the community are forgetfulness and disintegration. They are closely related. Disintegration—the loss of the center—is the result of forgetting what it was that constituted the community in the first place. This, at least (not to generalize too unwisely), seems clearly to be the malaise of Protestantism in North America. One church historian remarks that "the most conspicuous feature of American Protestantism as it moved toward the close of the nineteenth century had been its loss of identity."[19] I doubt if he would change his diagnosis today, as American Protestantism moves to the close of another century.

Confessions of faith are reminders. Their primary use is not to smoke out heresy but, through constant recollection, to preserve identity. They prevent disintegration by maintaining a common language, a community of discourse, without which the fellowship would suffer group amnesia and might dissolve in a babel of discordant voices. The common language is always recollective, not only in calling to mind the "faith of our fathers," but also, and above all, inasmuch as it goes back to the founding events that first brought the community into being. To *keep* the community in being, there must be continual remembering of these events that give meaning to the community's existence.

The recollective, community-forming role of creeds is unmistakably clear in those pre-Christian confessions of faith that we find already in the Hebrew Scriptures. They are firmly rooted in the Jewish consciousness of being made a people of God, and their function is to reaffirm this definitive consciousness by remembering and giving thanks. Deut. 26:1-11, for instance, might be described as a narrative credo for liturgical use. In content, it is a grateful recital of the redemptive deeds of God by which the people of Israel was once constituted, and still is: the making of a great nation from "a wandering Aramean," the deliverance from the Egyptian bondage, and the gift of the promised land. The credo is expressly designed as a liturgy for use in the sanctuary; it is to accompany the presentation of the "first fruits" of the land. "[You] shall celebrate with all the bounty that the Lord your God has given to you and to your house" (v. 11). The use of the pronouns "we," "our," and "us" strikingly underscores the fact that the worshiper identifies completely with the one historic community of faith: "*We* cried to the Lord, the God of our ancestors; the Lord heard *our* voice . . . . The Lord brought *us* out of Egypt" (vv. 7-8). Israel's world of meaning lies wholly in this history.

The ancient Christian creeds have an exactly similar form and function, rooted in the consciousness of the *ecclesia*—the people "called out" by the deeds of God in Jesus Christ. The heart of the Apostles' and Nicene creeds is recital of the story of Christ, already cast in summary form in several New Testament passages, in which it is understood as continuous with the Old Testament story of redemption (see, e.g., Acts 13:16-41; 1 Cor. 15:3-7). The Christian creeds rehearse the saving events on which the church is founded, the memory of which sustains the church's identity; and they, too, had their original use in a liturgical setting. The Apostles' Creed grew out of the baptismal confession of the Roman church; the Nicene Creed came to be used in both the Eastern and the Western churches as a eucharistic confession. In the context of worship, the creeds become acts of thankful celebration that gather the community around the crucified and risen Lord and renew its existence as his church. However elaborately the primitive Christian formula may be developed, the confession that makes and remakes the church has always been: "Jesus is Lord (or Christ)."

Christians are who they are because they are persuaded that light and life came into the world in Jesus Christ. They live *anno Domini*, in the last times, and their confession is celebration of the advent of Christ. This is the critical moment that constitutes the history of them all—this "crisis of the world," to use an expression from the Fourth Gospel (John 12:31). Nonetheless, we must surely add, they do not all have the same history. They belong to the one Church only by belonging to one of the churches. The reason that they have their particular, as well as common, confessions is that they have their particular histories, which lead them to speak in different ways about the one foundation. Some of the differences may well be anachronistic, ready for the museum or the scrap heap. But differences there will always be. Their inevitability need not be deplored, any more than we regret the variety of witness to Christ that we find already in the New Testament. What must be deplored in our day is the lingering illusion that one way of recalling the common heritage is absolutely right, and not merely one contribution to the family conversation.

It was never the intention of the Lutheran Reformers, for example, to set aside the ancient creeds. On the contrary, their *Book of Concord* (1580) expressly reaffirmed them as the "chief symbols" of the Christian faith,[20] and one might well say that the Reformation began as a defense of one article in the Apostles' Creed: "I believe . . . in the forgiveness of sins." The young Martin Luther became convinced that both the practice and the theology of the church in his day endangered the catholic confession of forgiveness, which, if it means anything at all, is a work of God's free grace in Jesus Christ. At the heart of the Reformation creeds is the rediscovery of the gospel of the glory and grace of God as (in Luther's memorable phrase) "the real treasure of the Church."[21] No doubt, the special emphasis of the Augsburg Confession (1530), dictated by the needs of the time, imparted a distinctive character to the Lutheran church within the Christian family. But the confession did not question the catholic faith; it judged abuses in the church by the norm of the gospel.[22] Though not a liturgical confession, it was, and is, a safeguard against forgetfulness; as such, it fits the basic use of Christian creeds and belongs, in a sense, to us all, whether we are Lutherans or not.

Much the same thing can be said of the creeds and confessions of other churches. In intention, at least (and it is not my purpose to comment on their success), they are reminders: they correct, shape, and sustain the consciousness of the believing community by recalling the one foundation that constitutes the history of *all* the churches. "For no one can lay any foundation other than the one that has been laid; that foundation is Jesus Christ" (1 Cor. 3:11). That is a simple historical fact, and each builder, as the Apostle says, "must choose with care how to build on it" (v. 10). Time will show how well each has built. "The Day will disclose it" (v. 13).

A Confessional Theology

If my case so far has been sound, then the justification for confessions of faith is sociological: they are part of the socializing activity by which the community remains true to itself and by which faith is both imparted and nurtured. The anticredalists, however understandable their protest may be, focus too narrowly on the use of confessions as tests of orthodoxy. We can turn the edge of their criticism if we insist that this is by no means the primary use of confessions, gladly conceding that tests of orthodoxy risk a misleading reduction of faith to beliefs. And we will point out that anticredalism, in turn, has its own risk: in its plea for liberty of conscience, or freedom of expression, it may weaken the social context of faith and move religion too far into the private domain. The church as a historic community may then dissolve into transient associations for the sharing of individual experiences or concerns.[23] We do not need to say: This, our confession, is the Catholic Faith, "which Faith except every one do keep whole and undefiled, without doubt he shall perish everlastingly."[24] But we do insist that there cannot be a Christian faith without a confessing church that lives by looking to the rock from which it was hewn (cf. Isa. 51:1).

Confessions are not, of course, the only means by which a religious community preserves its common language. Churches that have no formal creeds may have the functional equivalent in their favorite hymns, for example; one may well speak of the Christian hymn as a "sung confession of faith."[25] In the broad sense in which I have been describing it, a "confessing church" can exist without creeds in the strict sense of written and officially authorized statements of faith. All I have done is to show how written confessions of faith can have a place in the life of the church, along with other means of spiritual formation, without necessarily falling under in the condemnation of the anticredalists. If it is once conceded that the very survival of a church depends on preserving its identity through recollection, then a legitimate function for confessions of faith is assured. Neither does the absence of confessions guarantee the absence of intolerance. Even the noncreedal churches may operate with unwritten creeds, and they can be, in practice, quite intolerant of deviations from the approved language.

This, then, is the argument so far. It has left a great deal unsaid. I have not looked, for example, at the different types of creed or confession, which reflect a variety of uses subordinate to the regulative use of preserving identity. My excuse is that I have written about the nature and history of Christian creeds elsewhere.[26] If one were to peruse that history, it would become clear that Christian creeds had their original place in a liturgical, rather than a legal, setting, and that they serve the church's regular, day-to-day needs. The view one often hears that a creed is a response to some urgent crisis in the life of the church proves to be as one-sided as the view that creeds are tests of correct belief. Every historical confession of faith was certainly addressed to some particular moment in the community's situation. But the "crisis" from which they all derive their power and urgency is the event they recall, and the church is summoned to proclaim it "in season and out of season" (2 Tim. 4:2).[27]

The diverse uses and occasions of Christian creeds are reflected in the traditional titles they bear. An affirmation of communal identity having the official sanction of a church might be called "creed," "confession," "articles of faith," "canons," "decrees," "catechism," "declaration," "covenant," "consensus," "platform," "apology," and so on. Arguably, however, it is the original liturgical setting that best conveys the basic function of identity maintenance. Worship brings the life of the community to a "ritual focus."[28] In the course of the liturgy (or service of worship), the Apostles' Creed, say, and a sermon on the catechism might take their place alongside hymns and prayers, the reading of Scripture, and the celebration of the Eucharist as the church's cumulative affirmation of the redemptive events by which it lives.

If this is the meaning of a confessing church, what does it imply about the task of a confessional theology? It should go without saying by now that when I venture to reply by stating the position of my own church, I do not pretend to offer anything more than a contribution to the forum of ecumenical debate. Even for someone who agrees with what I have said about a confessing church, there is more than one possible way to turn next in defining a confessional theology. It should also go without saying that the road I myself take is not marked "For Presbyterians Only." I simply ask for the privilege of speaking out of my own small corner in the expectation that others will do likewise, as they should. As I see it, then, to do confessional theology is to accept at least two fundamental obligations: to work always out of the confessional heritage of the church, and sometimes, as the occasion arises, to work toward a new confession of faith. In the brief remarks that follow, I want to look first at the *presupposition* of a confessional theology, so understood; second, at one recent *product* of it. The presupposition is what we might call "open confessionalism," and the product I shall take by way of illustration is the Brief Statement of Faith adopted in 1991 by the Presbyterian Church (U.S.A.).

Open Confessionalism

The Reformed churches have never had a single preeminent creed like the Augsburg Confession, or a closed symbolic collection like the *Book of Concord*.[29] Their symbolic library has always been "open." In origin, they were a more diverse and international family than the Lutherans, and they did not seal their common allegiance with a common creed. As the Reformed faith spread, it gave birth to new, indigenous statements of faith. Family resemblances can certainly be identified, and an early attempt was made to demonstrate a common mind by means of a "harmony" of extracts from the Reformed confessions, arranged topically. The full title of the work was *A Harmony of the Confessions of Faith of the Orthodox and Reformed Churches That Purely Profess the Sacred Doctrine of the Gospel in All the Chief Kingdoms, Nations, and Provinces of Europe*.[30] The time of its publication, in 1581, made the *Harmony* a Reformed answer to the Lutheran *Book of Concord* (1580). (The compilers actually presumed to include the Augsburg Confession, albeit in the revised version of 1540.) The differences from Lutheran confessionalism are immediately clear. None of the Reformed confessions used for the

Harmony was ever given universal authority; neither did any of the Reformed churches confer symbolic status on the *Harmony* itself, as the Lutherans did on their *Book of Concord*. To the contrary, the *Harmony* in effect sanctioned particularity and (within limits) pluralism. From the first, every Reformed confession was understood to belong to a particular time and place.[31]

A glance at the individual confessions shows a willingness to draw the natural inference from historical particularity: several of them expressly acknowledge their own reformability. Indeed, they invite criticism and correction, pointing to the Scriptures as the higher authority by which they wish to be judged. Most winsome is the preamble to the Scots Confession (1560), which makes this request:

> . . . if any man will note in our Confession any chapter or sentence contrary to God's Holy Word, that it would please him of his gentleness and for Christian charity's sake to inform us of it in writing; and we, upon our honour, do promise him that by God's grace we shall give him satisfaction from the mouth of God, that is, from Holy Scripture, or else we shall alter whatever he can prove to be wrong.[32]

Confessions have unquestionably functioned in the Reformed church as the hermeneutic lens through which Scripture is read, but only as long as the church is persuaded that they interpret the Scriptural norm correctly. In a sense, the latest Presbyterian confession has obliged the Scots with at least one demand for alteration. The Scots Confession asserts that "the Holy Ghost will not permit [women] to preach in the congregation."[33] The Brief Statement says that the Spirit "calls women and men to all ministries of the Church."[34] The change arises from the conviction that it would be a mistake to transfer to our own world the biblical injunction that women should be silent in the churches (1 Cor. 14:34-35).[35]

The Reformed confessions disclaim infallibility. Similarly, they disclaim finality. Even if they *were* perfectly free from error (which they do not pretend to be), there would still be a need to keep the book open simply because history refuses to stand still, and what is said truly today is not always said appropriately for another day. In effect, Calvin's offspring have applied to their confessions of faith the rules Calvin proposed for judging church synods or councils, which, after all, are the authorizing source of creeds and confessions. Calvin acknowledged that what the pastors or bishops of the church decide in council must have greater weight than whatever an individual thinks up at home or a group of individuals puts together in private.[36] But in reading the judgments of a council we must always take due account of the time when it met, the issue under discussion, and the intention and qualifications of the people who were present. Then we are ready to examine the issue in the light of Scripture.[37] In other words, not only are the pronouncements of a church council subordinate to the word of God; they are also to be understood historically. And Calvin thought that even the best councils have their limits, because even the best human beings have their limits: sometimes they lack the necessary expertise; sometimes they are carried away by their emotions; and we can hardly expect them to foresee every problem that will arise later. A council's decision has the force of a *praejudicium*, by which Calvin did not mean a prejudice, but a provisional judgment, pending further reflection.[38] As Karl Barth said, a Reformed confession holds good *bis auf weiteres*, "for the time being."[39]

This does not mean that Reformed confessions are scrapped every year or two. It means, rather, that the old confessions have their influence on the mind of the church in large measure indirectly, through the church's leaders. For the Reformed theologian, the Westminster Confession, say, read historically, can be just as much a present guide as the Augsburg Confession is to the Lutherans. And, as a matter of fact, the confessions do not all grow old at the same rate. Some, such as the incomparable Heidelberg Catechism (1563), seem ageless. The Catechism is as durable as its opening question and answer. "What is your only comfort, in life and in death?" Answer: "That I belong—body and soul, in life and in death—not to myself but to my faithful Savior, Jesus Christ."[40] Other confessions (I will not say which) it seems unkind to inflict even on the elders and deacons of the church. But the Presbyterian Church (U.S.A.) has shown good sense, I think, in including some of both sorts in its *Book of Confessions*. Its ministers are not required to discriminate between them but to answer the questions: "Will you be instructed and led by those confessions as you lead the people of God?" and, "Will you be a minister of the Word and Sacrament in obedience to Jesus Christ, under the authority of Scripture, and continually guided by our confessions?"[41] In a sense, the pledge to be continually guided by the confessions is stronger than simply to affirm that you think they are right.

But the task of shaping the common language of the community cannot be wholly indirect—turned over to the professionals, who are trained to think historically. There is surely a need for a confession *of the church*. And the dilemma of a confessional (not just confessing) church is that in time even the noblest creed, taken as a whole and not merely quoted by favorite parts, loses its ability to speak directly to the congregation or, better, to articulate the living voice of the congregation—

to rally the assembled company and to renew its sense of identity and purpose. One of the ironies of church history is that by clinging to the Westminster Confession Presbyterians almost lost the confessional character of their church. As a whole, it simply could not serve any longer as the banner around which the church could muster. Its champions, afraid of apostasy, seemed to defend it only as a token or for one or two items that it conveniently enshrined. An open confessionalism means that the confessing church must be ready to draft a new confession—to address the needs of the day in the idiom of the day. And it is the task of a confessional theology, working deferentially out of the heritage of the past, to work toward this end. A confessional church, if I may so put it, ventures to produce a new confession only when it has first admitted (with the prophet Elijah) that we are not better than our forebears. It is just that the world has changed: things have happened that our forebears could not have foreseen, and the church is summoned to think afresh about the ecclesial identity its confessions are designed to secure. Which brings me to the Brief Statement of Faith.

A Brief Statement of Faith

Others have given an account of the making of the newest Presbyterian confession, and there is a line-by-line commentary on it.[42] I want to confine my observations to just one point: the way in which the Brief Statement reflects and furthers the direction Reformed confessionalism has taken in the twentieth century. A turning point came in 1967, when the United Presbyterian Church in the U.S.A. adopted a confession on reconciliation. Ingeniously, it was titled "The Confession of 1967," or "C-67" for short. One Presbyterian theologian remarked: "*C-67 recaptures and intensifies the understanding of faith* held by Luther and Calvin. Everything else in the Confession hangs on this one accomplishment."[43] By this he meant faith, not as assent to a system of doctrine, but rather as response to the reconciling activity of God in Jesus Christ. Similarly, one of our church historians suggested that C-67 marked a redefinition of "confession," not as the affirmation of beliefs, but as witness to the grace of God in Christ. "That witness," he adds, "was decisively oriented toward the world." Hence: "C-67 moved toward a functional or mission-oriented understanding of confessionalism."[44] A confession was no longer a catalog of beliefs; it was a commitment to Jesus Christ and to the ministry of reconciliation that this commitment entails. The church is required, by consequence, to speak out on all those conflicts—between one race and another, nation and nation, rich and poor, male and female—

that divide the human community and threaten to tear it apart. The Brief Statement moves confessionalism in exactly the same direction.[45]

The statement is intended for use as a liturgical confession. It remains to be seen how well it works in the context of worship. (Everyone admitted it is too long, and everyone could think of something else that just *had* to be added.) But the question is: Why a liturgical creed at all, since we already have the Apostles' and Nicene creeds? There is no desire to *replace* the old creeds; that could be seen as presumptuous and even schismatic (as our Roman Catholic consultants rightly warned us). The design, rather, is to *add* the new confession to the old ecumenical creeds. Why? Because the old creeds, while they seek to protect the church's confession of Jesus Christ, do not say as much as needs to be said in our day about the church that confesses him.

What calls for enlargement is the bare affirmation, "I believe in . . . the holy Catholic Church, the communion of saints." Presbyterians do so believe. But unless it is added that the communion of saints is turned outward to the world, not inward on itself, then the old "Noah's ark" mentality may prevent the saints from being the church, which is not a shelter from the rain but the body of Christ at work in the world. It is not the purpose of the confession to furnish the church with an itemized program—any more than an itemized list of beliefs. But it must impress on the church the self-understanding from which its mission comes, which is: to seek first the rule of God and God's justice (Matt. 6:33). This, in my opinion, is one of the most important things the new confession tries to say. And it is closely linked with another important emphasis: on the ministry of Jesus, as the Gospels portray it.

The Apostles' Creed developed in a time when it was critical to affirm the genuine humanity of the Redeemer. This, the scholars tell us, is why the second article contains an apparent redundancy: the Lord "suffered . . . was crucified, dead, and buried." Calvin's catechism asks: "Why do you jump straight from his birth to his death, leaving out the story of his entire life?" And the pupil is expected to reply: "Because nothing is dealt with here but what belongs strictly to the substance of our redemption."[46] Should Calvin have known better, since he tells us in his *Institutes* that Christ redeems us "by the entire course of his obedience"? "In short," Calvin there says, "he began to pay the price of liberation for our redemption from the moment when he took on the form of a servant."[47] But even in the *Institutes*, Calvin makes nothing of the ministry of Jesus.

The Brief Statement, by contrast, moves from the ministry of Jesus to the mission of the church. The self-understanding of the church is grounded in the redeeming words and deeds of Jesus' life. If it is the church's mission "to hear the voices of people long silenced, and to work with others for justice, freedom, and peace," the reason is that "Jesus proclaimed the reign of God: preaching good news to the poor and release to the captives."[48] In this, after all, Calvin is on my side. He tells us that the purpose of the eucharistic service, in which the confession of our faith has its place, is to impart to us the life of Christ. And he adds: "The life of Christ consists in this: to seek and to save the lost."[49]

The question with which I ended chapter 3, "How do those who have it actually come by their faith in God?" has led, with some guidance from the sociologists, to a reappraisal of Christian creeds. To the "enlightened," a creed is plain evidence that faith is mindless surrender to authority. For ourselves, who take faith to be the perception of meaning in one's life, creeds or confessions are a natural token of the fact that faith, in this sense, is given in community. Moreover, the appearance of inflexibility that the antidogmatists deplore in a church's fidelity to old creeds is mollified by recognition that confession is a never-ending task because the situation of the believing community changes and gives rise to new demands and new insights. A confessional theology, on which I shall have more to say in the final chapter, is always oriented to this task.

By now we can venture something like a concluding definition of a confession of faith, or, better perhaps, a redefinition. As far as it goes, there is little wrong with the old definitions, which make a confession an official codification of the faith of the church, or the faith of *a* church. But we will avoid the identification of "faith" with "beliefs," and our redefinition will be functional and mission-oriented: *A confession of faith is an official codification of a church's world of meaning that seeks, through recollection of the founding events, to reaffirm the historical identity of the church and to reformulate its mission in a new day.* As such, a confession is one of the means by which faith is imparted and confirmed.

There are, no doubt, difficulties in this understanding of confessions. It is intended as a *via media* between rigorous adherence to the old creeds and total rejection of any creeds whatever; and, like every mediating view, it is liable to objections from both sides. Anticredal churches have other means of socialization, and churches that are less willing than mine to admit the reformability of their creeds (perhaps having less need to do so) prefer to adapt their confession to the new day by pronouncements and teaching aids, not new creeds. The decided anticredalist will suspect that, sooner or later, the old tyranny will return, while a stricter confessionalist will protest that reformable creeds are no creeds at all. On the one side is the admonition that any attempt to define the identity of the community will drive many out of it; on the other, the accusation that a flexible definition explains why so many have left already. The debate goes on.

My own conviction is that creeds or confessions, in the sense defined, certainly belong to the well-being of the church, if not to its very being; it is hard to imagine how we might do without them. And while I am eager to learn from the great systems of doctrine embodied in some of the Reformation confessions, I think that the best creeds are those that teach the churches to get their priorities straight, even at the cost of leaving a few things out. If the real treasure of the church is the gospel of the grace of God, Ulrich Zwingli began well enough when he wrote the first Reformed confession of faith: "The sum of the Gospel is that our Lord Jesus Christ, the true Son of God, has made known to us the will of His heavenly Father, and by His innocence has redeemed us from death and reconciled us unto God. . . . All who regard another doctrine as equal to or higher than the Gospel err and do not know what the Gospel is."[50]

To keep our own priorities straight, we must ask what it means to confess, with Zwingli, that salvation rests on faith in the gospel of Jesus Christ. This, our last question, requires us to shift into the dogmatic mode. We have to show, first (in chapter 5), where faith in Jesus Christ fits in a system of doctrine, and we have to ask, second (in chapter 6), what can finally be said about the connection of faith with Jesus Christ in the light of our conclusions on the nature of faith, its social matrix, and the task of a confessional theology. And it may be as well to recall what I said in my preface. I am not constructing a linear argument but building a case for a particular way of interpreting faith in Christ. The question of faith in Christ has been present from the outset, even if not always evident. My procedure has not required of me a strict *remotio Christi*, as Anselm might put it—leaving Christ entirely out of view—but only a change of perspectives, the last of which will be expressly dogmatic.[51]

Chapter 5
THE DOCTRINE OF FAITH

Where the idea of the whole rules throughout, you have a system.
Immanuel Kant

We will exhaust the entire range of Christian doctrine if we consider the facts of the devout self-consciousness, first, as they are presupposed by the antithesis [of sin and grace] expressed in the concept of redemption; second, as they are determined by it.
Friedrich Schleiermacher

God is not far from each one of us.
Acts 17:27

In the first three chapters, I looked at only a very small fragment of the literature on faith. But the results were complex enough, if not confusing, because I tried to move beyond the customary oversimplifications. The prevailing view, I suspect, still takes faith to be "firm or unquestioning belief in something for which there is no proof." "Faith" certainly may have that meaning; I am simply quoting sense 2,a,1 in *Webster's Third New International Dictionary*. And from this definition, or something like it, academic discussions tend to move quickly to the question whether faith, so understood, can be justified: whether one is, or may be, within one's epistemic rights in holding something to be true "on faith." Church folk are generally less worried than professors about the epistemological status of faith, more interested in its content: they want to hear about the beliefs they hold, or are supposed to hold, as Christians. But by and large they, too, assume that faith is believing certain things, taking them on trust: that God exists, that Jesus was God, that there is a life after death, and so on.

Such a conception of faith, we can now say, is an oversimplification. As John Calvin remarks: "We must understand that the meaning of the word 'faith' is ambiguous."[1] He had in mind only the meaning or meanings of "faith" in the Bible, and the linguistic data are even more ambiguous as soon as we venture outside the Old and New Testaments. Calvin's definition of "faith" resembles Martin Luther's but differs strikingly from Thomas Aquinas's, though they all thought they were defining Christian faith. If Martin Buber was right, Christianity would represent (in the main) another type of faith altogether than the faith of Judaism, and Jesus' faith would be more Jewish than Christian. Friedrich Karl Forberg thought that genuine religious faith is a matter not of what you believe, but of how you behave; you can leave beliefs to theologians and philosophers. Wilfred Cantwell Smith, who also contrasts faith with intellectual belief, thinks it possible to view faith as a unifying bond between religions, but he does not argue that faith is exactly the same in all of them. And finally—to draw the list to a close—in F. H. Jacobi and James Fowler, as in Smith, the word "faith" does not necessarily carry a religious connotation at all. You might possibly wish to argue that something like "conviction without proof" is a common element in all these accounts of faith. But to *reduce* faith to such a narrow definition would be singularly unhelpful.

As we went along, however, I tried to show that the diversity does not leave us with sheer chaos and confusion. Sometimes what appear to be sharply opposed definitions of Christian faith turn out to be more a matter of different emphases. And I have argued, quite simply, (1) that Christian or "saving" faith is one instance of comprehensive meaning construction, and (2) that it presupposes certain inevitable beliefs that Christians hold in common with everyone else around them. In this way, it has proved possible to weave a number of distinct strands into what begins to emerge, I hope, as a clear pattern. I have represented saving faith not as something totally unique—in a class by itself—but as one of the ways in which persons construe their experience religiously. Moreover, Christian and non-Christian faiths do not simply take their place alongside one another as exclusive alternatives; with some of them Christian faith overlaps inasmuch as they, too, hold the theistic conception of God as transcendent creator and preserver of the world. And Christian faith overlaps even with nonreligious constructions of meaning insofar as they, too, share a certain elemental faith in the order of the world we all inhabit together.

If, then, we concentrate now on these three—elemental, theistic, and Christian faith—the question naturally arises: What more can be said of the relationship between them from a strictly theological point of view? Or can Christian theology set this question aside and confine itself wholly to "saving," Christian faith? I want to try to show in this chapter not only that clarification of the various concepts of faith is a necessary prerequisite of dogmatic theology but also that the structure of dogmatics itself may be so conceived that it turns on the relationship between what I am calling "elemental," "theistic," and "Christian" faith. And, in the final section of the chapter, I will illustrate some of the ways in which the dogmatic model I propose can be both intellectually responsible and of practical use in the ministry of the church.

The Shape of Christian Dogmatics

By "dogmatics" I mean the division of theological studies that seeks to present the whole faith of the church, or of a church, in its systematic coherence—the way it all holds together. I recognize the problems under which such a discipline must labor. It is not merely that the very word "dogmatic" has acquired derogatory associations, so that I would gladly use another if a better one were available.[2] "Dogmatic" suggests an obstinate and overbearing insistence on one's own opinions—a pathetic remnant of the age of authority. More serious: we still live to some extent with the legacy of the 1960s, when the death of God was announced in the public news media and a period of impressive theological construction came to an end. Even those who did not turn their backs on the theological task were inclined to admit that the times were not right for theological construction on the grand scale; many in the theological guild spoke rather of an "occasional" theology that would be content to address the most urgent issues one at a time. This, I believe, was a mistake. Theology, if it wants to be taken seriously, cannot permit its questions to arise haphazardly. Moreover, the very meaning of the beliefs in which the Christian community gives expression to its faith can be understood only in their relation to one another: they form a "system." And if this system is not to remain esoteric, ghettoized, it must somehow be brought into relation with the beliefs entertained more generally outside the Christian community.

When I first began to study theology, I must admit that, like most beginners in the field, I had no conception of Christian doctrine as an organic whole. Beginners, as a rule, mean by "systematic theology" joining the conversation on the latest topic of theological interest, whatever it happens to be. A little education moved me quickly beyond that exhilarating delusion, and I realized that systematic theology had to be systematic. Even then, I took this to mean simply "comprehensive" or "all-inclusive." I would begin at the beginning and keep going until I reached the end, checking off *every* topic and not just talking about the newest and hottest one. It took a while longer before it occurred to me that there might be a difficulty in deciding where to begin, and where to move next. The cumulative practice of the past seemed to make any such questions an unnecessary waste of time. You do what everyone else seems to have done: you begin by establishing the sources of dogmatics, then run chronologically through the works of God—past, present, and to come. But is it really that easy?

Calvin's "Institutes"

It was John Calvin who first brought home to me the possibility that dogmatics might be something more than a complete assemblage of Christian beliefs. It is true that Calvin himself, no doubt under the influence of the Lutheran theologian Philipp Melanchthon, at first saw it as his task in the *Institutes* to run in turn through all the main topics in what he called "the Christian philosophy." But by the time he came to make the final revision of the work (1559), he had evidently had some interesting second thoughts about the arrangement of the material. First, the entire work is now prefaced with the fascinating discourse (first introduced into the 1539 edition) on piety and the nature of religion. Second, a new ordering principle is introduced: the twofold knowledge of God as creator and redeemer. There has been endless scholarly debate about the significance of both of these features of Calvin's 1559 *Institutes*, and initially they may not strike the reader as worth so much argument. They show, however, that Calvin had moved beyond the method of topics (theological *loci* or "commonplaces") to a more organic conception of how the parts of a dogmatic system fit together. He himself indicates that the new arrangement was important to him, and the changes are well worth a closer look.[3]

After the famous opening chapter on the two correlative parts of wisdom (knowledge of God and knowledge of self), Calvin actually begins his *Institutes* neither with the authority of Scripture nor with the doctrine of creation, but—surprisingly, perhaps—with a discussion of innate human religiousness. On the basis of common experience—and with a great deal of help from the Roman philosopher-statesman Cicero (106–43 B.C.E.)—he offers what we might call a description of the religious consciousness as the capacity that distinguishes humans from the rest of the animal kingdom. Calvin's remarks on the inborn "sense of divinity" are not as crystal clear as one would like them to be. One may well ask what they are doing there at all, especially since they are so heavily dependent on a pagan philosopher of religion (*ille ethnicus*, as Calvin describes him: "the well-known pagan"). Whatever happened to *scriptura sola*?

Some interpreters argue that Calvin assigns no other function to the sense of divinity than to establish the common guilt of humanity, none of whom, though they knew God, honored God as God. The seed of religion, implanted in all, has remained barren and fruitless. Hence, it is said, in this roundabout way Calvin *is*, in fact, simply making the case for the necessity and authority of Scripture. But this, I am convinced, cannot be all he intends. The saving knowledge revealed in the word, when it comes, attaches itself to a remnant of the natural knowledge of God; if it were not so, Calvin's famous comparison of the word to a pair of spectacles, which bring to clear focus an otherwise confused knowledge, would make no sense.[4] The innate awareness of God, though suppressed or perverted into idolatry, remains, we must surely say, as the condition for the possibility of revelation—the point of contact between the gospel and the mind warped by sin.

When Calvin finally turns to the doctrine of creation, he seems at first sight to settle into much more conventional lines of thought. In premodern dogmatics, the place of creation was automatically dictated by the assumption that the creation was act one in a sequence of divine acts. The order was supposedly historical or chronological. Implementing the eternal decrees, God first created the world and humans; then, when Eve and Adam fell through disobedience, God intervened in human history by the election of a chosen people; in the fullness of time, God became human in Jesus of Nazareth, now continues to establish God's rule through the spread of the church, and in the end will bring the sequence of temporal events to its conclusion with the Day of Judgment. If we remove the divine decrees beyond time, the creation appears as the first act in a divine drama, and Calvin would have needed no lengthy reflection to make the knowledge of God the creator the theme of book one of the *Institutes*. In the temporal sequence of divine works, creation is where it all begins; redemption and eternal bliss are where it is going, at any rate for the privileged elect.

Take a closer look, however, and you find another way in which Calvin relates knowledge of the creator and knowledge of the redeemer, reversing the priority. In the quasi-historical order, knowledge of the creator is naturally first: Adam and Eve enjoyed a relationship with their maker that would have led them to blessedness, had they remained innocent. But they fell, and the path back to the maker leads by way of the cross. Knowledge of the redeemer must now come first, because only believers in Christ—the church, the elect—see the world through the spectacles of the word.[5] In the order of individual experience, then, since the fall, those who have first been redeemed can alone have knowledge of God the creator—or at least sound, unconfused knowledge. The doctrine of redemption actually has dogmatic priority over the doctrine of creation, which entirely depends upon it: a genuine awareness of God as creator is strictly a function of being redeemed, albeit this did not lead Calvin to talk about redemption first.

Schleiermacher's "Christian Faith"

The dogmatic relationship between creation and redemption that first impressed me in reading Calvin was confirmed later in my reading of Friedrich Schleiermacher, who, I think, furnishes much clearer terms for it and frees it from Calvin's parochialism. For Schleiermacher, dogmatics is *Glaubenslehre*, the "doctrine of faith"; it is about the Christian "way of believing," in which everything is determined by the redemption accomplished by Jesus of Nazareth. In other words, faith in redemption is the proper subject matter of Christian theology: it constitutes the second, or main, part of Schleiermacher's dogmatic work *The Christian Faith* (1821–22, 1830–31^{2}). The introduction begins from the innate awareness of God, which Schleiermacher calls "the feeling of absolute dependence," and part one is on the doctrines of creation and providence, or (as he prefers to say) creation and "preservation," in which the feeling of absolute dependence is expressed. The sequence—creation, preservation, redemption—is once again conventional. But the reasons for it are not. The doctrines are not supposed to be in chronological order, as though God first made the world, then preserved it, and finally redeemed it. The heading Schleiermacher gave to the first part of his system is carefully and precisely formulated: "First Part of the Doctrine of Faith: Elucidation of the Religious Self-Consciousness as It Is Always Presupposed, but Also Always Contained, in Every Christian Religious Affection."

"Presupposed" and "contained" are the key words. First, Christian faith in the redemption brought about by Jesus Christ *presupposes* certain things about the way one sees the world and its relation to God, and these presuppositions form the proper subject matter of the doctrines of creation and preservation. In a nutshell: Christian faith presupposes a world whose course is absolutely reliable because it is wholly dependent on a single absolute causality, which is what is meant by a Creator-God. But this is not only a logical presupposition. The point is also, so to say, psychological: it is a matter of how the believer in Jesus Christ actually experiences the created order and construes it as wholly dependent on a Creator-God. Because she sees it as the stage or theater of redemption, she trusts its progress as absolutely reliable. Second, then, belief in creation and preservation is not only presupposed by but *contained in* Christian belief in redemption. Christians perceive the world as a divinely-governed system because, to them, it is the place where God in Christ is redemptively at work.

I will try to indicate later why these interesting reflections of Schleiermacher seem to me of immense theological importance. For now, we can surely view them as a development of Calvin's insistence on the dogmatic priority of redemption over creation, though there are certainly differences between the two dogmaticians, which I will not try to spell out here. Christian "redemption faith" presupposes and contains within itself a "creation faith," but not because only the elect have clear vision. On the contrary, Schleiermacher thinks that Christians hold an understanding of the world that is shared, in essentials, by Jews and Moslems. That is why I suggested that he not only clarifies the relationship between the Christian doctrines of creation and redemption but frees them from Calvin's parochialism. Calvin, it is true, had a stronger sense of the community of Christians with Jews than Schleiermacher did, because Calvin held to the unity of the two testaments in a single covenant of grace. ("Who, then," he asks in one place, "would dare to make the Jews destitute of Christ?")[6] But he had no interest in acknowledging the common ground between Christianity and Islam in the doctrine of creation. The Turks, he remarks, proclaim at the tops of their lungs that the creator of heaven and earth is their God, but in repudiating Christ they put an idol in the place of the true God.[7] Schleiermacher no longer views all non-Christian faiths as idolatrous products of human sinfulness. He recognizes that under the heading "creation and preservation" there will be at least some statements that express monotheism in general, even though in a Christian dogmatics we must not think of them as detached in actual experience from faith in Christ.[8]

A Revised Model of Dogmatics

There is one respect, however, in which I have presumed to suggest a modification of Schleiermacher's scheme—or, if you like, a further development of Calvin's model.[9] It is an oddity, perhaps a defect, of Schleiermacher's argument that when he tries to press back to a still more general definition of what unites the various ways of believing, including the monotheistic faiths, the word "faith" does not itself play the decisive role. In fact, readers of this work, which is devoted to Christian faith, may be surprised to discover just how little Schleiermacher's *The*

Christian Faith actually has to say anywhere about the concept of faith. Instead, we hear of "the religious self-consciousness," "the religious affections," "piety," and "the feeling of absolute dependence," the last of which seems to correspond to Calvin's "sense of divinity." If the subject matter of dogmatics is Christian faith as a way of believing, then it surely makes the best sense to begin with the question: What is faith, or what does it mean to believe?

Schleiermacher actually came very close to so phrasing the first question of dogmatics in the earlier edition of his work, when he wrote: "There is something common to every kind of faith (*in allen Glaubensweisen*) by virtue of which we put them all together as kin, and something peculiar in each, by virtue of which we separate it from the rest."[10] He no doubt had in mind the historical religions, of which Judaism and Islam were the two that, along with Christianity, most interested him. But to communicate what Christian dogmatics is about, it seems to me a natural enough move to press back, beyond the historical religions, to less explicitly religious ways of believing, including that "inevitable belief," as A. J. Balfour called it (or "elemental faith" as I propose we call it), that we inhabit an orderly world. We can then try to see if this elemental faith might be taken to perform somewhat the same dogmatic function as Calvin's "sense of divinity" and Schleiermacher's "feeling of absolute dependence."

The actual presentation of Christian dogmatics will then incorporate all three of the kinds of faith from which I began: elemental faith, theistic or creation faith, and distinctively Christian or redemption faith. But the three will not be related like the foundation, the first story, and the second story of a house; they will be related rather as simultaneous moments of consciousness. It is *because* Christians believe in Jesus Christ that they trust the reliability of the natural order; *because* they see nature as the theater of redemption, they are reassured that human existence is not chaotic but ordered and meaningful. A dogmatic system, then, is not a complicated proof in which one first lays a philosophical foundation, then erects a full-blown natural theology upon it, and lastly finishes off the building with the truths of revelation. It is an attempt to uncover descriptively or phenomenologically the layers of a complex mode of consciousness, moving in presentation from the most abstract content to the most concrete: that is, from elemental faith (in the introduction), through theistic creation faith (in part 1), to the Christian redemption faith (in part 2) in which the other two kinds of faith are contained.

Dogmatic Theology in the University and the Church

So far, I have tried to sketch the task and shape of dogmatic theology, as I understand it. I take dogmatics to be a kind of excavation or archaeology, if you like, of the Christian consciousness: it seeks to uncover the layers of faith in the mind of a believer in Christ. But, admittedly, I have presented the data somewhat formally and abstractly, and the impatient reader may be wondering: What's the point? Why do I think it worthwhile to develop this model of dogmatics? The answer is twofold. If I read the signs of the times correctly, we are presently in danger of developing two antagonistic types of theology: one in the university, and one in the seminary. I would wish to claim that my dogmatic model has a legitimate place in both contexts, and that it can—for this reason—provide a needed link between the two. These, I admit, are broad generalizations and large claims; they need a great deal of refinement. But let's take them as at least a point of departure. Consider first the university context.

Dogmatics in the University[11]

In the university, the theologian is often perceived as a kind of fifth columnist—the agent of a foreign power, engaged in sabotage. The security of the university depends on unswerving loyalty to the disinterested pursuit of truth by means of universally accessible methods of inquiry. And it is widely assumed in the academy that theologians are advocates of exclusive and esoteric truths, which are not open to public assessment. Theology, in this view, is the ideology that underwrites the cause of the churches, or whatever causes the churches are currently promoting, and the appeal to revelation serves to forestall the kind of critical scrutiny that is directed routinely at any other truth claims. The ultimate loyalty of the theologian is to the churches and their values, not to the university and the values of the academic community. Hence, if theology still has a place in the university—simply for now-obsolete historical reasons—it no longer belongs at the center of the intellectual enterprise: it has become marginalized, moved out to the fringes of an enterprise that in our time rightfully falls to the natural and social sciences and the humanities. As Robert Maynard Hutchins (1899–1977) so bluntly put it in 1936, when he was president of the University of Chicago: "Theology is banned by law from some universities. It might as well be from the rest. Theology is based on revealed truth and on articles of faith. We are a faithless generation and take no stock in revelation. Theology implies orthodoxy and an orthodox church. We have neither."[12] And in case there should be any doubt about it, Hutchins later explained that he meant dogmatic theology, "which rests upon faith, or supernatural knowledge."[13]

Hutchins was never, I think, antireligious, though he gradually left his boyhood religion behind him. His father was a Protestant minister and professor of homiletics. Hutchins was still a communicant in good standing when, at the age of 30, he was made president of the University of Chicago—to become one of the foremost educational theorists in America. His biographer tells us that, as he entered his thirties, "the voice of the Calvinist God, or any other, was no longer clearly audible to him."[14] Hutchins recalled the exact moment when the cord finally broke. At first, he regularly attended the university chapel. But one Sunday morning the dean's sermon opened with the attention-getting sentence: "Yesterday I was on the golf course and as I teed off I was reminded that we must follow through in life." Hutchins acquired a weekend hideaway and never attended chapel again. Not that what he heard in the chapel was untrue, but he said that he had heard such truths sufficiently often and "sometimes in a better literary framework."[15]

Now the revelation that came to the dean on the golf course was not exactly what Hutchins had in mind when he described theology as "based on revelation." He meant the old, authoritarian kind of dogmatic theology that was put forward as the science of supernaturally communicated truths—the kind that answered to the concept of faith as compliance with the voice of the church. I agree with Hutchins that a discipline so defined has no place in the modern, secular university. The theologian of today, if she works in a university context, cannot stand at the podium and say: "This is the Catholic Faith, which except a man believe faithfully, he cannot be saved."[16] But, like the university itself, theology has moved on. In the model I have advocated, the university theologian says more modestly: "This, as I understand it, is the way one important part of the human family believes." And she welcomes dialogue with those who have an insider's understanding of other ways of believing. In the academy, the old humanistic motto holds good: "I am a human: I count nothing human foreign to me."[17]

Ideally, the university then becomes the home of an interfaith dialogue that is limited only by our finite resources, not by special pleading for one way of believing to the exclusion of others. Back in the 1960s, the decisive step forward was taken in some of the state universities, which had previously banned theology on the grounds of the separation of church and state. The Constitution of the United States, in the First

Amendment (1791) of the Bill of Rights, was taken to prohibit the preference of one religion above the rest but not the study of religions impartially. The strategy adopted at that time was to make room for complementary appointments in Roman Catholic, Protestant, and Jewish thought, and it was quickly extended to the study of Far Eastern religions as well. More recently, if we learned anything at all from the turbulent 1980s, it was surely the urgent need to understand, in addition, the religion of Islam. The ignorance of our political leaders during the Iranian hostage crisis was a source of much embarrassment. We are told that a leading authority on the faith of Islam was flown weekly to Washington to give the State Department a crash course on what Moslems believe—and what they don't believe, such as the separation of religion and politics.

Dogmatics in the Church

The urgency of a global perspective is bound to transform the seminary curriculum, too, in the decades ahead. The old field of missiology (the study of Christian missions) cannot be simply abandoned; it has to be transformed into a genuine interfaith conversation, in which the church actually listens to those it once condescendingly named "heathen" and "infidels." But how does the theological model I propose serve the more immediate needs of the pastor in an American congregation? Unfortunately, while the academy doubts whether church theology is a serious intellectual discipline, the churches, for their part, are often suspicious of the academic theology that goes on in the university. They perceive it as addressed to the wrong audience—to colleagues in other departments of the university, who have put the theologian on the defensive. Academic theology is assumed, by consequence, to serve theoretical rather than practical ends and to have lost touch with the real business of the church.[18]

I suppose that no system of theology has been more sharply judged in this respect than Schleiermacher's *The Christian Faith*, which is forbiddingly dense and demanding. It is true that Schleiermacher did address one of his books—his first—to the cultured despisers of religion: his famous *Speeches*, which appeared in 1799. It is also true (or so I have argued elsewhere)[19] that even if there were no pastors to be educated for the ministry of the church, he could still have defended dogmatics (in his modern version of it) as a humanistic discipline in the university. But he himself in fact taught and wrote dogmatic theology as a church discipline for preachers: no less than Calvin's *Institutes*, Schleiermacher's *The*

Christian Faith was intended for candidates for the ministry; and no less than Barth's fourteen volumes, it was a church dogmatics. He knew well that none of his students would be able to quarry ready-made sermons from his dense paragraphs. He did not wish them to. But he wanted each of them, as future ministers, to assimilate the work for himself.[20]

The result was no doubt different from Calvin's *Institutes* or Barth's later *Church Dogmatics*. What Schleiermacher offered the Protestant minister might be called a "manual on the dynamics of faith": a description of the way Christian believing actually functions, designed for those whose task it is to nurture it. Ernst Troeltsch described Schleiermacher's *Christian Faith* as a "technical" book, not in the sense of being academically esoteric and inaccessible, but rather because its goal is mastery of the "technical" means by which the religious sensibility is represented and stimulated.[21] This, I think, is entirely correct, and it presents a conception of the dogmatic task with which I fully agree. To back this opinion adequately would, of course, take a great deal more discussion than I can offer now. (It would take nothing less than a completed dogmatic system.) But let me try to illustrate the pastoral significance of dogmatics, so understood, for each of the steps I have outlined.

Elemental Faith. The minister of the gospel must know, to begin with, what the gospel is addressed to. The traditional Protestant answer has been that the Christian proclamation speaks to human sinfulness and guilt, so that where guilt is not present it must be induced: the bad news of the law must precede the good news of the gospel. But if my case so far has been sound, we must admit that this understanding of the gospel's function does not quite hit the mark. It is much more context-bound than Protestants have been ready to admit. A message of guilt and inexcusability may have suited Paul's or Luther's struggle with false religion, and I do not doubt that it will always have its place in the proclamation of the word. But the actual point of contact for the gospel is surely elemental faith: confidence in an order that gives meaning to our existence. The gospel comes with the reassurance that this confidence is not a delusion, whatever forces in our life may seem to cast a shadow of doubt over it.

Consequently, I see it as the initial, introductory task of dogmatics to explore the character of this elemental faith: to uncover what it is in the depths of our humanity that resonates with the gospel of Jesus Christ. To carry out this task, the dogmatic theologians need all the insight they can find, not in Scripture alone, not in the tradition of the church alone, but also in the psychologists and the philosophers—and, of course, in those master physicians of the soul who have been there before us.

I have spoken already of at least a few of the psychologists and philosophers from whom I have learned. Among the physicians of the soul, my favorite is that troubled, deeply sensitive genius, F. W. Robertson (1816–53), who became one of the greatest preachers of the Anglican Church, but who first had to pass through a total loss of his Christian faith. In retrospect, Robertson wrote:

> It is an awful moment when the soul begins to find that the props on which it has blindly rested so long are, many of them, rotten, and begins to suspect them all. . . . In that fearful loneliness of spirit, when those who should have been his friends and counsellors only frown upon his misgivings, and profanely bid him stifle doubts . . . I know but one way in which a man may come forth from his agony scathless [sic]; it is by holding fast to those things which are certain still—the grand, simple landmarks of morality. In the darkest hour through which a human soul can pass, whatever else is doubtful, this at least is certain. If there be no God, and no future state, yet, even then, it is better to be generous than selfish, better to be chaste than licentious, better to be true than false, better to be brave than a coward.[22]

This is not a watertight proof for the existence of God—far from it. But it was one man's way of rediscovering the coordinates of *his own* existence. And this elemental faith provided him with the point of contact for renewed faith in God. His subsequent preaching in Trinity Chapel, Brighton, shows the power with which he could stir the same elemental faith in a Christian congregation. Witness, for example, his famous sermon on John 7:17: "Anyone who resolves to do the will of God will know whether the teaching is from God. . . ." It must be one of the laws of nature, Robertson inferred, that *obedience* is the organ of spiritual knowledge.[23] In our terms: he saw deeply into at least one aspect of elemental faith—what I have called "practical belief"—and he knew how to use his insight, born out of his own experience, in his pastoral ministry.

Creation Faith. The first part of dogmatics proper deals with what I have termed the "creation faith" presupposed by faith in Jesus Christ. Here the main point I want to make, by way of illustrating my dogmatic model, is that it ought to lay to rest the anxieties that churchgoers still bring to their pastors about the creation story in Genesis. The problem is especially acute in well-educated congregations, in which the members will have learned a great deal about geology and evolution in school and college and will very likely have concluded that textbook science and biblical religion are in conflict with each other. The conflict flared up as recently as the 1980s with the debate over so-called creation science. Of course, not all working scientists are Darwinians. One of the intriguing facts that emerged in the Arkansas creationism trial in 1981 was that the witnesses on the creationist side were mostly scientists—holders of higher degrees in the natural sciences, occupying academic posts in recognized university faculties. Their adversaries, on the other hand, who spoke against compulsory teaching of creation science in the public schools alongside of evolution, were mostly representatives of religion. Langdon Gilkey reports that in one leading university he discovered four tenured creationists in the natural sciences faculty, none at all in the department of religion.[24] Such interesting data ought to make the educated public wonder about the supposed warfare of science and religion: the warfare appears to be between two rival scientific communities, not between scientists and believers. But the Arkansas trial generated a furor that revealed again the surprising extent to which the creation story of Genesis remains a source of perplexity to many Christians.

From our point of view, the perplexity arises out of a mistaken view of revelation and faith. Revelation is not information, supernaturally communicated, about things that lie outside our experience, such as the way the world began; it is God's *self-disclosure* to us precisely in the midst of our own existence. Faith is our *recognition* of God in this self-disclosure. Genesis 1, therefore, is not to be taken as a revealed account of the beginning of the world; it presents in story form the way the world *is* to the eyes of faith, not how it *began*. Faith perceives the world as wholly under the governance of God, who directs its course to determined ends. This is not at all to depreciate the Genesis narrative but rather to restore it to its original use. Scholars these days are almost unanimously agreed that the literary genre of the creation story is myth: it expresses an understanding of human existence in the form of a narrative about origins.[25] To transform myth into revealed science is a mistake. The common objection that to term the Pentateuchal account "mythical" is to deny its truth actually turns things upside down: the account may very well be true as myth, but it is not true science. It serves to nurture confidence in a world order that is absolutely reliable because wholly under the direction of the creative power of God. Faith can leave it to the scientists to frame hypotheses about how the universe began. The creation faith presupposed by faith in Jesus Christ affirms only that the world, as the theater of redemption, must be orderly, not totally chaotic, in its progress.

So far from being in conflict with natural science, then, Christian faith presupposes what the scientific enterprise itself presupposes. Working scientists, it is true, do not usually like to employ the words "faith" or "belief," which they assume to be religious and alien to objective inquiry.

They are likely to insist that their own confidence in the regularity and predictability of nature is just a working assumption. It has worked nicely for a very long time and probably will continue to do so; if it does not work tomorrow morning, there will be good reason to worry about it then, not now.[26] But the natural scientist whose being is not totally reducible to his or her research is, I think, more likely than the rest of us to wonder at cosmic order. One of our leading astrophysicists, though an agnostic from his youth, recently expressed his awe at "how well everything in the universe works together," and remarked: "I'm beginning to realize there's something out there."[27] That is not a confession of faith in God, but it is interesting to note how readily the sense of cosmic order can generate the thought of "something out there." Like Robertson's hitting the rock bottom of moral obligation, this, too, is one of the ways in which talk about God is occasioned or justified.

It may even be that the scientist, like the religious believer, presupposes that in our corner of the universe order is also moral. We are much less likely these days to insulate scientific inquiry from questions of value, or even of right and wrong.[28] Our research may be carried through with the most rigorous and impersonal scientific procedures; but if, say, the virus was borrowed from somebody else's laboratory (without acknowledgment), we still assume that what is going on is bad science. The presuppositions of religion and science coincide more than is commonly recognized. To show that this is so falls to the task of Christian dogmatics, part one: the doctrine of creation.

Redemption Faith. The theme of redemption brings us back again to where we started—with "saving" faith—and my remarks cannot be anything more than a brief but necessary postscript. The difficulty is that in the doctrine of redemption, more than anywhere else, the interconnectedness of everything is most evident, and the strictly dogmatic task is therefore most urgent: part two has to be treated as a single whole. Wherever you break the circumference, you have to trace the entire circle. What you think of the church will depend on what you think of Christ; how you understand Christ's person will depend on what you believe he did (or does) to redeem you; what you take redemption to be will necessarily correspond with the way you interpret the sin or estrangement that calls for redemption; and so on. Hence I know that I invite other problems when, to head off one problem, I confine myself to a single point: that faith, in the end, is a gift of grace. Nothing I have said so far about faith as meaning construction must be taken to place in doubt this cardinal point of Christian belief.

I have tried to show that the Christian message resonates with an elemental human confidence in an ordered and meaningful environment, a confidence that the doctrine of creation both stirs and articulates. Anyone who looks with Christian eyes at this elemental faith—and at the will-to-meaning that it attests—will be bound to see it as evidence for Paul's assertion at Athens: that God has made the entire human race to search for and find God (Acts 17:26-27). Theologically interpreted, the search for meaning is a search for God, in whom we live, and move, and have our being (v. 28).[29] But Paul's point is not, by any means, that the search is successful.

The problem is that elemental faith, though it appears in thought to be a matter of inevitable belief, in actual experience continually fails and slips away from us. If everyone all the time perceived the environment as structured and therefore meaningful, and if everyone all the time construed the environment as a secure moral order, then we might well ask: What need is there to speak of redemption? Does Christian faith merely fill in the details, telling us more about an order we already trust? Alas, it is not so simple! The will-to-meaning struggles and flounders in what Frankl called "the existential vacuum which is the mass neurosis of the present time."[30] The gospel is addressed to an elemental confidence in the depths of the human self, but it is a confidence assailed by doubts and tired by life's contradictions. It fluctuates and sometimes is overwhelmed; it needs reassurance and healing. The Redeemer, accordingly, is presented not as a teacher who provides more information to his well-informed students but as a physician who brings healing to the sick and helpless (Matt. 9:12, Mark 2:17, Luke 5:31). There is, no doubt, a measure of truth in the existentialist motto "We make ourselves," because the transformation of the self is always through the understanding and the will: it calls for personal insight and resolve. But Christian faith nonetheless confesses that it is the grace of Christ that is the source of healing. Paul's question, "What do you have that you did not receive?" (1 Cor. 4:7), applies to the confidence the Christian has in the meaning of his or her existence, as to everything else. And it is the confession of total dependence on the grace of Christ that forms the core of dogmatics, part two.[31]

Christian dogmatics, in the model I am proposing, is a three-tiered investigation of the phenomenon of Christian faith. It begins with an introduction on elemental faith, then lays out in turn the doctrines of creation and redemption, under which all the themes of church doctrine are subsumed. The movement of thought, however, presents not successive steps in a logical argument but simultaneous moments in a particular mode of religious consciousness, the last of which contains and qualifies the other two. In sum: *Christian dogmatics is the doctrine of Christian faith—a faith that answers to the deepest drives of the human self, makes religion and science allies rather then adversaries, and, above all, is acknowledged as wholly the gift of grace in Jesus Christ.* It is the final member of this description that must occupy us next. The heart of the Christian confession is this: "By grace you have been saved through faith, and this is not your own doing; it is the gift of God. . . . We are what he has made us . . ." (Eph. 2:8-10). To *Christian* faith, at any rate, this—and not "We make ourselves"—must be the last word. Our reflections on the nature and shape of Christian dogmatics thus lead us on ineluctably to inquire more closely about faith and Jesus Christ.

But how do we proceed with this, the final task? What are the criteria by which we might claim to speak truly about Jesus Christ—or, for that matter, about any other dogmatic theme? Many students of theology will find it natural enough to open the latest book or article on the subject and to take it from there. This is not necessarily wrong: insofar as it expresses the need to do theology in full awareness of the present situation, it is entirely right. But if the latest proposal is invested with an authority that time alone can properly confer, there is a risk of misrepresenting the nature of dogmatic reflection. I have tried to show (in chapter 4) that Christian dogmatics, like Christian faith itself, has an inescapably "social" character: it is the handing on of a sacred heritage within a believing community, which lives by *keeping faith* with its own past. The difficulty, however, is that keeping faith with the past can never mean simply repeating it.

Chapter 6
FAITH AND JESUS CHRIST

Here we take our stand with Schleiermacher: redemption is simply faith—being made sure of God by the impression the image of Christ makes on us.

Ernst Troeltsch

We must . . . run with resolution the race for which we are entered, our eyes fixed on Jesus, on whom faith depends from start to finish.

Hebrews 12:1-2 NEB

A confessional tradition is more than its creeds or confessions of faith; it includes hymns and histories, the biographies of heroes and the treatises of theologians, reports and pronouncements of church assemblies, inherited forms of worship and polity, and—along with everything else—an intangible *ethos* that is easier to recognize than to define. (A Lutheran friend once remarked that he could spot a Calvinist a mile off, but he didn't say how he did it.) The diversity and mass of a confessional tradition resist reduction to a formula or two, to which unquestioning assent might be given. In Ernst Troeltsch's apt phrase, tradition is "not a legally binding authority, but a body of material to be worked through freely."[1] Keeping faith with tradition, then, is not at all being bound by the letter of the law; it is more a matter of the company you keep—or the books you reach for first—when you want to do your best thinking. Even though you reduce the pertinent materials of tradition to a church's authorized confessions, you still have to exercise freedom in the midst of faithfulness if your own church prescribes *several* confessions of faith for your guidance, every one of them inescapably limited by the situation that produced it. Not only is it unwise, it is impossible (except in science fiction) to transport yourself back to another time. "You cannot step twice into the same rivers, for fresh waters are ever flowing in upon you." The aphorism of Heraclitus is exactly right.[2] It follows that tradition is not an immovable rock that rises majestically above the stream: it is the stream itself. And to do dogmatics is to direct the inevitable passage of the waters, as far as possible, by the free activity of informed and responsible thought.

Clearly, the task of the dogmatic theologian is a peculiarly difficult one. It might be easier just to tell the world what you think about God, humanity, and the cosmos, not troubling yourself with the labor of working through all the forbidding material of tradition. But that is not an option for dogmatics, which, by definition, is *church* dogmatics. A church is tied, for good and for ill, to its history; for a church is something quite other than a special-interest group, which comes into existence to deal with an urgent issue and dissolves again when the issue is settled, or loses its interest, or yields first place to some other urgent problem. The dogmatician pledges fidelity to the church as church, not to some party or other within it, and this necessarily entails deference to the confessional tradition. But the task is made all the more difficult by the fact that if the tradition is manifold and mobile, not simple or static,[3] then faithfulness can be exercised only through the exercise of critical judgment: by determining, as best one can, what it is in the immense resources of the past that most needs to be made effectual in the present. Caught between the old tradition and the new situation, the church theologian must be ready to judge the past by the present but also to judge the present by the past—and to judge both by the Scriptures, to which the confessions themselves defer. The church that binds its theologians to the confessions will accordingly permit, indeed require, them to read the confessions critically for the sake of a future, better confession.[4]

This is the view of the dogmatic task that must lead us through the final question, about faith and Jesus Christ. It is a view that will always vex those who see tradition in simpler, more static terms, whether because they think it too perfect to tamper with or because they suppose it to be dead. Others may even judge it un-Protestant to talk about tradition at all, seeing that "the Bible only is the religion of protestants."[5] Troeltsch, it is true, thought that his understanding of tradition as "material to be worked through freely" was in fact distinctively Protestant.[6] But he meant *liberal* Protestant. He took it to be a by-product of the modern idea of development, whereas the original Reformers intended to rely on the Bible alone. In this, however, Troeltsch was mistaken. To speak once more from my own ecclesiastical corner: The notion of a developing tradition was not at all foreign to John Calvin, at least, who can hardly be invoked to support the principle *scriptura sola* if it means that the theologian, to do theology, needs nothing but an open Bible in her lap.

Calvin not only made constant use of the humanistic learning of his own day; he was also anxious to preserve lines of dogmatic continuity with the fathers and even the medieval schoolmen. A formidable patristic scholar, he seeded all his arguments with liberal citations from the fathers, above all from Augustine; and he did not deem all the schoolmen equally benighted but discriminated among them. On God's initiative in the justification of the ungodly, for example, he claimed that not his beloved Augustine alone but the "sounder" schoolmen, too, were on his side.[7] And while he freely rejected some scholastic concepts, he just as freely availed himself of others. Others again he managed to keep by reinterpreting them. He assured Bullinger, for instance, that the sacraments really do "contain" and "confer" grace, as the schoolmen said; for the sacraments confer grace by arousing faith, and grace is contained in them as Christ is contained in the gospel.[8]

The conservative use Calvin made of the Latin theological tradition is something more than an apologetic strategy for refuting the charge of heresy. It serves a constructive purpose in his theological reflection, though its implications for a Protestant theological method are seldom noticed. It was by no means an inconsistency or a lapse on the part of an otherwise exemplary Protestant. On the contrary, Calvin worked with an appreciative understanding of tradition: he did not reject it, but held that it ought to be submitted to criticism. Since genuine tradition is nothing but the "handing down" (*tradere*) of the word of God, our duty is to test it by the word of God.[9] And Calvin recognized that what passes the test may still need to be said better. For this reason, he dismissed the taunt of Albert Pighius (ca. 1490–1542), a Roman Catholic controversialist, that what he, Calvin, was saying on free will was not at all what Martin Luther had said. Calvin admits that some of Luther's outbursts on the bondage of the will were exaggerations. But the times cried out for them: "[Luther] saw the world so stupefied by a false and pernicious confidence in works, as if by a fatal lethargy, that what was needed was not voice and words, but the blast of the trumpet, thunder, and lightning."[10] In any case, there is no reason that we ourselves, who agree with Luther in substance, should not try to say things better, or more appropriately, than he did. "If Pighius does not know it, I want to make this plain to him: our constant endeavor, day and night, is to put into the form we think will be best whatever is faithfully handed on by us."[11]

A better formulation of the dogmatic task than that would be hard to find: the dogmatic theologian hands on the heritage of the past by "re-forming" it in a new day. Notice that Calvin not only affirms the legitimate claims of a tradition subordinate to the word of God but has also begun to think in terms of a Protestant tradition, in which Luther is held to have spoken the first word, not the last. To take Calvin's understanding of tradition seriously, we shall, of course, have to admit that Calvin didn't have the last word either. And *our* last word, too, can only be partial and provisional as we turn to our final question: What is the connection of faith with Jesus Christ? Like Calvin, we must try to answer this and every other dogmatic question by placing ourselves between the historical tradition and the present situation. But, for us, neither the tradition nor the situation is what it was for him. Both have moved on.

Christology at the Crossroad

It makes little difference whether one begins with the old tradition or the new situation, if the task is to mediate between the two. My instinct is to start with the sacred history, so to say. But because I have been talking about tradition for most of my life, let me reverse the order this time and ask, without further ado: What, if anything, in our modern world separates our thoughts about Jesus Christ from Luther's and Calvin's and therefore calls for reformation?[12] "Crisis" is an overworked word. But few will deny that there is a crisis today, if anywhere, in "christology," the doctrines of Christ's work and person. What is not always so clearly recognized is just how long the crisis has been in the making. It is the product, in part, of two characteristics of our modern habits of historical thinking: relativism and historical skepticism. For Luther and Calvin, there could only be one Savior of the world; outside of faith in Christ, they could see nothing but idolatry and the willful suppression of God's witness to Godself. And they had no serious doubts about the historical reliability of what the New Testament says of Christ. Whether true or false, neither of these two assumptions—the uniqueness of Christ and the historical reliability of the Gospels—can be taken for granted anymore.

Relativism and the Uniqueness of Christ

It is astonishing to find doubts on the first assumption as early as the seventeenth century, in the confessions of a model Puritan. Here is John Bunyan's testimony in *Grace Abounding*:

> The Tempter would also much assault me with this: How can you tell but that the Turks had as good Scriptures to prove their *Mahomet* the Saviour, as we have to prove our *Jesus* is; and could I think that so many ten thousands in so many Countreys and Kingdoms, should be without the knowledge of the right way to Heaven (if there were indeed a Heaven)

> and that we onely, who live but in a corner of the Earth, should alone be blessed therewith? Everyone doth think his own Religion rightest, both *Jews*, and *Moors*, and *Pagans*; and how if all our Faith, and Christ, and Scriptures, should be but a think-so too?[13]

Bunyan's temptation expresses an early tremor of Christian complacency in a world not only of confessional pluralism but of religious pluralism, too: he has looked at the alarming possibility that all religions, Christian and non-Christian, are alike no more than "think-so," none of them having any special right to be set apart as alone true, or even placed on top as the truest there is. We remember, of course, that it was the Devil who put these unnerving thoughts into Bunyan's mind. But what to him was a passing insinuation of the Tempter became for the English Deists, who followed him, a sustained assault on any revelation addressed to all humankind from corners, as Anthony Collins ironically put it.[14] And for the present-day Christian theologian it has become a sober, unavoidable theological question: Is there only one mediator between God and humankind? If there are many candidates, how can we adjudicate between them? Or does religious pluralism necessarily imply a religious relativism, in which what is good and true for us may not be good and true for everyone?

As the travels of seventeenth- and eighteenth-century Europeans opened up new worlds, there was good reason for the anxiety that afflicted Bunyan to grow worse. The horizon expanded, and the moral and religious perspective of the West began to change—albeit slowly, here and there. Even "primitive" peoples (as we called them) were allowed, up to a point, to speak back to a Christendom that was still self-satisfied after the horrors of the religious wars. Take, for example, *The Life and Strange Surprising Adventures of Robinson Crusoe, of York, Mariner*, which Daniel Defoe (1660–1731) published in 1719. It is a grand yarn (not for children only!), but its author, once intended for the dissenting ministry, seems to sprinkle in a little preaching. Crusoe is an honest Englishman, condescending to the "savages," and only slightly less condescending to other Europeans. After his first encounter with cannibalism, he devoutly thanks God that he was born in a civilized, Christian land. But when he thinks it over, it occurs to him that perhaps the heathen do not so much lack virtue as have a code of virtue different from his: cannibals are not murderers.[15] And along with the same rational and moral capacities as providence has given to Englishmen, the cannibals also, it seems, have religion.

Delighted to learn that his man Friday believes in a god—"one old Benamuckee, that live[s] beyond all"—Crusoe undertakes to instruct him in the saving knowledge of the true God. Priestcraft, he discovers, is not peculiar to the Roman church but a common feature of religion, and he decides to "clear up this fraud" in Friday's mind. But the savage is permitted to ask the Christian difficult questions, which Crusoe finds himself ill-equipped to answer. For instance: "But if God much strong, much might as the devil, why God no kill the devil, so make him no more do wicked?"[16] Sophisticated theologians and philosophers had puzzled over that one back home, in Christendom. Crusoe has to learn that it casts an initial shadow of implausibility over Christian faith in the eyes of a simple religious outsider.

In *The Farther Adventures of Robinson Crusoe*, published later the same year, the gentle questioning turns into sharp, if indirect, criticism. Crusoe finds the most earnest Christian piety in, of all people, a Roman Catholic, although he is "first, . . . a Papist; secondly, a Popish priest; and thirdly, a French Popish priest." The priest insists that the English adventurers must make honest women out of their native companions, and this requires that they must undertake to convert the women first. Until now, however, the men have not mentioned God except in profanity. "Lord, sir," says the scoundrel Will Atkins to Robinson Crusoe, "how should we teach them religion? . . . Folks must have some religion themselves before they pretend to teach other people." Atkins fears that if the English try to teach their native companions about God, Jesus Christ, and heaven and hell, they are likely to be asked where they themselves expect to go. Sure enough, his own native companion is astonished to hear that the English, too, believe in a god. "And she has preached such a sermon to me," Atkins reports, "as I shall never forget while I live."[17]

Defoe's point is that the "horrid lives of Christians" hinder the conversion of the heathen, who, when they do convert, make better Christians than those who preached to them. Will the savage be converted, then, and the instrument of his conversion cast away?[18] A second point is that the mission to the heathen unmasks the folly of all those squabbles about niceties of doctrine and schemes of church government that have plunged England into civil war: "They were all," Crusoe admits, "perfectly useless to us; as, for aught I can yet see, they have been to all the rest in the world."[19] Defoe is not questioning the church's duty to evangelize the non-Christian world. He is simply showing what a foreign mission should mean for the churches back home—shaming their moral corruption and relativizing their cherished dogmas. Others went further and wondered why, or whether, the rest of the world needed converting at all.

Theories constructed to assimilate the new data about other religions sometimes adjusted the old theology, sometimes broke with it; either way, a new theological agenda was quietly taking shape for the future. Richard Baxter (1615–91) argued that if all nations of the world have some kind of religion, then all may hope to obtain mercy for their sins. "Those that know not Christ nor his redemption, are yet his Redeemed."[20] A staunch Puritan, Baxter could not suppose that the salvation of pagans nullifies the need for atonement; it must mean, rather, that the efficacy of Christ's saving work extends to some, at least, who have never heard of him. Christian theology thus retains its priority over the evidences of natural religion, which are simply incorporated into the old scheme with a minimal adjustment—an adjustment, by the way, that was not without precedent in the theology of the Reformation era.[21] But the English Deists reversed the priorities: they incorporated Christianity into a general understanding of religion.

The Deists were not all of one mind. But we find repeatedly in their writings the view that a pure religion is accessible to all by nature and that Christianity, like every other historical religion, partly exhibits the religion of nature, partly obscures and corrupts it. The familiar scheme of Protestant orthodoxy is turned upside down. Revelation does not, after all, clarify our confused natural knowledge of God; quite the contrary, our innate knowledge of God enables us to judge every pretended revelation and to sort out truth and error even in Christianity itself. Such a revolutionary shift of perspective, typical of the Deists, nurtured a fascinating body of subversive literature, which actually began even before the heyday of Deism.[22] Against Christian orthodoxy, it was variously argued that we should look to China to see natural religion preserved for a very long time in its original purity (John Webb); that in their authentic core Judaism, Islam, and Christianity are identical (John Toland); that Judaism and Islam are actually closer to the religion of Jesus and his first disciples than is present-day Christianity (Henry Stubbe); and so on.[23] Natural religion, or the religion of plain reason, was assumed to be an uncomplicated ethical monotheism, incompatible with trinitarian speculations and the imposition of other religious duties besides the duty to lead a virtuous life.

These are not, to be sure, the sentiments of the orthodox theologians, who poured out a flood of angry refutations in response. The vehemence of the establishment polemics may betray more anxiety than assurance. But if so, the nineteenth-century churches recovered their nerve, and the nettling questions of the Deists were brushed aside by the missionary zeal that accompanied colonialism. It may be that Robinson Crusoe's father was right: Crusoe would have been happier if he had stayed home.[24] He might not have lost his Christian innocence. But the encounter with other religions was an inevitable by-product of what Crusoe calls "the distemper of wandering,"[25] and it went on quietly under the temporary aegis of empire-building. Already in the nineteenth century, there were outsiders who judged that Christian confidence and missionary fervor rested as much on ignorance as it did on faith. Recall Ralph Waldo Emerson's (1803–82) reply to the zealous clergyman who quoted passages from the Gospels and declared that they could not be matched in the sacred books of any other religion: "The gentleman's remark only proves how narrowly he has read."[26] Well, it may have proved also how profoundly grateful the gentleman was to the Christ who had met him in the pages of the Gospels. But Emerson had a point.

In the early twentieth century, when imperialism was still at its height, another outsider, Ernst Troeltsch, observed that christocentrism is the theological counterpart of geocentrism and anthropocentrism in cosmology: an anachronistic absolutizing of our own contingent place in the scheme of things.[27] That the center of our own religious history is also the sole hope of salvation for the rest of humanity could be a miracle of divine election, but to the rest of the world it looks like another example of the Western will to dominate.[28] And now that the supporting ideology of colonialism has collapsed, the absoluteness of Christianity appears ready to collapse with it. Christians face the adherents of other religions on an equal footing; the dialogue begins, in effect, with Troeltsch's persuasion that the history of religions reveals several nodal points, not one absolute center.[29] And Christians must now ask: Is Jesus Christ the only redeemer, or are there many? This, however, is only the first reason that the present-day theologian has to rethink the meaning of Jesus Christ for faith. For what, in any case, can we claim to know about him?

Skepticism and the Historical Jesus

On this problem, too, the dividing line between the Reformers and ourselves fell in the eighteenth century, the period of the Enlightenment; and the pioneers were again the English Deists, who turned a skeptical eye to the wondrous events related in the Gospels. During the same period New Testament scholars, especially in Germany, began to reflect critically on the fact that the four Gospels do not yield a consistent, unified narrative of the life of Christ. Of course, Christians had noticed from the earliest times that the Gospels have individual characteristics and present the story of Jesus with wide variations. But this had not given rise to much serious doubt concerning their truthfulness. Even Calvin's ingenuity did not suffice for him to incorporate the Fourth Gospel into his *Harmony of the Gospels*; he commented separately on John. Yet he was confident that his arrangement of the Synoptics (as we call them) gave a generally accurate account of the words and deeds of Christ. Where the pieces seemed not to fit, he was content to shrug his shoulders and to grant that the Evangelists were not always concerned to provide a strict, chronological account. Neither was he bothered by what he admitted to be a few minor errors in the texts.[30]

We find ourselves in quite another world when we turn from Calvin to the notorious Wolfenbüttel Fragments, which G. E. Lessing (1729–81) began to publish in 1774, thereby launching the so-called quest for the historical Jesus.[31] H. S. Reimarus (1694–1768), the author of the fragments (not identified by Lessing), had been influenced by the English Deists and had decided that the Gospels were not merely inaccurate but fraudulent. Jesus announced the arrival of the messianic kingdom. But his predictions were mistaken, and his life ended in the tragedy of the cross. Unable to accept his failure, his disciples stole his body and pretended that he had miraculously risen from the grave. A true, historical account of Jesus is possible, according to Reimarus, only if we separate Jesus from what his disciples made of him.[32]

Others took the view that the Gospels were not so much conscious fabrications as the work of naive believers living in a pre-scientific age: their credulity led them to misconstrue the testimony of their own eyes. The miracles reported in the Gospels, once the cornerstone of Christian apologetics, had by now become an embarrassment. The solution was to establish that what really happened was not miraculous at all. According to one ingenious writer, Jesus did not walk on water but was standing on a raft; he did not multiply the loaves and fishes but had his back to a cave, from which hidden associates surreptitiously passed food out to him; he did not die on the cross but swooned after taking a potion prescribed by Luke the physician.[33] Another author, equally inventive, explained the feeding of the five thousand by suggesting that actually Jesus had brought his own lunch with him, shared it with those around him, and inspired others who had come similarly provided to do likewise. His apparent death was merely a coma, from which he was awakened in the tomb by the noise of the earthquake, and the earthquake also conveniently rolled the stone away from the entrance.[34]

The attempt of the early lives of Jesus to unearth plain facts, and to reassure Christians that the facts were not really miraculous, went nowhere. One commentator on one such interpretation remarks that it retained the husk and surrendered the kernel.[35] But the story of the quest for the historical Jesus is long, complicated, immensely fascinating—and still incomplete. We now have an Old Quest, a New Quest, and a Third Quest.[36] I cannot trace the story here. I simply venture to offer a theologian's comments on its apparent inconclusiveness. Occasionally, it is true, New Testament scholars have spoken of an agreed core of information about the words and works of Jesus. But the consensus, when it is predicted, does not arrive; or if it is achieved, it does not last.[37]

Recent years have seen an extraordinary flurry of new proposals, ranging from technical works of esoteric scholarship to racy publications that court a public sensation. Barbara Thiering's contribution, *Jesus the Man* (1992), attracted media attention chiefly by its argument that Jesus married Mary Magdalene, had three children with her (two boys and a girl), divorced her, and was remarried—this time to the Lydia of whom we read in the Acts of the Apostles. (Acts 16:14 tells us that "the Lord opened [Lydia's] heart," which, being interpreted, means they fell in love.) Naturally, this presupposes that Jesus did not die on the cross: poison given him as an act of mercy only left him unconscious. In the tomb Simon the magician, one of the two offenders who had been crucified with Jesus, was able to revive him with the spices left by the women. He lived to a ripe old age, but there is no record of his last days. "He was seventy years old in A.D. 64, and it is probable that he died of old age in seclusion in Rome."[38]

A banner headline in a British weekly caught my eye in October 1992: "Man and Myth—More Bad News for Believers." It was a review of several popular attempts, including Barbara Thiering's, to rescue the real Jesus from the church.[39] But it is, I think, easy enough for believers to brush aside the entire genre of popular Jesus books. A senior New Testament scholar may speak for most believers when he remarks that "Thiering's exotic fantasy would be a rollicking good joke, were it not so sad that the public, ignoring the Gospels, lap up this total rubbish."[40] The bad news for believers, if there is any, is surely the failure of the more sober scholars to reach a consensus on the historical Jesus: if they agree on anything at all, it is that the Gospels cannot be taken for historical or biographical accounts of what the Jesus of history said, did, and suffered. And where does *that* leave believers?

I admit that I am a mere dilettante in the historical field explored so closely by New Testament specialists. I can only stand by and watch as a church theologian intensely interested in the implications the quest has for faith. And if the significance of the Christian encounter with other religions is that it sets Jesus amid a crowd of competing redeemers, the significance of the many quests for the historical Jesus seems to be that they have taken away the Lord altogether: he disappears in a crowd of competing interpreters. Jesus is variously represented as a marginal Jew (John Meier), a Mediterranean Jewish peasant (John Dominic Crossan), a wandering Cynic preacher (Burton Mack), a Jewish revolutionary (S. G. F. Brandon), a Galilean holy man (G. Vermes), and so on.[41] And when we move from such general characterizations to matters of detail, it is again the lack of consensus that is most likely to strike the believer as bad news. Perhaps the best we can hope for are the results of Robert Funk's "Jesus Seminar," which has now classified all the sayings attributed to Jesus as certainly inauthentic, probably inauthentic, probably authentic, or certainly authentic. A sequel has followed on what Jesus really *did*.[42] A great deal of fun has been poked at the method of deciding historical matters by majority vote of a select conclave, although that is how the church has usually decided matters of dogma. But the real question (for a theologian) is this: Can faith survive the wait, as the words and works attributed to the Lord are passed through the sorting office? And if it can wait, will it then survive all the uncertainties about him that will inevitably remain?

The Christ of Faith

The two problems I have laid on the table are unavoidable. How deeply they have already affected Christians untroubled by a theological education is hard to say. A lot depends on where they live and where, or whether, they go to church. In England church attendance is slight, but religious pluralism and the quest for the historical Jesus have been strenuously debated in the public news media. There are signs of a growing public concern in America, too, where a much higher percentage of the population is connected with one or other of the churches. In any case, both the interfaith dialogue and the search for the real Jesus are gaining in intensity, and they promise to have repercussions in the churches not unlike the impact (in an earlier time) of the Darwinian controversy. Christian theology must clearly take up the new agenda, which is not in truth so new as is sometimes imagined.

Unfortunately, the problems are not only unavoidable; they are also difficult problems, in which Christian sensibilities are painfully exposed. I cannot hope to enter into conversation with all the various positions that are currently recommended, or even to say as much as I should like to say about my own position. I know the risks, but I will only try to point out an *approach* to christology, which, admittedly, is not itself a christology. The important thing, for now, is to make the experiment of continuing on the path we have been following thus far: that is, to address the two problems now before us out of conclusions already reached on the nature of faith and its social context in a confessing church. This means, above all, that we will be speaking of faith as a total orientation of the self, a way of existing or being human. Emil Brunner rightly maintains that Luther's greatness as a reformer was to have rediscovered exactly this, the true Pauline sense of faith.[43] Our question is, then: How is faith *in this sense* to be related to Jesus Christ, if we take to heart the problems of relativism and historical skepticism?

The Work of Christ

In the light of what we have already said, it is not, or not at the outset at least, a question of what Christians ought to believe about Christ. Perhaps the instinctive Christian reaction to relativism and to skepticism about the Jesus of history is to insist: "But Jesus was God in human flesh! We believe in his divinity. This is what separates our Christian faith from every other religion, and it isn't negotiable. Salvation depends on it."[44] However understandable the instinctive Christian response (if such it is) may be, it cannot be promoted to dogmatic status, or we will find ourselves back with faith as the Athanasian Creed understands it. The creed says: "The right faith is that we believe and confess that our Lord Jesus Christ, the Son of God, is God and Man. . . . This is the Catholic Faith, which except a man believe faithfully, he cannot be saved." The objection we have to register, first of all, is that faith as belief, and even as belief in the divinity of Jesus Christ, is something other than "saving faith" (as we have defined it).

But more than that: To begin with belief in the divinity of Jesus is also a dubious stand to take in the present situation of interfaith dialogue. It is dubious not simply because the tone of inflexibility tends to close off conversation, rather than to foster it, but also because the uniqueness of belief in Jesus as God-Man is one of the things that the conversation has placed in doubt. Elevation of the founder of a religion into a preexistent divine being, it will quickly be pointed out these days, has occurred also in Mahayana Buddhism.[45] Further, there are remarkably close parallels between the stories that celebrate respectively the birth of Jesus and the birth of Octavius (the emperor Caesar Augustus). John Dominic Crossan concludes: "Jesus' divine origins are just as fictional or mythological as those of Octavius."[46] The conclusion, I should think, goes beyond the evidence. The *stories* about the divine origins of Jesus and Octavius may be fictional, but either one of them, or both, could still be in some sense divine, or of a divine origin, as could also the Buddha. The point, rather, is that *belief* in the divinity of Jesus does not settle the question of Christianity and other religions, and it raises again questions about the truthfulness, or (better) the literary character, of the Gospels.

A third difficulty with going straight to Chalcedon, so to say, is that it immediately raises the question of the scriptural norm. Whether the New Testament teaches that Jesus was God, like nearly everything else in biblical scholarship, is keenly debated. The expression "Jesus is (or was) God" occurs nowhere in the Gospels, or anywhere else in the New Testament, although it has sometimes been made into the watchword of Christian orthodoxy. The overwhelming weight of the New Testament's way of speaking about Jesus is plainly on the side of distinguishing him from God. Paul's statement may be taken as an apt summary: "For us there is one God, the Father, . . . and one Lord, Jesus Christ" (1 Cor. 8:6). The sole uncontroverted instance of Jesus himself being named "God" is in doubting Thomas's confession, "My Lord and my God," addressed to the risen Lord (John 20:28); and the scholars will immediately tell us that this is probably a formula from the Evangelist's own time, made in response to the claim of the Emperor Domitian to be "our Lord and God." The case can certainly be made for a few other instances—with varying degrees of probability or improbability. But that only brings us back again to our harried believers, waiting anxiously for the latest news about the historical Jesus.[47]

For Roman Catholics, the problem is less painful than it is for Protestants. Raymond Brown begins an essay titled "Does the New Testament Call Jesus God?" by noting that he is not asking whether Jesus was in fact God. "This question," he says, "was settled for the Church at Nicaea. . . ."[48] Brown also points out—superfluously, I suppose—that the constitutional basis of the World Council of Churches, formulated by the Amsterdam Assembly in 1948, is acceptance of Jesus Christ as "God and Saviour." For Protestants, however, no decision of an ecclesiastical council is irreformable. It is true that the Protestant reformers and the Reformation confessions often endorsed the trinitarian and christological definitions of the ecumenical creeds and councils. But the grounds on which they did so must be clearly understood. The Reformers did not share the view of the Roman Catholic and Eastern Orthodox churches that the pronouncements of a synod of bishops have, or can have, the status of dogmas that are free from error and binding for all times. (That would be a theory of church government quite alien to those churches, in particular, whose historic stand has been against episcopacy.) The Reformers reaffirmed Nicene orthodoxy because they thought it agreeable to the word of God, and this logically implies the possibility of second thoughts if scriptural exegesis so requires. Otherwise, the descendants of the Reformers would find themselves in exactly the error of which Karl Barth so relentlessly accused the Church of Rome—not permitting the Bible to remain free, sovereign over all ecclesiastical interpretations of it, so that the church may be always and only a hearer, not the master, of the word of God.[49]

But suppose we begin, not where Athanasius ended, but where Athanasius himself began, with the actual experience of new life in Jesus Christ; and that we do our best to understand the new life with the resources available to us, as he did with the resources available to him. We would then, I think, be following much the same path that Luther and Schleiermacher were to take later. For Athanasius, the divine life that came into the church from the incarnate Word was imperiled when the Arians took God's Word to be something less than God: if he "deifies" us, the Son must be of the same substance as the Father.[50] Luther said in one of his sermons (in that carefree style that can make even a Lutheran nervous): "Christ is not called Christ because he has two natures. What is that to me?"[51] And in another sermon he said: "To believe in Christ does not mean to believe that Christ is a person who is both God and man. That helps nobody."[52] At first hearing, this may sound like a rejection of the christological orthodoxy that Athanasius had labored to secure. But Luther was certain that it was God he met in Jesus Christ because his conscience told him that his sins were no longer counted against him. Christ is revealed as God by doing God's work.[53] The scribes asked correctly: "Who can forgive sins but God alone?" (Mark 2:7).

I believe that Friedrich Schleiermacher discerned particularly well the logic of christological reflection exemplified in Athanasius and Luther. As I said in my little book on Schleiermacher: "He began neither with ancient dogmas nor with ancient history, but with what every Christian experiences, and he sought to give an honest account of it that would not run away from the intellectual problems of the modern world."[54] What Christians actually experience in their encounter with Jesus Christ, according to Schleiermacher, is a heightened awareness of God, which is symbolized and celebrated in the joy of Christmastime: they are drawn under the sway of Jesus' uniquely powerful sense of God. "To ascribe to Christ an absolutely powerful consciousness of God and to attribute to him a being of God in him," Schleiermacher concludes, "are entirely one and the same thing."[55] Naturally, I had to admit in the Schleiermacher book, and I admit it again now, that "what every Christian experiences" is a question-begging expression. But that is only to concede the limitations of the approach, not to doubt its fundamental soundness. Schleiermacher believed one could make headway in dogmatics only by inviting the hearer's or reader's participation in the inquiry. He took the question, "What does Christ actually do for the Christian?" to be, as we say, existential or self-involving: it invites the Christian's reflection on her own experience. He knew well that there are varieties of Christian experience. But he remained convinced that, on reflection, a common faith would be discerned in them all, and it held the clue to a sound understanding of Christ's person.

In the three testimonies we have just looked at, the key thought that brings it all together, so to say, changes: "life," "forgiveness," "the sense of God." But the question "What, as a matter of fact, does Christ do for Christians?" is still, I think, the crucial one to ask in any Christian community, if the christological project is to be duly launched. The proper approach, in short, is to begin not with the definition of Chalcedon (451), "truly God and truly man . . . in two natures," but with the actual experience of Jesus Christ that has led to the confession of his divinity, or of a unique being of God in him. Applying the same approach to our own progress so far, we are surely on firm ground if we assert that what Christians actually receive from Jesus Christ is saving faith (in the sense defined). "Saving faith," we said, " . . . is both (1) perceiving one's experience under the image of divine benevolence (*fides*) and (2) a consequent living of one's life out of an attitude of confidence or trust (*fiducia*)." The work of Christ, we can now add, is the gift of saving faith, which is not belief about Christ, but confidence in God through Christ—a confidence that rests on the perception of a pattern in the events of one's life.[56]

What is *believed* about Christ is the implication, not the precondition, of this gift of faith. Hence the primary or initial interest of christology is to understand the faith that actually occurs through Jesus Christ. I have no wish to cut off the traditional christological assertions any more than Luther or Schleiermacher did. It is the duty of the dogmatic theologian to understand and, as far as possible, to retrieve the doctrinal formulas of the past—at the very least, to show their point. But a proper order must be observed. The Chalcedonian definition is not the foundation of saving faith, and unless one accounts for it genetically, it is more likely to mystify than to enlighten us, or else to become a mere shibboleth of doctrinal correctness.

The Word of Christ

But how is the gift of saving faith given? The next step, obviously, is to look more closely at the actual phenomena of faith and repentance, the new birth and growth in grace, and to ask how the work of Christ is accomplished. How does it happen that someone comes to faith and has faith nurtured and strengthened? Here I have to recall a passing criticism I leveled earlier at Calvin,[57] even though I borrowed my definition of saving faith largely from him. In one place I cited, Calvin makes faith depend on a prior acceptance of divine truth, as though the order of experience were this: First I am persuaded of the authority of God's word, and then I come to know thereby of God's fatherly goodwill. This, it seems to me, is untrue to the usual pattern of Christian experience—and, indeed, out of harmony with Calvin's own concept of faith as "recognition."

That a person can have confidence in God is not a piece of information provided by an authoritative scripture: the confidence is given in the recognition of God's "fatherly face." To be sure, this happens through the word, as Calvin rightly says, but the word understood not as truth supernaturally communicated, but as the instrument of divinely corrected vision. The nature of the revelation must correspond strictly with the nature of faith, as it in fact does in Calvin's own simile of the spectacles of Scripture. What Calvin likes to call the *historia evangelica* (the "gospel story") functions as a lens that focuses a picture: in it the true image of God is presented, and through it God can be recognized everywhere else. And, of course, the simile of the spectacles presupposes that a confused vision was already there before the corrective lenses were put on.[58] But this is all, perhaps, too abstract. Let's try an example.

Take the familiar narrative of the crucifixion. To begin with, it has every appearance of a *tragedy* or a *failure*. Thus far Reimarus was right. The messianic hopes that Jesus has kindled end with the cruel joke "This is Jesus, the King of the Jews" (Matt. 27:37), and the terrible cry of dereliction, "My God, my God, why have you forsaken me?" (v. 46). "Then Jesus cried again with a loud voice and breathed his last" (v. 50). In Matthew and Mark, you might say, that is all (cf. Mark 15:22-37). Why, then, have Christians always found in the story such a powerful source of faith? The first thing one has to say is that no one answer can suffice: the four versions of the story, by their very differences, already invite more than one emphasis for construing its meaning. For all Christians, however, the narrative has always spoken of the cost of redemption; and for all, I submit, it nurtures faith by its powerful statement of a meaning and purpose that *incorporates* tragedy.

The narrative achieves its effect not only because the passion is seen in relation to the sequels—the earthquake and the resurrection—but also because the account of the crucifixion itself has been strikingly amplified by Luke and John, and the different versions are always fused together in the Christian's memory. Luke reports Jesus as saying, "Father, forgive them" (Luke 23:34),[59] "Today you [the thief] will be with me in Paradise" (v. 43), and, "Father, into your hands I commend my spirit" (v. 46). John adds Jesus' sayings to his mother and the beloved disciple (John 19:26-27), "I am thirsty" (v. 28), and the dramatic last words, "It is finished" (v. 30). In this fashion, the stark picture in Matthew and Mark is transformed: the tragedy is already a victory, before the resurrection, and John in particular wants us to believe that Jesus never quite relinquished control. In short, the crucifixion narrative awakens faith because it has become a story about faith. The face of God is still made out, albeit barely; or, to put it in my other language, the narrative stirs that deep, elemental human longing to be reassured that there is, after all, meaning—despite the appearances.

Obviously, I would have some difficulty proving that this is what every Christian experiences in reading or hearing the crucifixion story. I can only invite others to think about it, to go to church, and—most of all perhaps—to listen to the pastoral experience of Christian ministers. Well, one other thing I can do is try, as usual, to enlist the support of John Calvin. We have seen that Calvin defines faith as "steadfast knowledge of the fatherly goodwill of God." But he admits that this faith is always assailed by anxiety and doubt, so that we are tempted to imagine God is against us.[60] This is exactly what Calvin sees happening to Jesus on the cross, as he bore the penalties that were due to us. The cry of dereliction proves that even Jesus was tempted to think God opposed to him. But the cry was addressed to God, and Calvin assures us that it was still a cry of Jesus' faith, "by which he beheld the presence of God, of whose absence he complains."[61] Calvin thus perceived in the crucifixion not only the price of redemption, but also the archetype of faith as he understood it: seeing God even in the midst of agonies of body and soul, when every natural feeling cries out that God must be against me. It is impossible to doubt that Calvin's own faith was ratified and strengthened by this conformity with the faith of Christ.[62]

Although I have taken a narrative as my example, the power of the narrative, it seems to me, lies in the *words* of Jesus. What the soldiers did to him makes its brutal impact on the reader, but it is the words "Father, forgive them" that leap out and seize the attention. The story is in fact read from saying to saying. I can well understand another of Luther's provocative judgments: that if he had to do without either the works or the preaching of Jesus, he would rather do without the works. "For the works do not help me, but his words give me life, as he himself says [John 6:63]." And that, Luther tells us, is why John is the best Gospel.[63] By the "works" of Jesus, Luther no doubt intends the miracles he performed—such as the feeding of the five thousand, which in John (chapter 6) provides the occasion for the discourse on the bread of life. But a careful look at other narratives in *all* the Gospels will show how often the power lies in Jesus' words. In short: If the *work* of Christ is the gift of faith, then we must surely add, as a matter of plain observation, that he gives it through his *word*.

Naturally, when one moves outside the Gospels to other New Testament writings, it is the apostolic word *about* Christ, rather than the words *of* Christ, that mediates saving faith. One additional saying of Jesus, not mentioned in the Gospels, is indeed quoted in Acts: "It is more blessed to give than to receive" (Acts 20:35). But in the Acts of the Apostles, as in the Pauline epistles, faith is imparted by the proclamation *about* Jesus—the *kerygma*, as we call it, that points toward the second article of the Apostles' Creed. Recurring items in the *kerygma* include the statements: that Jesus was the promised messiah; that he was crucified, died, and was buried; that he was raised from the dead and exalted to God's right hand; that he will come again as judge.[64] Through the "foolishness" of this *kerygma* God has decided to save those who have faith (1 Cor. 1:21). It is interesting that in Rom. 10:17 Paul seems to think of Christ himself as speaking through his messengers, who proclaim the *kerygma*: "So faith comes from what is heard, and what is heard comes through the word *of Christ*."[65] In this sense, we might simply include the apostolic *kerygma* in the expression "the word of Christ." Or we could perhaps subsume both the word *of* Christ and the word *about* Christ under the term that has been so influential in modern theology since Schleiermacher: the "picture" (or "image") of Christ.[66] In any case, I have taken a narrative from the Gospels, rather than the apostolic *kerygma*, as my illustration of how faith is generated mainly because the Gospels pose the problem of historical veracity much more acutely.

It may seem obvious enough to conclude that saving faith, which is the work of Christ, is given by the image of him that the New Testament evokes through its account of his words and deeds and of the apostolic word about him. But this invites the questions: Is that the only way in which faith is given? and, Can the Christian know for sure that the New Testament image of Jesus shows Jesus as he actually was? We have now lent some greater precision to the problems of relativism and historical skepticism—and, we may hope, have shown the perspective from which they may be faced and resolved.

The Body of Christ

My intention thus far has been to bracket the problems of the other religions and the historical Jesus and simply to describe what makes a Christian believer. I have followed what I take to be the general logic of classical christological reflection and have applied it to the particular concept of saving faith defined in the first chapter, using the crucifixion narrative of the Gospels to illustrate the way this faith is generated and nurtured. I took the text just as it lies before us, neither comparing it with the scriptures of other religions nor asking which, if any, of the seven words from the cross may have actually been uttered by the Jesus of history. Now, an objector might grant that I have given a plausible enough account of how saving faith normally occurs, and still want to ask: Would it work like that if the brackets were removed?

It should be easy to remove the first brackets without disaster. To say that the Christian receives saving faith through the New Testament image of Jesus need not imply that faith cannot be had in any other way, or that no other religious faiths confer salvation.[67] Hence it does not preclude or impede open and honest interfaith dialogue but simply states the point from which, for the Christian, the dialogue begins. While genuine conversation is certainly inhibited by absolute and exclusive claims, there cannot be a conversation at all if the Christian has nothing to say, or no Savior to confess. Christians will begin the dialogue convinced that what has been given to them through Jesus Christ is for all humanity. But Jesus Christ may not be humanity's sole access to it; there is no way to know that in advance, before one has listened to the other parties in the conversation. Obviously, Christians need to pay attention to what the adherents of other religions are saying if it is to be decided whether the language of "saving faith" has its counterparts outside the church. And that is something I cannot even begin to talk about here. For now, it is enough to have shown how, in my opinion, the dialogue can be genuinely open.[68]

To remove the other brackets may seem, at first glance, much more troublesome. For suppose the preacher admitted in the course of her sermon on the passion narrative that, to be honest, we really don't know what Jesus said on the cross. Would it matter? Most Christians undoubtedly assume still that the Gospels give a generally accurate account of the words and deeds of Christ. The question is how far the efficacy of the New Testament's image of the crucified and risen Christ is dependent on preserving the assumption. Experience shows that believers are, as a matter of fact, sometimes anxious about bad news of the quest for the historical Jesus. But do they need to be? And is the remedy for them to pretend that they know more than they do about him? Like the man born blind in the Gospel, the Christian may be uncertain who this is who can restore the vision of the blind, but still say: "One thing I do know, that though I was blind, now I see" (John 9:25). To shift the attention from the healing word to the historical quest is to risk distracting faith from its actual foundation. If the believer's anxiety needs any further reassurance, beyond the experience of healed vision, it might be wiser to recall that Jesus evidently did give saving faith to his first disciples, and that their picture of him as the Christ has continued for two millennia to pass on the same gift to others. It is again simply a matter of observation that the efficacy of the healing word is partly dependent on the ecclesial context in which the "word of faith" (Rom. 10:8) is proclaimed. To change the metaphor: the race is run in the presence of the "cloud of witnesses" (Heb. 12:1).

In her book *Christ without Absolutes* (1988), Sarah Coakley takes issue with my views on the historical Jesus, indirectly set out in an article on Troeltsch.[69] But she does not quite pinpoint the crucial difference between us, as I tried to make clear in my review.[70] I agree entirely when Coakley writes: "The point is that . . . Troeltsch saw religious truth as mediated precisely *in* history." But I question her inference: "Does this not then provide a clear theological reason for faith's need to relate to the actual earthly Jesus?" I think her answer is: No, it doesn't. I would not quarrel with the inference if it were intended only to assert that to be related to the Christ of the New Testament *is* an indirect relation to the actual, earthly Jesus, however little we may be able to say of him with certainty. But that is not what Coakley means. She goes on to speak of "the desire to recover what one can about him through accurate research."[71] Historical "realism," she thinks (in agreement with Troeltsch), requires us to ground christology "in verifiable facts about Jesus of Nazareth."[72]

That invites the question "How many facts do you need, and what do you need them for?" Even Rudolf Bultmann, of whom Coakley is also critical, linked christology with one assured fact, *that* Jesus came announcing the kingdom of God, but he did not ground the present decision of faith in his one fact.[73] Coakley wants more, and for a different reason. She speaks approvingly of Troeltsch's supposition "that the Christian believer only attains real 'strength' and 'certainty' from the ideal presented in Jesus if he knows it as a *real* possibility," and this "demands contact with a historical actuality."[74] In response, I stand by my original assertion that

> what is crucial for the picture of Christ, if it is to qualify as a "historical" symbol, is not that it corresponds to the life once lived by a particular

> individual but that it exists, embodied in the corporate life of the Christian community, as the sacramental word by which the community is continually re-created. This is what makes it possible for faith to happen, to occur as an event of the present.[75]

Theological questers for the historical Jesus are not mistaken in seeking a historical anchorage for faith. The problem is that they look for it in the wrong place and hold faith captive to historical science, as the old doctrine of creation once held it captive to natural science. The historical anchorage is to be found in the life of the church, the confessing community in which the gospel is proclaimed—the body of Christ.

My view too, then, is that history mediates religious truth. The question is: *What* history, and *how*? Troeltsch, followed by Coakley, makes the security of faith rest, albeit only in part, on what the biblical scholars can reconstruct *behind* the Gospel picture of Jesus Christ, whereas I take the picture *itself*, as transmitted in the church, to be the actual medium that evokes faith; and I believe Troeltsch did, too, in his clearer moments. Perhaps I would think differently if I were more sanguine about the results of the quest. It is interesting that Coakley herself, having insisted on faith's need for verifiable facts about Jesus of Nazareth, does not display much optimism about the possibility of obtaining them. She admits that the sort of things most likely to be important to Christians, such as Jesus' agony in the garden and his "demeanor" during the crucifixion, are not likely to be substantiated by historical means.[76] This is surely right, and to my mind it focuses the theological question of the actual ground of faith, which has always been imparted by these two segments of the Gospels and presumably always will, whatever the New Testament scholars decide about their historical veracity. Historical studies since Coakley's book have concluded that none of the seven words from the cross could have been uttered by Jesus, and that his crucifixion—very likely part of a mass execution—would not have been witnessed by any of his disciples. If so, then the words tell us not how Jesus died but what his death meant to his followers, and this is the medium by which faith is transmitted in the church.[77]

Strictly speaking, of course, there is not one image of Jesus Christ in the New Testament; there are several, and they range all the way from the wandering teacher, who had nowhere to lay his head (Matt. 8:20, Luke 9:58), to the Cosmic Christ through whom and for whom everything in heaven and on earth was created (Col. 1:15-17). The image a religious community or a devout believer forms of Jesus Christ is always a construct, in which some particular characteristics the New Testament ascribes to him become dominant: he is the master in whose footsteps we are to follow (Mark 1:17, etc.), the Savior who loved me and died for me (Gal. 2:20), the Eternal Logos that enlightens every man and woman (John 1:9). These may not be exclusive or contradictory images of Jesus Christ, but they are not likely to be given equal rank in, say, a Baptist, a Lutheran, and a Greek Orthodox church. And other portraits of him may not be as firmly tied to the biblical witness at all.

Here, no doubt, lies one reason for theological interest in "verifiable facts about Jesus of Nazareth." They are needed, it will be said, to regulate the christological pluralism of the New Testament and, still more, to restrain the subjectivism that imposes fantasy on the text.[78] The history of the church abounds in demand-and-supply christologies, which make the long-suffering Christ the sponsor of whatever program or platform is currently in fashion.[79] True enough. But the problem with which we began is that the historical quest for the real Jesus has itself produced variety, not consensus, and hardly provides the norm for measuring the images of Christ entertained by theologians or naive believers. No one pretends that the quest has been free of subjective bias: often it has mirrored the quester's own thoughts on Jesus, religion, and the church. George Tyrrell's (1861–1909) familiar gibe about Harnack was that the Christ he saw, as he looked back through nineteen centuries of Catholic darkness, was "only a reflection of a liberal Protestant face seen at the bottom of a deep well."[80]

Unfortunately, it has proved much easier to detect theological bias in other people's images of Jesus Christ than to be wholly free of it oneself, despite professions of innocence. But the number of possible images is not infinite, and the image-forming mechanism is not merely willful or subjective. The possibilities are limited by the text, by the common mind of the individual community, and by mutual exchange between one community and another. The ecclesial context not only confirms the experience of *faith* but also restrains *belief* from becoming too eccentric. It is hard, perhaps finally impossible, to define the unity in all the portraits of the Christ. But, as Troeltsch put it in a striking simile, no one familiar with the series of testimonies to Christ in Christianity can doubt that the heartbeat of a powerful personality goes through it all, like the vibration of a ship's engine throughout the entire vessel.[81]

With these reflections on faith and Jesus Christ, I must bring to a close both the present chapter and my inquiry into the concept of faith. My explorations have led from a definition of the Reformers' "saving faith" to an appraisal of the Christian claim that Jesus is the "author and finisher" of faith (Heb. 12:2 KJV). I have argued that saving faith, as recognition plus confidence, is a particular instance of a generic concept of faith as meaning construction, and that other instances are "secular" in the stretched, double sense of either religious but non-Christian or not religious at all. *Some* instances, in fact, have the status of inevitable beliefs held in common by us all, and no faith is purely private: faith is always a social construction. To this extent, having faith is not as such unnatural, irrational, or odd, although there may be good arguments (not explored here) against entertaining one specific faith rather than another.

Christian theology likewise, I have maintained, is not a private activity. It is practiced within a confessing community, whose faith it seeks to articulate, and I have defended the approach of a confessional theology that looks to written creeds as normative expressions of the collective mind. But if the systematic drive is to direct theological reflection, as I think it should, it will not be sufficient merely to thematize Christian doctrines; there will be, besides, an interest in displaying their connection with one another and with other kinds of discourse both inside and outside the Christian community. It is precisely here that my circuitous route to the last two chapters has its point. The various instances of meaning construction are not wholly external to one another; they overlap, and the task of Christian dogmatics is not only to present the distinctively Christian belief in redemption through Jesus Christ, but also to interpret it, in part, by exhibiting its connection with other religious faiths and with those inevitable beliefs presupposed in all meaning construction, religious or not.

Obviously, this is to sketch no more than the bare skeleton of a Christian dogmatics, which must eventually put flesh on the bones by reviewing *all* the traditional dogmatic themes. Neither have I attempted here to locate the dividing lines between Christian faith and other religious faiths. I have only wished to show why, in my opinion, the church's confession of Jesus Christ does not foreclose the question whether "saving faith" may have its counterparts, perhaps differently symbolized, in other religions. And this, of course, is not to disregard whatever is distinctive or unique in any one of them.

I can now sum up the conclusion to the present chapter and indicate what it does, and does not, imply. The church's confession is that *saving faith, which is confidence in God through the perception of a parent-like goodwill in all the events of one's life, is the gift of God given in the presentation of the New Testament picture of Jesus Christ.* But here I must return to our sociological retrieval of the old high-church motto, "Outside the church there is no salvation." The Christian need not invoke it to assert that there is no saving faith outside the church—much less that there is no salvation outside *my* church. Rather, it attests to the crucial importance of holding faith and community together. The church is the essential link between the Christian believer and the Jesus of history: the church is the work of Christ, part two. To the question whether it is necessary to move on from the benefits of Christ to the Holy Catholic Church, Calvin's catechism answers: "Yes, indeed, unless we want to make Christ's death ineffective (*ociosam*) and count as nothing all that has been related so far. For the one effect of it all is that there should be a Church."[82] An unintended work of Christ, it may be! As Roman Catholic historian Alfred Loisy (1857–1940) observed: "Jesus foretold the kingdom, and it was the Church that came."[83] But Loisy's elegant aphorism rightly affirms that there is continuity as well as discontinuity in the move from the proclamation of the kingdom to the existence of the church. A better formula for the continuity between the Jesus who inspired faith in the hearts of his disciples and the Christ who still gives faith today would be hard to devise.

I do not mean that this is the only possible way of establishing the link between the Christ of faith and the Jesus of history. Logically, perhaps, faith *could* live with the news that there is a radical disharmony between the church's Christ and the real Jesus, or even—the ultimate bad news?—that Jesus never existed. But it doesn't *need* to. The extreme hypothetical cases are of interest only insofar as they provoke the theological question: Is faith really at the mercy of the latest report on the quest for the historical Jesus? If my argument has been made good, then just how much we know of the Jesus of history can be left to the early church historians as an open question. The history that saving faith depends on is the life of the church, which confesses that grace has been revealed "through the appearing of our Savior Jesus Christ" (2 Tim. 1:10). Whatever the historians decide about the event so confessed, it is the confession itself that mediates faith. The Christian assertion that saving faith is the gift of God in Christ Jesus (Eph. 2:4-10) is not a claim to know more about the past than historians can know, any more than it is a claim to possess a salvation from which the greater part of humanity is excluded. It is the outward attestation of an inner conviction nurtured in the communion of saints. In the words ascribed to the Apostle Paul in the Second Letter to Timothy: "I am not ashamed, for I know the one in whom I have put my trust, and I am sure that he is able to guard until that day what I have entrusted to him" (2 Tim. 1:12). That, and not *Extra ecclesiam nulla salus* (narrowly meant), is the authentic expression of Christian assurance.

ABBREVIATIONS

ABD *Anchor Bible Dictionary*. Ed. David Noel Freedman et al. 6 vols. New York: Doubleday, 1992.

BC *The Constitution of the Presbyterian Church (U.S.A.), Part I: Book of Confessions*. Louisville, Ky.: Office of the General Assembly, 1994.

CC Philip Schaff, *Bibliotheca Symbolica Ecclesiae Universalis: The Creeds of Christendom with a History and Critical Notes*. 4th ed. 3 vols. New York: Harper & Brothers, 1919.

CELC *The Book of Concord: The Confessions of the Evangelical Lutheran Church*. Trans. and ed. Theodore G. Tappert et al. Philadelphia: Fortress Press, 1959.

CF Friedrich Schleiermacher, *The Christian Faith*. Eng. trans. of the second edition of Schleiermacher's *Der christliche Glaube* (abbreviated *CG*). Ed. H. R. Mackintosh and J. S. Stewart. Edinburgh: T. & T. Clark, 1928.

CG Friedrich Schleiermacher, *Der christliche Glaube nach den Grundsätzen der evangelischen Kirche im Zusammenhange dargestellt*. 7th ed., based on the 2d (1830–31). Ed. Martin Redeker. 2 vols. Berlin: Walter de Gruyter, 1960. Cited by section (§) and subsection. For the Eng. trans., see *CF*.

CG^{1} The first edition of *CG* (1821–22). *Kritische Gesamtausgabe* (the critical edition of Schleiermacher's works), division 1, vol. 7, in three part-vols. Ed. Hermann Peiter and Ulrich Barth. Berlin: Walter de Gruyter, 1980–84.

CO *Ioannis Calvini opera quae supersunt omnia*. Ed. Wilhelm Baum, Eduard Cunitz, and Eduard Reuss. 59 vols. *Corpus Reformatorum,* vols. 29–87. Brunswick: C. A. Schwetschke and Son (M. Bruhn), 1863–1900.

CR B. A. Gerrish, *Continuing the Reformation: Essays on Modern Religious Thought* (Chicago: University of Chicago Press, 1993).

IDB *The Interpreter's Dictionary of the Bible: An Illustrated Encyclopedia*. Ed. George Arthur Buttrick et al. 4 vols. Nashville: Abingdon Press, 1962. Supplementary volume. Ed. Keith Crim et al. Ibid., 1976.

Inst. John Calvin, *Institutio Christianae Religionis,* 1559 edition. Cited by book, chapter, and section. I use the text in *OS* 3–5. The standard English translation is *Calvin: Institutes of the Christian Religion*. Ed. John T. McNeill and trans. Ford Lewis Battles. 2 vols. LCC 20–21. Philadelphia: Westminster Press, 1960.

JR *The Journal of Religion*.

JW *Friedrich Heinrich Jacobi's Werke*. Ed. Jacobi, Friedrich Köppen, and Friedrich Roth. 6 vols. 1812–25. Reprint, Darmstadt: Wissenschaftliche Buchgesellschaft, 1980.

KJV The Authorized (King James) Version of the Bible.

LCC Library of Christian Classics. Ed. John Baillie et al. 26 vols. London: SCM Press, Philadelphia: Westminster Press, 1953–66.

LW *Luther's Works,* American Edition. Ed. Jaroslav Pelikan and Helmut T.

Lehmann. 55 vols. St. Louis, Mo.: Concordia Publishing House, Philadelphia: Fortress Press, 1955–86.

NRSV The New Revised Standard Version of the Bible.

OPN B. A. Gerrish, *The Old Protestantism and the New: Essays on the Reformation Heritage.* Chicago: University of Chicago Press, Edinburgh: T. & T. Clark, 1982.

OS *Ioannis Calvini opera selecta.* Ed. Peter Barth, Wilhelm Niesel, and Doris Scheuner. 5 vols. Munich: Chr. Kaiser Verlag, 1926–52.

PE *Works of Martin Luther*. Philadelphia Edition. Ed. and trans. Henry Eyster Jacobs et al. 6 vols. Philadelphia: Muhlenberg Press, 1930–43.

RSR *Religious Studies Review.*

RSV The Revised Standard Version of the Bible.

ScG Thomas Aquinas, *Summa contra Gentiles.* Cited by book, chapter, and paragraph.

ST Thomas Aquinas, *Summa theologiae.* Cited by part (or subpart), question, article, and (where appropriate) response to an objection. "Eng. trans." refers to the American edition. *Summa Theologica.* Trans. Fathers of the Dominican Province. 3 vols. New York: Benziger Brothers, 1947–48.

TT *Calvin's Tracts and Treatises.* Trans. Henry Beveridge. 3 vols. Edinburgh, 1844–51. Reprinted, Grand Rapids, Mich.: Wm. B. Eerdmans Publishing Co., 1958. Also included as vols. 1–3 in *Selected Works of John Calvin: Tracts and Letters.* 7 vols. Grand Rapids, Mich.: Baker Book House, 1983.

WA *D. Martin Luthers Werke: Kritische Gesamtausgabe.* Weimarer Ausgabe. Weimar: Hermann Böhlau [and Successor], 1883–. Cited by volume (or part-volume), page, and line.

WADB Ibid. *Deutsche Bibel.* 12 vols. 1906–61.

WATR Ibid. *Tischreden.* 6 vols. 1912–21. When an entire entry is pertinent, it is cited by number rather than page and line.

NOTES

1. Saving Faith

1. Sydney Cave, *The Doctrine of the Person of Christ* (London: Duckworth, 1925), 139.

2. Martin Luther, *Lectures on Galatians* (1535), pref., WA 40^2.33.7; *LW* 27:145. Unless otherwise noted, my Luther quotations in English are from *LW*.

3. Ibid., WA 40^2.37.23; *LW* 27:30.

4. Ibid., WA 40^2.34.10; *LW* 27:28.

5. Ibid., WA 40^1.255.30; *LW* 26:147.

6. Luther took the Habakkuk text to mean that the just (or justified) shall live by faith. The verse from Deuteronomy reads in the old KJV: "I will hide my face from them . . . for they are a very froward generation, children in whom is no faith." In both texts the correct translation is not "faith," but "faithfulness" or "steadfastness." The Greek word *pistis* sometimes has this sense in the New Testament (in Rom. 3:3 it is used for the faithfulness of God); sometimes also it has the sense of *fides quae creditur*, "the Christian faith" (e.g., in 1 Tim. 4:1,6). For a fuller summary of the pertinent linguistic data on *emunah* and *pistis* and their cognates, see *IDB* 2:222–34, together with the articles in the supplement (pp. 329–35), and *ABD* 2:744–60. Frequently, of course, the New Testament speaks of faith as directed to Christ rather than God, but, as Bultmann says, this does not mean that the relationship with God is pushed into the background: the faith is directed to God's deed in Christ, or the God who meets the believer in Christ. See Rudolf Bultmann and Artur Weiser, *Faith*, Bible Key Words from Gerhard Kittel's *Theologisches Wörterbuch zum Neuen Testament*, no. 10, trans. Dorothea M. Barton (London: Adam & Charles Black, 1961), 86. I do not need to go into the more controversial question whether the phrase *pistis Christou* in Paul may be taken to mean "the faith [or faithfulness] *of* Christ" (subjective genitive) rather than "faith *in* Christ" (objective genitive). There is a useful discussion of the question in Richard B. Hays, *The Faith of Jesus Christ: An Investigation of the Narrative Substructure of Galatians 3:1-4; 11*, Society of Biblical Literature Dissertation Series, no. 56 (Chico, Calif.: Scholars Press, 1983), chap. 4. The third article under "Faith" in *ABD* (2:758-60) is also devoted to the phrase *pistis Christou*.

7. See James Barr's critique of linguistic arguments for the alleged contrast between Hebrew and Greek ways of thinking in *The Semantics of Biblical Language* (Oxford: Oxford University Press, 1961), especially chap. 7.

8. Martin Buber, *Two Types of Faith*, trans. Norman P. Goldhawk (1951; reprint, New York: Collier Books, 1986), 44.

9. Ibid., 58–65. In the original German, Buber's theme was *Zwei Glaubensweisen*.

10. Ibid., 7–9, 96–98.

11. See Bultmann and Weiser, *Faith*, 70–76. Bultmann also lays heavy emphasis on the connection of *pistis* with obedience (ibid., 63–64; cf. Rom 1:5, 16:26).

12. Buber, *Two Types*, 11.

13. Ibid., 8.

14. The special status assigned to Thomas by Leo XIII (*Aeterni Patris*, 1879) and Pius X (*Doctoris Angelici*, 1914) has been qualified since the Second Vatican Council (1962–65) by the similar recognition of other doctors of the Roman church. But his *Summa theologiae* (hereafter *ST*) retains its authority as a systematic presentation of Roman Catholic faith.

15. Thomas, *ST* II–II, qq. 1–16.

16. Ibid., q. 2, art. 1; q. 4, art. 2; q. 2, art. 9.

17. Ibid., q. 1, arts. 4–5; q. 1, art. 2; q. 2, art. 1; q. 4, arts. 1, 8.

18. Ibid., q. 1, arts. 8–10; q. 2, arts. 5–6.

19. Ibid., q. 8, art. 4, ad 2; Eng. trans., 2:1206.

20. Ibid., q. 5, art. 3; q. 10, art. 8; q. 11, arts. 3–4. Thomas actually distinguishes three kinds of unbelief—in the pagan, the heretic, and the apostate, respectively (ibid., qq. 10–12).

21. Ibid., q. 4, art. 1; cf. art. 5. On confession as the outward act of faith, see q. 3; on the concept of a theological virtue, see *ST* I–II, q. 62.

22. Thomas, *ST* II–II, q. 4, art. 3; q. 23, art. 1; q. 82, art. 2, ad 1.

23. Ibid., q. 4, art. 3, ad 1; q. 2, art. 9; q. 4, art. 4 (cf. q. 6, art. 2, ad 3); q. 1, arts. 1–2. The Latin of q. 4, art. 3, ad 1, says simply that love "informs" (*informat*) the act of faith; "quickens" in the Eng. trans. (2:1192) is perhaps borrowed from the next article, where faith formed by love is decribed as *formata et vivens*.

24. Terence Penelhum, "The Analysis of Faith in St. Thomas Aquinas," in Penelhum, ed., *Faith* (New York: Macmillan Publishing Co., 1989), 113–33; quotation on 123–24.

25. A major source of the criticism has been the work of Hartmann Grisar (1845–1932). See the one-volume condensation of his great Luther study: Hartmann Grisar, *Martin Luther: His Life and Work*, trans. from the 2d German ed. by Frank J. Eble (Westminster, Md.: Newman Press, 1950), 487–88. The issue is much more complex than I need to show here, not least because the word *fiducia* in Luther's usage sometimes implies "trust," sometimes "certainty," and he can state the object of certainty as a proposition to which assent is required (i.e., *fides*). The Catholic objection is perhaps less accurately conveyed by Grisar's "fiduciary faith" than by Paul Hacker's "reflexive faith": that is, a faith in which the ego bends back upon itself. See Hacker, "Martin Luther's Notion of Faith," in Jared Wicks, ed., *Catholic Scholars Dialogue with Luther* (Chicago: Loyola University Press, 1970), 85–105. Whichever term is used, most Luther scholars will judge the criticism one-sided, even if they concede that it may contain a grain of truth.

26. This was one of the major issues in Luther's hearing before Cardinal Cajetan at Augsburg (1518). The "Proceedings at Augsburg" will be found in WA 2.6-26; *LW* 31:259-292. See esp. WA 2.13.6-16.12; *LW* 31:270-75. Note that the term Luther uses is *fides* rather than *fiducia*, and he understands *fides* as belief in the word or promise of Christ or God.

27. Luther, *Galatians*, WA 40^{1}.26.11-25; *LW* 27:22-23.

28. Ibid., WA 40^{1}.285.20; *LW* 26:168. Cf. James 2:19.

29. Luther, *A Brief Explanation of the Ten Commandments, the Creed, and the Lord's Prayer* (1520), WA 7.215.1-8; the trans. is taken from PE 2:368 (emphasis is

the translator's). With this contrast Thomas's remarks on *belief about* God and *belief in* God, or believing a proposition and believing a reality, in *ST* II–II, q. 1, art. 2, ad 2, where the distinction is not at all between mere assent and trustful surrender. Cf. ibid., q. 2, art. 2, on the distinction between believing God, believing in a God, and believing in God.

30. Luther, *The Blessed Sacrament of the Holy and True Body of Christ, and the Brotherhoods* (1519), WA 2.753.19; *LW* 35:66. Here not to believe (*wer nit glaubt*) is not to trust (*nit trawet*).

31. Luther, "Preface to the Epistle of St. Paul to the Romans" (1546 [1522]), WADB 7.11.16; *LW* 35:370.

32. Luther, *Galatians*, WA 40^{1}.228.33-229.30, 602.18-603:13; *LW* 26:129-30, 396. Harnack thought it a serious flaw in the *Summa theologiae* that Thomas treated the entire doctrine of grace before the doctrine of the person of Christ and accordingly could not make the connection between grace and "the impression produced by the person who awakens spirit and life, certainty and blessedness." Adolph [Adolf von] Harnack, *History of Dogma*, trans. from the 3d German ed. by Neil Buchanan et al., 7 vols. (London: Williams & Norgate, 1894–99), 6:300, n. 2. The criticism, made from a Lutheran standpoint, is not without substance. But more needs to be said: the apparent remoteness of Christ must be attributed partly to the exigencies of a systematic presentation, which is bound to treat separately things that are not separate in fact. Nobody will doubt that Thomas believed, for instance, in Christ's eucharistic presence.

33. Luther, *Galatians*, WA 40^{1}.376.23; *LW* 26:238. Note that Luther qualifies this right thinking as a "knowledge of the heart (*cogitatio cordis*)."

34 Luther, *Sermons on the Gospel of St. John Chapters 6–8* (1530–32), WA 33.506.35 (*LW* 23:316); *Table Talk*, WATR 3, no. 2935 (1533; *LW* 54:182).

35. The controversies peaked in the 1960s. See my 1963 article, revised and reissed in *OPN*, chap. 4.

36. Luther, *Galatians*, WA 40^{1}.488.25; *LW* 26:315.

37. Ibid., WA 40^{1}.91.23, 298.13-299.28, 602.18-603.13; *LW* 26:38, 177-79, 396.

38. Ibid., WA 40^{1}.605.15; *LW* 26:397.

39. Ibid., WA 40^{1}.603.12; *LW* 26:396.

40 John Calvin, *Institutes of the Christian Religion*, 1559 edition (hereafter *Inst.*), 3.2.8; LCC 20:551. Except where otherwise noted, my Calvin quotations in English follow the wording of the translation in LCC 20-21.

41. *Inst.*, 3.2.13; LCC 20:558.

42. *Inst.*, 3.2.17: LCC 20:562. For explicit appeals to experience, see, for example, secs. 4, 11, and 12.

43. Thomas, *ST* II–II, q. 4, art. 8, ad 1.

44. *Inst.*, 3.2.7 (trans. mine).

45. *Inst.*, 3.2.14; LCC 20:560. Calvin notes that John, however, uses "knowledge" (*scientia*) rather than "recognition" (*agnitio*) in speaking of faith. The English word "recognition" (from the Latin *recognitio*), unlike *agnitio*, implies the identification of someone previously known. But the implication is entirely in harmony with Calvin's view of revelation as bringing to focus a knowledge of God that is given to everyone but has become confused. See my article, "Errors and Insights in the Understanding of Revelation: A Provisional Response," *JR* 78 (1998): 64–88. There is a very interesting exploration of the theme of recognition in sacred and secular narratives, brought to my attention after the present chapter was written, in Diana Culbertson,

The Poetics of Revelation: Recognition and the Narrative Tradition, Studies in American Biblical Hermeneutics, no. 4. (Macon, Ga.: Mercer University Press, 1989).

46. *Inst.*, 3.2.2; LCC 20:545.

47. "Tota Christianorum vita, quaedam pietatis meditatio esse debet" (*Inst.*, 3.19.2). "Nam haec demum vera pietatis regula est, distincte tenere quisnam sit Deus quem colimus" (Comm. on Acts 17.24, *CO* 48:410).

48. Comm. on Isa 42:14, *CO* 37:69-70; Comm.on Isa 49:15, *CO* 37:204.

49. *Inst.*, 3.2.2 (trans. and emphasis mine).

50. *Inst.*, 3.2.28; LCC 20:574. Calvin's wording is influenced by the Latin (Vulgate) version, "Et ostende faciem tuam, et salvi erimus," which he puts into the third person. On faith and the divine fatherhood in Calvin's theology, see further B. A. Gerrish, *Grace and Gratitude: The Eucharistic Theology of John Calvin* (Minneapolis: Fortress Press, Edinburgh: T. & T. Clark, 1993), 22–31, 38–41, 62–71. Perhaps Calvin's most striking affirmation on faith as the recognition of God's fatherhood comes in his chapter on free justification, in which he states that "as Paul attests, faith is not true unless it asserts and brings to mind that sweetest name of Father—nay, unless it opens our mouth freely to cry, 'Abba, Father.'" This, he explains, is the faith by which alone we are justified (*Inst.*, 3.13.5; LCC 20:768).

51. *Inst.*, 3.2.36; LCC 20:583.

52. *Inst.*, 3.2.28; LCC 20:574.

53. *Inst.*, 3.2.15; LCC 20:561.

54. Calvin, *Catechism of the Church of Geneva* (1545), q. 111, *OS* 2:92: "Sic autem definire licet [sc. fidem], ut dicamus certam esse ac stabilem cognitionem paternae erga nos Dei benevolentiae." Trans. mine; cf. *TT* 2:53.

55. *Inst.*, 3.2.20, 2.28, 7.10, 19.5, etc.; LCC 20:566, 574, 701, 837.

56. Here and elsewhere I have put "saving" in quotation marks to remind the reader that I am simply referring to what church theologians have traditionally *called* "saving faith." It will become clear in my final chapter that I do not assume at the outset that only professed Christians can have a faith that saves.

2. Secular Faith

1. See for example Thomas, *ST* II–II, q. 10, art. 5.

2. Even these variations do not exhaust the range of meanings assigned to faith and its opposites in the New Testament. From the Letter to the Hebrews, for instance, one exegetical tradition has inferred that faith is a venture, even a risk, and its opposite a futile clutching after security in the things or situations that appear to be subject to our control.

3. Thomas, *ScG* I, chap. 6, paras. 1–3.

4. Calvin, *Inst.*, 3.2.6.

5. Wilfred Cantwell Smith, *Towards a World Theology: Faith and the Comparative History of Religion* (Maryknoll, N.Y.: Orbis Books, 1981).

6. Wilfred Cantwell Smith, *Faith and Belief* (Princeton, N.J.: Princeton University Press, 1979), 8–9, 166.

7. Ibid., 12.

8. Ibid., 116, 120, 166; Wilfred Cantwell Smith, *Belief and History* (Charlottesville: University Press of Virginia, 1977), 41, 45–46, 65–66, 96. In my conclusion to chap. 1 I allowed for a distinction also between *belief in* and *beliefs* (plural): that is,

a multitude of *beliefs that*. It is the second sense of "belief" that Smith intends when he contrasts "belief" and "faith."

9. Smith, *Faith and Belief*, 12–13, 129–30, 133. Note the hesitant turn of phrase when Smith writes: "Faith, then, so far as one can see as one looks out over the history of our race, is an essential human quality. One might argue that it is *the* essential human quality: that it is constitutive of man as human . . ." (p.129; his emphasis). The hesitancy ("one might argue that") is appropriate, and because I myself am skeptical of historical or empirical arguments for what constitutes humanity, I do not wish my own concept of "generic faith" in the present chapter to be taken as including a strictly universal claim. The transition to philosophical argument in my next chapter will open up the possibility of a stronger claim. My limited purpose, at this stage, is simply to propose that Christian faith is best understood if it is not treated as the sole instance of a unique class of one. Granted the variations in the concept of Christian faith, I do not rule out the possibility that there might in fact be more than one generic model under which it could plausibly be subsumed. Against Smith's view of faith as universal and generically human, one recent study (not available to me when I wrote the present chapter) proposes six models of faith: William Lad Sessions, *The Concept of Faith: A Philosophical Investigation* (Ithaca, N.Y.: Cornell University Press, 1994).

10. Smith, *The Meaning and End of Religion: A New Approach to the Religious Traditions of Mankind* (New York: Macmillan Co., 1963), 188–89. The subtitle on the cover of the paperbound reprint (San Francisco: Harper & Row, 1978) announces "a revolutionary approach to the great religious traditions."

11. Huston Smith, "Faith and Its Study: What Wilfred Smith's against, and for," *RSR* 7 (1981): 306–10; see 307.

12. Ibid., 308–9.

13. Smith, *Faith and Belief*, 177, n.3. Elsewhere Smith writes of Friedrich Schleiermacher's earlier work *On Religion: Speeches to Its Cultured Despisers* (first published in 1799) as apparently "the first book ever written on religion as such . . . on religion itself as a generic something" (*Meaning and End*, 45). Although Schleiermacher's legacy was the inclusion of the nonintellectual element in the concept of religion (p. 46), and for this he is to be commended, Smith thinks the word "religion" is no substitute for "faith" (p. 50). In a later book he acknowledges that Schleiermacher's *Christian Faith* is indeed about Christian piety "and *other forms* of faith" (*World Theology*, 114; emphasis in the original). But in general the great liberal theologian remains under a cloud, in Smith's thinking, for turning theology in upon the religious subject. Whether Smith's own term "faith" is any the less anthropocentric is another question, on which Langdon Gilkey has made some telling comments: Gilkey, "A Theological Voyage with Wilfred Cantwell Smith," *RSR* 7 (1981): 298–306.

14. The quotation from Schleiermacher I used as my first epigraph at the beginning of this book follows his statement of intent in the first edition of *The Christian Faith* to compare Christianity with other *Glaubensarten* (*CG*[1] §§ 6–7). Trans. mine.

15. Gilkey, "Voyage with Smith," 306, n.2. It must of course be granted that if Smith uses Christian—even Protestant—categories, he does not do so to perpetuate exclusive Christian claims. On the contrary, he can affirm eloquently that the adherents of non-Christian religions, too, have been saved by faith—"saved from nihilism, alienation, anomie, despair; from the bleak despondency of meaninglessness" (*World Theology*, 168).

16. See for example Smith, *Faith and Belief*, 12, 139, 163, 166.

17. Smith, *World Theology*, 154–55. By a "big-bang theory" Smith does not mean the exclusive claim of any one religion to possess the sole revelation but rather the tendency to interpret every religion as though it lived entirely out of the one great "seismic event" of its origin. Moreover, in *Faith and Belief* Smith certainly acknowledges that faith has what he calls an "intellectual dimension": faith is "recognition of truth, insight into reality," and its conceptualization is belief. But he goes on to set aside the concept of revelation (p. 169), whereas we have seen that for Calvin recognition and revelation ("the word") are correlates. It is interesting, however, that Smith's exploration of "belief" as "recognition that" leads him very close to Calvin. He writes: "No one should believe in God who has not personally encountered Him. . . . Believe in God only insofar as you see Him and know Him, dimly or vividly, or can discern His acting in history or in your own life . . ." (*Belief and History*, 79). On Schleiermacher's understanding of revelation, see Walter E. Wyman, Jr., "Revelation and the Doctrine of Faith: Historical Revelation within the Limits of Historical Consciousness," *JR* 78 (1998):38–63.

18. Viktor E. Frankl, *Man's Search for Meaning: An Introduction to Logotherapy*, 3d ed., trans. Ilse Lasch and Gordon W. Allport (New York: Simon & Schuster, 1984), 11. The first edition of the English translation was titled *From Death-Camp to Existentialism: A Psychiatrist's Path to a New Therapy* (Boston: Beacon Press, 1959). The book was first published in Austria as *Ein Psycholog erlebt das Konzentrationslager* (1946).

19. Frankl, *Search for Meaning*, 12, 74, 104, 106, 108, 115, 140, 146–47, 151.

20. Ibid., 75.

21. Ibid., 19.

22. Ibid., 91, 136.

23. Ibid., 148.

24. Ibid., 51, 85, 113, 145.

25. See, for instance, the report by Roy Larson, "Psychiatrist Has Words of Hope," *Chicago Sun-Times*, 15 April 1984.

26. Frankl, *Search for Meaning*, 48–50, 68, 109–10.

27. Ibid., 81–84. Elsewhere, Frankl was by no means reticent about matters of religion, though he insisted on the distinction between psychiatry and theology. In *The Unconscious God: Psychotherapy and Theology* (New York: Simon & Schuster, 1975 [German ed., 1948]), he suggests that religion may be defined as "man's search for *ultimate* meaning," belief and faith as "*trust* in ultimate meaning" (p. 13; Frankl's emphasis). There is an "unconscious religiousness" in everyone, to be understood as a "latent relation to transcendence" (p. 61), and it is the task of logotherapy "to re-mind [*sic*] the patient" of this unconscious religiousness (p. 67). In *The Will to Meaning: Foundations and Applications of Logotherapy* (1969; expanded ed., New York: New American Library, 1988), Frankl expressly asserts that faith in the ultimate meaning, or "supra-meaning," is "preceded by trust in an ultimate being, by trust in God" (p. 145), and he has some interesting remarks about "basic trust in an ultimate meaning" (p. 150)—a notion to which I return in chap. 3. The individual religions and beliefs (plural), he suggests, are different languages about the ultimate (pp.153–56) . But I am not aware of any place where Frankl shows plainly how the pieces fit together or offers a thorough analysis of the concept of "faith," which he sometimes appears to distinguish from "belief" (for instance, in his preface to Donald F. Tweedie, Jr., *Logotherapy and the Christian Faith: An Evaluation of Frankl's Existential Approach to Psychotherapy* [Grand Rapids: Baker Book House, 1961]). Hence we need to carry

the quest for a psychological concept of faith further than Frankl takes us. See also, among his other pertinent writings, *The Doctor and the Soul*, trans. from the German *Ärztliche Seelsorge* (1952) by Richard and Clara Winston (1955; expanded ed., with the subtitle *From Psychotherapy to Logotherapy*, New York: Alfred A. Knopf, 1965); and *Psychotherapy and Existentialism: Selected Papers on Logotherapy* (New York: Washington Square Press, 1967).

28. Frankl, *Search for Meaning*, 120–21. If we venture to describe this logodrama as an instance of meaning construction, it does not follow that, for Frankl, meanings are entirely subjective and relative. Though he insists that there is no such thing a "universal meaning of life," he speaks of meanings or values that are shared across society and are about the human condition as such, and he invites confusion by calling them "meaning universals" (*Will to Meaning*, 55–56; cf. *Unconscious God*, 119–20). Meanings are discovered, he says, not invented; and the intuitive capacity to find the meaning of a situation is what Frankl means by "conscience" (*Will to Meaning*, 63; *Unconscious God*, 113–15).

29. James W. Fowler, *Stages of Faith: The Psychology of Human Development and the Quest for Meaning* (San Francisco: Harper & Row, 1981), 164, 294. Fowler acknowledges that the influence of Erik Erikson on his development theory has been more pervasive than the influence of Jean Piaget and Lawrence Kohlberg, but more subtle and harder to "put on paper" (p. 110).

30. J. Harry Fernhout, "Where Is Faith? Searching for the Core of the Cube," in Craig Dykstra and Sharon Parks, eds., *Faith Development and Fowler* (Birmingham, Ala.: Religious Education Press, 1986), 65–89; see p. 86. See also Sharon Daloz Parks, "The North American Critique of James Fowler's Theory of Faith Development," in James W. Fowler, Karl Ernst Nipkow, and Friedrich Schweizer, eds., *Stages of Faith and Religious Development: Implications for Church, Education, and Society*, Eng. trans. of *Glaubensentwicklung und Erziehung* [1988] (New York: Crossroad, 1991), 101–15.

31. Fowler, "Faith and the Structuring of Meaning," in Dykstra and Parks, *Faith Development,* 15–42; quotation on 15.

32. Fowler, *Stages*, 4.

33. Ibid., 24–25.

34. Fowler, "Structuring of Meaning," 25–26 (italics and phrasing in the original).

35. Fowler, *Stages*, 104. Cf. ibid., xiii; Fowler, "Structuring of Meaning," 15–16.

36. Fowler, *Stages*, 293 (my emphasis).

37. Ibid.

38. Ibid., 17. The unpublished manuscript by Niebuhr to which Fowler refers (*Stages*, 34, n. 4) has since been made available by Niebuhr's son: H. Richard Niebuhr, *Faith on Earth: An Inquiry into the Structure of Human Faith*, ed. Richard R. Niebuhr (New Haven: Yale University Press, 1989). Fowler also acknowledges his debt to H. Richard Niebuhr, *Radical Monotheism and Western Culture* (New York: Harper & Row, 1960).

39. Fowler, *Stages*, 18–23; "Structuring of Meaning," 18.

40. Fowler, "Structuring of Meaning," 23.

41. See chap. 3 below.

42. Obviously, Calvin would not have needed to justify the use of faith language indirectly by appeal to the notion of loyalty contained in his term *fiducia*. For him, faith as *fides* is already the appropriate epistemological term for an authentic relation to God because it denotes knowledge by recognition. But it is not my intention

to impose Calvin's concept of faith on a more general one: on the contrary, I want to show how *his* concept can be subsumed under a *generic* concept arrived at by another route.

43. Dykstra and Parks, *Faith Development,* 9 (in their editorial introduction).

44. Dykstra, "What Is Faith? An Experiment in the Hypothetical Mode," in Dykstra and Parks, *Faith Development,* 45–64; see esp. p. 56–57. See also Richard R. Osmer, "James W. Fowler and the Reformed Tradition: An Exercise in Theological Reflection in Religious Education," in Jeff Astley and Leslie J. Francis, eds., *Christian Perspectives on Faith Development: A Reader* (Grand Rapids, Mich.: William B. Eerdmans Publishing Co., 1992), 135–50.

45. John Wood Oman, *The Natural and the Supernatural* (Cambridge: Cambridge University Press, 1931), 175. Cf. John Hick: "Our knowledge of [God by faith] is thus, like all our knowledge of environment, an apprehension reached by an act of interpretation; but it differs from the rest of our knowing in that in this case the interpretation is uniquely total in its scope" *(Faith and Knowledge: A Modern Introduction to the Problem of Religious Knowledge* [Ithaca, N.Y.: Cornell University Press, 1957]), 165. In his subsequent work, Hick has made use of Ludwig Wittgenstein's reflections on "seeing as." See, for example, John Hick, "Seeing-as and Religious Experience," reproduced from the *Proceedings of the Eighth International Wittgenstein Symposium* (1983) in Terence Penelhum, ed., *Faith,* (New York: Macmillan Publishing Co., 1989) 183–92.

46. Fowler, *Stages*, 92–93.

47. Fowler, "Structuring of Meaning," 15, 18; cf. Fowler, *Stages*, 4, 24.

48. This is the point of my second epigraph to this chapter (from Acts 14:17). I must admit that even friends sympathetic to my thinking have been reluctant to see construction and revelation, or construal and recognition, as anything other than exclusive concepts. (One of them thought "construal" an acceptable term, but not "construction," although the dictionaries allow both words, which are of course etymologically related, to denote an act of interpretation.) I may not be able to satisfy them fully here. I must be content to offer just two remarks. (1) The language of construal is by no means a novelty in the present-day theological discussion. It appears, for example, in Calvin's likening of revelation to corrective lenses that effect a clear knowledge of God (*Inst.*, 1.6.1; note his use of the word *contexere*). (2) Once it is granted that the mind is not passive in cognition, there cannot be an absolute contrast between disclosure and construal; there can only be disagreement about *how much* and *what* is to be attributed to the activity of the mind. To pursue the question further would inevitably take us into contemporary discussions not only about "construction," but also about critical realism, projection, and the religious imagination. See further the article referred to in chap. 1, n. 45, above and the contributions listed in the Bibliography by Ian Barbour, Garrett Green, Van Harvey, and Gordon D. Kaufman.

49. Luther, *Lectures on Romans* (1515–16), WA 56.392.28ff., 446.31; *LW* 25:382-83, 438-39.

50. Fowler, *Stages*, 196.

51. Calvin, *Inst.*, 4.16.19.

52. Ibid., 4.19.13.

53. Fowler, *Stages*, 302. See also ibid., 210, 281–91; Fowler, "Structuring of Meaning," 27.

54. Fowler, *Stages*, 201.

55. In Calvin's "saving faith," of course, the perception of meaning follows from

recognition of the object of loyalty. My point is simply that the mental operation of having generic faith includes both a cognitive activity of discernment and a volitional state of trustful commitment. The two are, I think, dialectically related in the sense that each acts and reacts on the other.

3. The Justification of Faith

1. Martin Luther, *The Large Catechism* (1529), *CELC* 365.

2. Heinrich Bullinger, *The Second Helvetic Confession* (1566), chap. 16. The Latin text is reproduced in Philip Schaff, *CC* 3:233–306. With one change, I have followed the translation by Arthur Cochrane, adopted in the *Book of Confessions* of the Presbyterian Church (U.S.A.), *BC* 53–119 (see p. 83). Arthur C. Cochrane, ed., *Reformed Confessions of the Sixteenth Century* (Philadelphia: Westminster Press, 1966), 257. Cochrane renders *fiducia* as "trust," for which I have substituted "assurance" because Bullinger plainly intends an intellectual, rather than a volitional, act. Other Reformed confessions preserve the balance of belief and trust much better, though without following Calvin's thought that belief, as recognition, is itself a matter of personal relationship. See, for example, the Heidelberg Catechism (1563), q. 21, and the Westminster Confession (1647), chap. 16: *BC* 31–32, 141.

3. Thomas, *ST* II–II, q. 2, arts. 9–10, q. 5, art. 2.

4. See Roland H. Bainton, *The Travail of Religious Liberty: Nine Biographical Studies* (Philadelphia: Westminster Press, 1951), 94; Bainton, *Hunted Heretic: The Life and Death of Michael Servetus, 1511–1553* (Boston: Beacon Press, 1953), 212–14.

5. Sebastian Castellio [Sébastien Castellion or Châteillon], *On the Art of Doubting*, bk. 2, chap. 2, trans. in Roland H. Bainton, *Concerning Heretics, Whether They Are to Be Persecuted . . . Together with Excerpts from Other Works of Sebastian Castellio and David Joris* (New York: Columbia University Press, 1935), 304. For information on Castellio, I am mainly indebted to Bainton, *Travail of Religious Liberty*, chap. 4, and the critical edition of *De arte dubitandi* by Elisabeth Feist Hirsch (see Bibliography).

6. Trans. Bainton, *Concerning Heretics*, 121 (also in Bainton, *Travail of Religious Liberty*, 110).

7. John Locke, *An Essay Concerning Human Understanding* (1690), ed. Peter H. Nidditch (Oxford: Clarendon Press, 1975), bk. 4, chap. 18, sec. 2 (p. 689).

8. Immanuel Kant, "What Is Enlightenment?" (1784), trans. Lewis White Beck in Kant, *On History*, ed. Beck (Indianapolis: Bobbs-Merrill Company, 1963), 3–10; quotation on 3. The Enlightenment's principle that belief must be proportionate to the evidence underwent a rebirth in the nineteenth-century "ethics of belief" debate. See Gerald D. McCarthy, ed., *The Ethics of Belief Debate*, American Academy of Religion Academy Series, no. 41 (Atlanta, Ga.: Scholars Press, 1986). Present-day antifoundationalists (or anti-evidentialists) have sharply criticized the principle. See, for example, Nicholas Wolterstorff, *John Locke and the Ethics of Belief*, Cambridge Studies in Religion and Critical Thought, no. 2 (Cambridge: Cambridge University Press, 1996), and nn.15 and 33 below.

9. The expression "inevitable belief" is borrowed from Arthur James Balfour, and my first epigraph to the present chapter will be found in his first series of Gifford Lectures, *Theism and Humanism* (New York: George H. Doran Company, 1915), 263. I have written more fully on Jacobi and Forberg in essays reprinted

in *CR,* chaps. 4 and 6. The essay on Jacobi first appeared in a volume honoring Schubert Ogden, whose analysis of "basic confidence" is the most interesting and persuasive case in current theological literature for what I am calling "inevitable belief." See Philip E. Devenish and George L. Goodwin, eds., *Witness and Existence: Essays in Honor of Schubert M. Ogden* (Chicago: University of Chicago Press, 1989). In Ogden, the argument for inevitable belief clearly does not rest on an empirical (or historical) survey of human experience but on conceptual analysis of the presuppositions of experience. For this reason, it can plausibly be claimed that the argument is about a strictly universal element in being human. Cf. Viktor Frankl's remarks on "basic trust in an ultimate meaning," which he takes to be transcendental "in the strict sense of Immanuel Kant's transcendentalism" (*Will to Meaning*, 150; cf. Frankl's two illustrations of his point on pp. 151–52). I am not concerned here to counter the objection that human experience is itself culturally specific and therefore implies culturally specific presuppositions. I must be content, for now, to locate the language of Christian faith on a *larger* map, whether or not it is a purely *human* map.

10. Goethe, conversation with F. v. Müller, 26 January 1825, in Johann Wolfgang Goethe, *Gedenkausgabe der Werke: Briefe und Gespräche*, vol. 23 (Zurich: Artemis, 1950), 372.

11. See Ronald Gregor Smith, *J. G. Hamann 1730–1788: A Study in Christian Existence* (London: Collins, 1960).

12. Jacobi is referring to David Hume, *Enquiry Concerning Human Understanding*, the 1770 edn., sec. 12, pt. 1.

13. Friedrich Heinrich Jacobi, *David Hume über den Glauben, oder Idealismus und Realismus: Ein Gespräch*, 2d ed. (1815), JW 2:163–66. The text of the revised ed. occupies pp. 125–288; Jacobi furnished it with a long introduction on pp. 3–123. Translations of Jacobi are mine.

14. Ibid., 204–5, 225–28, 267–71.

15. A colleague suggests that we ourselves might say, with Alvin Plantinga, "a properly basic belief" where Jacobi says "an original conviction," since both intend a belief that does not require proof by inference from other beliefs. It does sound very much like Jacobi when Plantinga asserts that testimony confers a *prima facie* right to believe. But a basic belief in his sense is not, or not necessarily, inevitable in Jacobi's or Balfour's sense but only in the sense that I am not obliged to stop believing simply because I cannot come up with sufficient evidence from other, cognitively secure beliefs. In particular, belief in God may be properly basic, but for Plantinga it isn't inevitable. Still, I am naturally intrigued by his appeal to Calvin's *sensus divinitatis*, apparently to explain why lots of people do believe in God, and all should. See, for example, Plantinga, "Reason and Belief in God," in Alvin Plantinga and Nicholas Wolterstorff, ed., *Faith and Rationality: Reason and Belief in God* (Notre Dame: University of Notre Dame Press, 1983), 16–93. I think I too can appeal to Calvin, not only for his definition of Christian, saving faith, but also for his notion of the light that still dwells in fallen humanity. It consists, he says, of two parts: first, all possess by nature some seed of religion; second, the distinction between good and evil is engraved on their consciences (Calvin, Comm. on John 1:5; *CO* 47:6).

16. Jacobi, JW 2:58–60.

17. Ibid., 107–8.

18. Jacobi, *Über die Lehre des Spinozas, in Briefen an Herrn Moses Mendelssohn* (1785), JW 4,1:223.

19. Just what to make of the doubts mystics, skeptics, and subjective idealists have entertained about the material world is a question that need not be pursued here. See the interesting observations of John Oman, "The Sphere of Religion," in *Science, Religion, and Reality*, ed. Joseph Needham (New York: Macmillan Co., 1925), 259–99, esp. 280–84. It is striking how consistently "antifoundationalist" Oman's religious epistemology was, long before the term itself was coined.

20. Arthur Schopenhauer, *The World as Will and Idea* (1819), trans. R. B. Haldane and J. Kemp, 3 vols. (New York: Charles Scribner's Sons, 1883), 1:xiv.

21. Jacobi, JW 2:44, 120.

22. Fritz Medicus. See Medicus, ed., *Johann Gottlieb Fichte: Die philosophischen Schriften zum Atheismusstreit, mit Forbergs Aufsatze "Entwickelung des Begriffs der Religion"* (Leipzig: Felix Meiner, 1910), iv.

23. Friedrich Karl Forberg, "Entwickelung des Begriffs der Religion" (1798), most conveniently accessible in Medicus (see n.22 above) or Hans Lindau, ed., *Die Schriften zu J. G. Fichte's Atheismus-Streit* (Munich: Georg Müller, 1912), 37–58.

24. Lindau, *Atheismus-Streit*, 59–88.

25. Fred. Chas. Forberg, *Manual of Classical Erotology (De figuris Veneris)*, Latin text and Eng. trans. by Julian Smithson (1884; facsimile ed., 2 vols. in 1, New York: Grove, 1966).

26. *Friedrich Karl Forbergs der Philosophie Doctors und des Lyceums zu Saalfeld Rectors Apologie seines angeblichen Atheismus* (Gotha: Justus Perthes, 1799), 22, 25. Translations from Forberg's apology are mine.

27. Ibid., 35–36.

28. Ibid., 160–63. Among our present-day philosophers, R. M. Hare comes closer to Kant's own position when he argues that "no practical morality could do without an ample faith that events will not frustrate its ends." Such faith, which he finds it natural to express in religious terms, "saves moral endeavor from futility." See R. M. Hare, "The Simple Believer," in Gene Outka and John P. Reeder, Jr., eds., *Religion and Morality: A Collection of Essays* (Garden City, N.Y.: Anchor Press/Doubleday, 1973), 393–427; quotations from 413–14.

29. Forberg, *Apologie*, 127–30, 136.

30. Ibid., 145.

31. See further my article "Toward a Moral Theology: Forberg on Practical Belief," *Criterion* 29 (1990): 10–13, esp. 12–13. It is an interesting fact, documented many times over, that even the inmates of prisons commonly presuppose, not only the difference between "ought" and "ought not," but also a scale of "ought nots": at the bottom (or worst) end of the scale come molestation and murder of little children, so that the perpetrators of these crimes must fear retribution from their fellow prisoners.

32. The fact (often pointed out to me) that many criminals remain wholly untroubled by remorse is not, I think, a persuasive argument against the existence of moral order, any more than the fact that motorists are passing me at eighty-five miles an hour proves there is no speed limit. We identify the former as sociopaths and the latter as traffic violators.

33. Balfour, *Theism and Humanism*, 32–33; see also Balfour's second series of Gifford Lectures, *Theism and Thought* (New York: George H. Doran Company, 1924), 232–40. Although one reader saw in my present chapter an adumbration of "basic belief" (n.15 above), another thought he detected a whiff of the very theological foundationalism against which the concept of basic belief has been developed: the view that a person's religious beliefs are justified for her only if she can derive them

from propositions that are either self-evidently true, or evident to the senses, or direct reports of her own states of consciousness. But while I think it obvious that religious beliefs are in fact confirmed (not demonstrated) as one sees their harmony with what one otherwise believes, and in particular with what everyone else seems to believe too, I am not arguing that Christian beliefs can be *deduced* from elemental faith, which, therefore, cannot logically serve as their *foundation*. This is a species of coherentism perhaps, but not foundationalism. In chap. 5, I return to elemental faith as the shared *logical* presupposition of scientific inquiry and Christian faith and argue that, in actual *experience*, elemental and Christian faith stand in a reciprocal relationship to each other.

34. Thomas, *ST* II–II, q. 3, art. 4. How I understand the relationship between confession, confessions, and confessionalism will be clearer in the next chapter.

4. The Confession of Faith

1. Ernst Troeltsch, *Protestantism and Progress: The Significance of Protestantism for the Rise of the Modern World* (first published with the subtitle *A Historical Study of the Relation of Protestantism to the Modern World*, 1912; reprinted in the series Fortress Texts in Modern Theology, Philadelphia: Fortress Press, 1986), 54.

2. The fact that the Lutherans have the gospel in their small corner, however, won't prevent the arrival of the day of judgment. Luther, *Table Talk*, *WATR* 5, no. 5239 (1540); *LW* 54:402.

3. In *The Sacred Canopy: Elements of a Sociological Theory of Religion* (Garden City, N.Y.: Doubleday & Co., 1967), Peter L. Berger writes: "The pluralistic situation is, above all, a *market situation*" (p. 137). This militates against religious traditionalism, although, he says, a measure of "product loyalty" may persist (p. 144). Further, as others have pointed out, the full consequences of disestablishment in America were obscured as long as the old English denominations continued to enjoy cultural and religious hegemony. See Milton J.Coalter, John M. Mulder, and Louis B. Weeks, *The Re-forming Tradition: Presbyterians and Mainstream Protestantism*, a volume in the series The Presbyterian Presence: The Twentieth Century Experience (Louisville, Ky.: Westminster/John Knox Press, 1992), 37–41. On "the predicament of pluralism," see ibid., chap. 4.

4. Robert Wuthnow, "The Restructuring of American Presbyterianism: Turmoil in One Denomination," in Milton J. Coalter, John M. Mulder, and Louis B. Weeks, eds., *The Presbyterian Predicament: Six Perspectives*, Presbyterian Presence series (Louisville, Ky.: Westminster/John Knox Press, 1990), 27–48.

5. Membership figures are given on the *Yearbook of American Churches*, since 1973 the *Yearbook of American and Canadian Churches* (Nashville: Abingdon Press).

6. See James K. Cameron, "Scottish Calvinism and the Principle of Intolerance," in B. A. Gerrish, ed., in collaboration with Robert Benedetto, *Reformatio Perennis: Essays on Calvin and the Reformation in Honor of Ford Lewis Battles*, Pittsburgh Theological Monograph Series, no. 32 (Pittsburgh: Pickwick Press, 1981), 113–28.

7. See B. A. Gerrish, *Tradition and the Modern World: Reformed Theology in the Nineteenth Century* (Chicago: University of Chicago Press, 1978), chap. 3; quotation on p. 74.

8. Gerrish, *Tradition and the Modern World*, 79.

9. Ibid., 78–79.

10. I say "reckless use" because I certainly do not deny a church's privilege to measure the public teaching of its leaders by the official standards, nor do I assume that the dissident is always right. The point rather is that since history shows how yesterday's orthodoxy sometimes becomes today's heresy, and today's heterodoxy sometimes (not always!) becomes tomorrow's orthodoxy, the church dare not silence dissent by foreclosing theological discussion and assuming that dogmatic definitions cannot be improved.

11. One source of the aphorism may be the first of Luther's *Eight Wittenberg Sermons* (1522), the opening paragraph: WA 10^3.1.7-2.3; *LW* 51:70.

12. Calvin, *Inst.*, 4.1.1, 4 (my trans.).

13. Quoted from Wesley's preface to the first Methodist hymn book (1739) by J. Wesley Bready, *England before and after Wesley: The Evangelical Revival and Social Reform* (London: Hodder & Stoughton, 1938), 202.

14. See Peter L. Berger and Thomas Luckmann, *The Social Construction of Reality: A Treatise in the Sociology of Knowledge* (Garden City, N.Y.: Doubleday, 1966), passim. In his *Sacred Canopy*, Berger maintains that a socially constructed world provides an order (*nomos*) by which the individual can make sense of his or her biography, and that the distinctive role of religion is to give assurance that the order is ontologically grounded in a sacred cosmos. Berger has never understood his sociological account of religion reductionistically (*Sacred Canopy*, 88–89, 180–81). But he recognizes that religion, precisely by sanctifying the social order, can be an oppressive "agency of alienation" (p. 87), and he sometimes speaks of glimpses of transcendence coming to the solitary individual *despite* the given, socially constructed world (see especially *A Far Glory: The Quest for Faith in an Age of Credulity* [New York: Free Press, 1992]). Other important contributions to the discussion of community and identity formation have been made by George Lindbeck, Charles Taylor, and Robert Bellah et al. (see Bibliography). See also my review of Lindbeck's *Nature of Doctrine* in *JR* 68 (1988):87–92.

15. Berger and Luckmann, 158.

16. See the perceptive reading of Bunyan's *Grace Abounding* in Henri A.Talon, *John Bunyan: The Man and His Works*, trans. Barbara Wall (London: Rockliff Publishing Corporation, 1951), 131–40.

17. Friedrich Schleiermacher, *On Religion: Speeches to Its Culture Despisers*, trans. John Oman from the 3d German ed. [1821] (1894; reprint, Louisville, Ky.: Westminster/John Knox Press, 1994), 223–24. The German expression is *sich niederlassen*: see *Friedrich Schleiermacher's Reden über die Religion*, ed. G. Ch. Bernhard Pünjer (Brunswick: C. A. Schwetschke and Son [M. Bruhn], 1879), 257.

18. Karl Barth, "The Doctrinal Task of the Reformed Churches," in Barth, *The Word of God and the Word of Man*, trans. Douglas Horton (London: Hodder & Stoughton, 1928), 218–71; quotation from 227 (my emphasis).

19. Winthrop S. Hudson, *American Protestantism* (Chicago: University of Chicago Press, 1961), 135.

20. *CELC* 17–21; cf. 465, 504.

21. Luther, *Ninety-Five Theses* (*Disputation on the Power and Efficacy of Indulgences*, 1517), thesis 62, WA 1.236.22; *LW* 31:31.

22. See Gerrish, "The Chief Article—Then and Now" (1983), reprinted in *CR*, chap. 1.

23. On the role of "the special purpose group," see Wuthnow, "Restructuring of American Presbyterianism," 37–39, 46–48. In his book *The Restructuring of American*

Religion: Society and Faith since World War II (Princeton, N.J.: Princeton University Press, 1988), Wuthnow maintained that the American denominations "have become to a greater extent diverse federations of special purpose groups" (p. 125) and that the local churches serve as "holding companies" for them (p. 127).

24. The Athanasian Creed.

25. Geoffrey Wainwright, *Doxology—The Praise of God in Worship, Doctrine and Life: A Systematic Theology* (New York: Oxford University Press, 1980), 183.

26. B. A. Gerrish, "Christian Creeds," *The Encyclopedia of Religion*, 16 vols. (New York: Macmillan, 1987), 4:140–50; Gerrish, ed., *The Faith of Christendom: A Source Book of Creeds and Confessions* (Cleveland, Oh.: World Publishing Company, 1963).

27. Barth may have been correct when he included creed making among "things which one dares do and can do only if he must do them" (Karl Barth, "The Desirability and Possibility of a Universal Reformed Creed," in Barth, *Theology and Church: Shorter Writings 1920–1928*, trans. Louise Pettibone Smith [London: SCM Press, 1962], 128). But this cannot mean that a creed is essentially a reaction to some new crisis; essentially, a creed is a response to an old crisis, as I have indicated, and as such arises out of the day-to-day mandate of the church.

28. Wainwright, *Doxology*, 8.

29. I have addressed the distinctiveness of Reformed confesionalism elsewhere. Besides the titles in n. 26 above, see Gerrish, "The Confessional Heritage of the Reformed Church," *McCormick Quarterly* 19 (1966): 120–34; and "The New Presbyterian Confession," *Christian Century* 83 (1966): 582–85. See also "Confessional Nature of the Church: Report and Recommendations," in the *Minutes* of the 198th General Assembly of the Presbyterian Church (U.S.A.), part 1, *Journal* (New York and Atlanta, Ga.: Office of the General Assembly, 1986), 516–27, and the titles listed in the Bibliography under Edward A. Dowey, Jan Rohls, Jack Rogers, and Lukas Vischer.

30. *CC* 1:354.

31. Bullinger and Leo Jud (1482–1542) wanted one of the earliest Reformed confessions to carry an express disclaimer beginning: "In no way is it our wish, with these articles, to prescribe a single rule of faith for all churches" (First Helvetic Confession [1536], *CC* 1:389, my trans. from the German; cf. Arthur C. Cochrane, ed., *Reformed Confessions of the Sixteenth Century*, [Philadelphia: Westminster Press, 1966], 97–98). It was a new departure in 1967 when the United Presbyterian Church in the U.S.A. authorized a *Book of Confessions (BC)*. But the intention was precisely to acknowledge variety, not to exclude it, and the book remained open to subsequent additions. Naturally, the broad contrast I have drawn between Lutheran and Reformed attitudes to creeds and confessions is not intended to deny the existence of debate about the nature of confessionalism within each of the Reformation churches. The Lutheran Formula of Concord (1577) itself views the "symbols" as products of particular circumstances (*CELC* 465). But I must leave further details to the literature already cited.

32. Scots Confession (1560), pref.; Cochrane, ed., *Reformed Confessions*, 164–65. Cochrane reproduces the modernized English version of James Bulloch.

33. Ibid., chap. 22; *BC* 23. Cf. Second Helvetic Confession, chap. 20; *BC* 104.

34. A Brief Statement of Faith—Presbyterian Church (U.S.A.), line 64; *BC* 276.

35. The note on these verses in NRSV draws attention to the apparent discrepancy with 1 Cor 11:5, reports that some take them to be an editorial insertion, and refers to the similar prohibition in 1 Tim 2:11-12.

36. Calvin, *Inst.*, 4.9.13.

37. Ibid., 4.9.8.

38. Ibid., 4.9.10; 9.8 (*sitque instar praeiudicii*).

39. Barth constrasts the Reformed *bis auf weiteres* with the Lutheran *ad omnem posteritatem*: "The Lutheran *Augustana* (Augsburg Confession) is to be, according to the Formula of Concord [of 1577], the authority for the correct interpretation of Scripture 'for all posterity' (*ad omnem posteritatem*)" ("A Universal Reformed Creed," 114–15). Actually, the Formula refers to *itself* as a testimony *ad omnem posteritatem*, and what it attests is simply the decisions made in the Lutheran controversies of the day (*CELC* 507; trans. from the German).

40. *BC* 29.

41. *The Constitution of the Presbyterian Church (U.S.A.), Part II: Book of Order* (Louisville, Ky.: Office of the General Assembly, 1997), G-140405(b). This is not the place to discuss the complicated history of "subscription" in the Presbyterian churches, on which I can refer to the items in the Bibliography by Leonard Trinterud, Thomas Schafer, Lefferts Loetscher, and (for pertinent documents) Maurice Armstrong et al.

42. William C. Placher and David Willis-Watkins, *Belonging to God: A Commentary on A Brief Statement of Faith* (Louisville, Ky.: Westminster/John Knox Press, 1992).

43. Arnold B. Come, "The Occasion and Contribution of the Confession of 1967," *Journal of Presbyterian History* 61 (1983): 13–32; quotation on p. 21 (emphasis Come's).

44. James H. Moorhead, "Redefining Confessionalism: American Presbyterians in the Twentieth Century," in Milton J. Coalter, John M. Mulder, and Louis B. Weeks, eds., *The Confessional Mosaic: Presbyterians and Twentieth-Century Theology*, Presbyterian Presence series (Louisville, Ky.: Westminster/John Knox Press, 1990), 59–83; quotations on 68.

45. The texts of C-67 and the Brief Statement will be found in *BC*, nos. 10 and 11 (261–70, 275–76).

46. Calvin, *Catechism*, q. 55, *OS* 2:82 (trans. mine); cf. *TT* 2:45.

47. Calvin, *Inst.*, 2.16.5 (trans. mine).

48. Brief Statement, lines 9–11, 70–71.

49. Calvin, *The Form of Prayers*, etc. (1542), *OS* 2:1–58; quotation on 42. For an English translation of the pertinent section of Calvin's liturgy, see "Calvin's 'Essay on the Lord's Supper' from *The Form of Prayers*, 1542 and 1545," in *Calvin's Ecclesiastical Advice*, trans. Mary Beaty and Benjamin W. Farley (Louisville, Ky.: Westminster/John Knox Press, 1991), appendix 1, p. 168.

50. Zwingli, *Sixty-Seven Articles* (1523), arts. 2, 5; trans. Cochrane, *Reformed Confessions*, 36.

51. The allusion is to the preface of Anselm's *Cur Deus Homo*.

5. The Doctrine of Faith

1. See chap. 1, n. 41.

2. This may appear to be a sufficient reason for dropping the suspect name "dogmatics" and using "systematic theology" instead. But though dogmatics must be systematic, it is only a part of the systematic enterprise (along with apologetics and Christian ethics), and the word "dogmatics" at least has the merit of identifying the

object of inquiry as the teaching of a church, even if church "dogmas" are not taken to be irreformable or impervious to outside influence.

3. For more detail and documentation than I can offer here, see my article "From Calvin to Schleiermacher: The Theme and the Shape of Christian Dogmatics" (1985), reprinted in *CR,* chap. 8.

4. Calvin, *Inst.*, 1.6.1. See also chap. 2, n. 48, and chap. 3, n.15, above.

5. Calvin, *Inst.*, 2.6.1.

6. Ibid., 2.10.4. For Schleiermacher, by contrast, the transition from Judaism to Christianity was a transition to a different religion (*CG* §12.2). Translations from *CG* in this chapter are mine. For an English version of the entire work, see *CF* in the list of Abbreviations.

7. Calvin, *Inst.*, 2.6.4. The reason for this harsh verdict is that, apart from Christ, there are no grounds for the persuasion that God is father.

8. Schleiermacher, *CG* §29.2. My second epigraph for the present chapter is the "proposition" (*Leitsatz*) with which *CG* §29 begins. The first epigraph is from Immanuel Kant, *Vorlesungen über die philosophische Religionslehre*, ed. Karl Heinrich Ludwig Pölitz, 2d ed. (1830; reprint, Darmstadt: Wissenschaftliche Buchgesellschaft, 1982), 4 (trans. mine).

9. See further my article "Nature and the Theater of Redemption: Schleiermacher on Christian Dogmatics and the Creation Story" (1987), reprinted in *CR,* chap. 9, esp. 211–15.

10. CG^1 § 7. Cf. chap. 2, n.14, above.

11. See my article "*Ubi theologia, ibi ecclesia*? Schleiermacher, Troeltsch, and the Prospect for an Academic Theology" (1992), reprinted in *CR,* chap. 12.

12. Robert Maynard Hutchins, *The Higher Learning in America* (New Haven: Yale University Press, 1936), 97.

13. Hutchins, pref. to William Adams Brown, *The Case for Theology in the University* (Chicago: University of Chicago Press, 1938), p.vi.

14. Harry S. Ashmore, *Unseasonable Truths: The Life of Robert Maynard Hutchins* (Boston: Little, Brown & Co., 1989), 88.

15. Ibid., 89.

16. The Athanasian Creed. Cf. chap. 4, at n. 24, above.

17. Terence (ca. 195–ca. 159 B.C.E.), *The Self-Tormentor*, act 1, scene 1.

18. See also Gerrish, "Tradition in the Modern World—The Reformed Habit of Mind," in David Willis and Michael Welker, eds., *Toward the Future of Reformed Theology: Tasks, Topics, Traditions* (Grand Rapids: William B. Eerdmans, 1999), 3–20.

19. Gerrish, "*Ubi theologia, ibi ecclesia?*" 262–67.

20. Friedrich D. E. Schleiermacher, *On the Glaubenslehre: Two Letters to Dr. Lücke* (1829), trans. James Duke and Francis Fiorenza, American Academy of Religion Texts and Translations series, no. 3 (Chico, Calif.: Scholars Press, 1981), 80.

21. Ernst Troeltsch, "Schleiermacher und die Kirche," in Troeltsch et al., *Schleiermacher der Philosoph des Glaubens*, Moderne Philosophie, no. 6 (Berlin-Schöneberg: Buchverlag der "Hilfe," 1910), 9–35; see 27. In my essay "*Ubi theologia, ibi ecclesia?*" I tried to show that Troeltsch's emphasis on the practical *end* of Schleiermacher's dogmatics, though in itself correct, led him to underestimate Schleiermacher's insistence on its scientific *status.* See also Gerrish, "The Possibility of a Historical Theology: An Appraisal of Troeltsch's Dogmatics" (1976), reprinted in *OPN,* chap. 13; esp. pp. 211–12. Whereas Troeltsch says that Schleiermacher made dogmatics a part of practical theology, Schleiermacher himself asserts that he has no

desire to write a "practical dogmatics" because it is a scientific presentation that future pastors need (*On the Glaubenslehre*, 58–59).

22. Stopford A. Brooke, ed., *Life and Letters of Frederick W. Robertson* (London: Smith, Elder & Co., 1865), 82.

23. *Sermons by the Rev. Frederick W. Roberston Preached at Brighton*, 2d series, People's Edition (London: Kegan Paul, Trench, Trübner & Co., 1904), serm. 8 (2 March 1851), 94–105.

24. Langdon Gilkey, *Creationism on Trial: Evolution and God at Little Rock* (Minneapolis: Winston Press, 1985), 238–39, n. 3; cf. 254, n.11.

25. There is an extensive—and often controversial—scholarly literature on the nature, function, and varieties of myth. For a recent review, see the articles "Myth and Mythology" and "Myth in the OT" by Robert A. Oden Jr., *ABD* 4:946–56, 956–60.

26. Such an account of scientific research does not adequately differentiate between a hypothesis and the underlying faith that drives the inquiry and generates the hypothesis. If a hypothesis or explanation is not confirmed by observation and experiment, the researcher goes back to the drawing board, as we say, and begins again, confident that there *must be* an explanation. The scientific enterprise does not founder when a particular project founders. In this respect, the scientist's faith is not unlike religious faith. As R. M. Hare observes: "In fact, we may say that the belief of the scientist is one kind of religious belief—a kind, moreover, which is not incompatible with what is called Christian belief, for it is part of it" (Hare, "Simple Believer," 405).

27. David N. Schramm in a conversation reported in the October 1980 issue of *Chicago* (the magazine of the University of Chicago), p.173. Others have argued at length that the scientific enterprise rests not only on faith in an ordered world but also on the standpoint of a moderate or critical realism in our attempt to understand it. See, for instance, Stanley L. Jaki, *The Road of Science and the Ways to God* (Chicago: University of Chicago Press, 1978); and Ian G. Barbour, *Myths, Models and Paradigms* (1974; paperback ed., New York: Harper & Row, Publishers, 1976).

28. See Langdon Gilkey's reflections on "scientific culture" in *Creationism on Trial*, chap. 7.

29. The classical affirmation of the innate human quest for God is Augustine's (354–430): "You have made us for yourself, and our heart is restless till it rests in you" (*Confessions*, I, 1). The conviction of Cambridge Platonist Ralph Cudworth (1617–88) that *all* human teaching is "but maieutical, or obstetritious," may be too bold a generalization; but it could well be taken to express an epistemological tradition for which teaching about *God*, at any rate, "is not the filling of the soul as a vessel, merely by pouring into it from without, but the kindling of it from within; or helping it so as to excite and awaken, compare and compound its own notions." I owe this intriguing Cudworth citation to Peter Harrison, *"Religion" and the Religions in the English Enlightenment* (Cambridge: Cambridge University Press, 1990), 38.

30. Frankl, *Man's Search for Meaning: An Introduction to Logotherapy*, 3d ed. (New York: Simon & Schuster, 1984), 131. Frankl thinks of the will-to-meaning as needing to be evoked by therapy "from its state of latency" (ibid., 110).

31. The argument of the present chapter should have confirmed the point made above in chap. 3, n. 33, that in actual experience elemental faith and Christian faith stand in a reciprocal relationship. In the minds of Christians, their Christian faith is the foundation of their belief in a moral order, but it sometimes happens that Christian faith, when lost or rejected, is perceived as worth a second look by someone who has been struck by the logical status of inevitable beliefs.

6. Faith and Jesus Christ

1. Ernst Troeltsch, *Glaubenslehre*, ed. Gertrud von le Fort (1925; reprint, Aalen: Scientia Verlag, 1981), 21 (trans. mine). Garrett E. Paul has translated Troeltsch's *Glaubenslehre* as *The Christian Faith*, Fortress Texts in Modern Theology (Minneapolis: Fortress Press, 1991); see 25–26 for the context of my citation.

2. Heraclitus (?–460 B.C.E.), fragment, trans. John Burnet, *Early Greek Philosophy*, 4th ed. (London: Adam & Charles Black, 1948), 136.

3. This, I showed in my fourth chapter, is the understanding of the confessional tradition in my own Reformed communion, which likes to style itself *ecclesia reformata, semper reformanda* ("the church reformed and ever to be reformed").

4. Cf. the apposite remarks in [Heinrich] Emil Brunner (1889–1966), *Dogmatics*, trans. Olive Wyon, David Cairns, and T. H. L. Parker, 3 vols. (London: Lutterworth Press, 1949–62), 1:57–58.

5. William Chillingworth's (1602–44) unfortunate dictum will be found in his book *The Religion of Protestants: A Safe Way to Salvation* (1638); see *The Works of W. Chillingworth*, 12th ed. in one vol. (London: B. Blake, 1806), 465. I have explained why I think the oft-quoted dictum "unfortunate" in my essay "Biblical Authority and the Continental Reformation" (1957), reprinted in *OPN*, chap. 3.

6. See n.1 above.

7. Calvin, *Inst.*, 3.14.11.

8. Calvin to Bullinger (25 February 1547), *CO* 12:483–84. Elsewhere Calvin rejects the scholastic concept of God's absolute power but appropriates the distinction between necessity of consequence and necessity of the thing consequent (for documentation see *OPN* 342, n. 69, and 343, n.78).

9. Calvin, *Defensio contra Pighium* (1543), *CO* 6:276–78. Translations from Calvin's book against Pighius are mine.

10. Ibid., 241, 250.

11. Ibid., 250. I have had more to say elsewhere about the idea of a developing tradition: besides *Tradition and the Modern World, Reformed Theology in the Nineteenth Century* (Chicago: University of Chicago Press, 1978), see *OPN*, chaps. 2, 11, 13, and the "afterword" to Mary Potter Engel and Walter E. Wyman Jr., eds., *Revisioning the Past: Prospects in Historical Theology* (Minneapolis: Fortress Press, 1992), 281–306.

12. "Old tradition" and "new situation" are, of course, abstractions; they do not denote objects as wholly distinct in reality as the terms might be taken to imply. The tradition shapes the situation, and is shaped by it. One might indeed speak of a "modern tradition," or "tradition of modernity," and in the remarks that follow I have taken care not to exaggerate the novelty of the situation in which we presently find ourselves.

13. John Bunyan, *Grace Abounding to the Chief of Sinners: Or, a Brief Relation of the Exceeding Mercy of God in Christ, to His Poor Servant, John Bunyan* (1666), sec. 97, in Bunyan, *Grace Abounding to the Chief of Sinners and the Pilgrim's Progress from This World to That Which Is to Come*, ed. Roger Sharrock (London: Oxford University Press, 1966), 33.

14. Quoted by Peter Byrne, *Natural Religion and the Nature of Religion: The Legacy of Deism* (London: Routledge, 1989), 74.

15. Daniel Defoe, *Robinson Crusoe*, Everyman's Library, no. 59 (London: J. M. Dent & Sons, 1906; reprinted 1929), 117, 121. This edition contains both the *Adventures* (pp. 1–236) and the *Farther Adventures* (pp. 237–453), to which I refer below.

16. Ibid., 155, 157.

17. Ibid., 318, 328–29, 335–36.

18. Ibid., 337, 342 (cf. 1 Cor 9:27).

19. Ibid., 158; cf. 346.

20. Richard Baxter, *Universal Redemption of Mankind* (1694), prop. 24, p. 37; quoted by Harrison, *"Religion" and the Religions*, 195, n.152.

21. In the sixteenth and seventeenth centuries, the grounds on which the stringency of the motto *Nulla salus extra ecclesiam* ("No salvation outside the church") could be mitigated, and sometimes was, varied from party to party. Those who were influenced by humanism were the most eager to find a place in heaven for virtuous pagans, but Protestant reluctance to identify the visible church with the invisible also provided a loophole for generosity of spirit; and the Calvinistic doctrine of election, commonly taken to be unpleasantly exclusive, could actually be pointed in the same liberal direction. The Westminster Confession, for example, asserts that elect infants dying in infancy and "all other elect persons, who are incapable of being outwardly called by the ministry of the word" will be saved by Christ "through the Spirit, who worketh when, and where, and how he pleaseth" (chap. 10, sec. 3). There are a number of interesting historical studies on *Nulla salus extra ecclesiam*: see the titles in the Bibliography under George Huntston Williams, Francis Sullivan, and Molly Truman Marshall; see also the excursus in Craig R. Thompson, ed., *Inquisitio de fide: A Colloquy by Desiderius Erasmus Roterodamus, 1524* (1950; 2d ed., Hamden, Conn.: Archon Books, 1975), 101–21.

22. For the old view, see Calvin, *Inst.*, 1.6.1; for the new, John Locke, *Essay Concerning Human Understanding*, bk. 3, chap. 9, sec. 23.

23. On John Webb (1611–72) and John Toland (1670–1722), see Harrison, *"Religion" and the Religions*, 154–55, 165–66; on Henry Stubbe (1632–76), see James R. Jacob, *Henry Stubbe, Radical Protestantism and the Early Enlightenment* (Cambridge: Cambridge University Press, 1983), esp. chap. 4. A mine of further pertinent information, with extracts from the sources, will be found in David A. Pailin, *Attitudes to Other Religions: Comparative Religion in Seventeenth- and Eighteenth-Century Britain* (Manchester: Manchester University Press, 1984).

24. Defoe, *Robinson Crusoe*, 3.

25. Ibid., 242.

26. Quoted in Robert O. Ballou, ed., *The Bible of the World* (New York: Viking Press, 1939), p. xvi. The incident took place in Boston at a meeting of the Free Religious Association of America. Emerson was in the audience.

27. Troeltsch, "The Significance of the Historical Existence of Jesus for Faith" (1911), in *Ernst Troeltsch: Writings on Theology and Religion*, trans. and ed. Robert Morgan and Michael Pye (1977; paperback ed., Louisville, Ky.: Westminster/John Knox Press, 1990), 189.

28. Troeltsch, *Christian Thought: Its History and Application*, ed. Baron F. Von Hügel (1923; reprint, New York: Meridian Books, 1957), 62.

29. Troeltsch, "Historical Existence of Jesus," 193.

30. See Gerrish, "Biblical Authority," *OPN* 63.

31. Hermann Samuel Reimarus, *Reimarus: Fragments*, ed. Charles H. Talbert, trans. Ralph S. Fraser, Lives of Jesus series (Philadelphia: Fortress Press, 1970). Only two of the fragments published by Lessing are translated in this volume: "On the Resurrection Narratives" (frag. 6, 1777) and the longer discussion in Reimarus's *Apology* from which it was taken, "On the Intentions of Jesus and His Disciples" (frag. 7, 1778).

32. Ibid., esp. 248–50.

33. Karl Friedrich Bahrdt (1741–92); see Albert Schweitzer, *The Quest of the Historical Jesus: A Critical Study of Its Progress from Reimarus to Wrede*, trans. from the 1st German ed. (*Von Reimarus zu Wrede*, 1906) by W. Montgomery (1910; 2d ed., London: Adam & Charles Black, 1911 and subsequent reprints), 38–44.

34. H. E. G. Paulus (1761–1851); see Schweitzer, *Quest*, 48–57.

35. Otto Pfleiderer (1839–1908), *The Development of Theology in Germany since Kant, and Its Progress in Great Britain since 1825*, trans. J. Frederick Smith (London: Swan Sonnenschein & Co., 1890), 212 (on H. E. G. Paulus).

36. See the surveys of the quest in W. Barnes Tatum, *In Quest of Jesus: A Guidebook* (Atlanta, Ga.: John Knox Press, 1982), and N[icholas] T. ("Tom") Wright, *Who Was Jesus?* (London: SPCK, 1992).

37. In the heyday of the Ritschlian theology, it was customary to assert that there was a consensus on the "basic features," at least, of Jesus' life and teaching, but it did not survive. See my essay "Jesus, Myth, and History: Troeltsch's Stand in the 'Christ-Myth' Debate" (1975), reprinted in *OPN,* chap. 14, esp. 233–34.

38. Barbara Thiering, *Jesus the Man: A New Interpretation from the Dead Sea Scrolls* (Sydney, Australia: Doubleday, 1992). The American edition carried the title *Jesus and the Riddle of the Dead Sea Scrolls: Unlocking the Secrets of His Life Story* (San Francisco: HarperSanFrancisco, 1992); the quotation is from 160.

39. Walter Schwarz, "Man and Myth—More Bad News for Believers," *Guardian Weekly*, 18 October 1992.

40. C. F. D. Moule, review of Wright's *Who Was Jesus?* (n. 36 above), *Theology* 96 (1993): 409.

41. See Bibliography.

42. Robert W. Funk, Roy W. Hoover, and the Jesus Seminar, *The Five Gospels: The Search for the Authentic Words of Jesus—New Translation and Commentary* (New York: Macmillan Publishing Company, 1993); Robert W. Funk and the Jesus Seminar, eds., *The Acts of Jesus: The Search for the Authentic Deeds of Jesus* (San Francisco: HarperSanFrancisco, 1998).

43. Brunner, *Dogmatics*, 3:140. But Brunner rejects any suggestion that such faith might be a generic concept: he takes it to be a possibility only through encounter with Jesus Christ.

44. Cf. Luther's remarks on the second article of the Apostles' Creed: "By this article our faith is set apart from all other faiths on earth. . . . On this article depends your life and salvation." Luther, *Heerpredigt wider den Türken* (1529), WA 30^2.186.15, 27.

45. John Hick, "Jesus and the World Religions," in Hick, ed., *The Myth of God Incarnate* (London: SCM Press, 1977), 168–71. Hick refers to the study by B[urnett] H. Streeter, *The Buddha and the Christ* (London: Macmillan, 1932; American ed., New York: Macmillan Co., 1933).

46. John Dominic Crossan, "A Tale of Two Gods," *Christian Century* 110 (1993): 1270–78; quotation on 1275. This article was adapted from Crossan's (then forthcoming) *Jesus: A Revolutionary Biography* (San Francisco: HarperSanFrancisco, 1994), chap. 1.

47. See Bibliography under Rudolf Bultmann (1955), Vincent Taylor, A. W. Wainwright, and Murray J. Harris.

48. Raymond E. Brown, "Does the New Testament Call Jesus God?" *Theological Studies* 26 (1965): 545–73.

49. Barth, *Church Dogmatics*, vol. 1, pt. 1, trans. G. W. Bromiley (Edinburgh: T.

& T. Clark, 1975), 257–67. For Barth it followed that the validity of a dogma had to be suspended and established afresh: even the most universally accepted dogmas *can* be corrected and transcended—including the decisions made at Nicaea (325) and Chalcedon (451) as well as the Lutheran Formula of Concord (1577) and the Reformed Canons of Dort (1618–19). Barth, *The Göttingen Dogmatics: Instruction in the Christian Religion*, ed. Hannelotte Reiffen, trans. Geoffrey W. Bromiley, vol. 1 (Grand Rapids, Mich.: William B. Eerdmans Publishing Co., 1991), 39, 247.

50. For Athanasius, the cardinal point of soteriology—and therefore of his unyielding stand against the Arians—was that the Word "was made man that we might be made God [deified]" (*On the Incarnation of the Word* [ca. 318]; LCC 3:107).

51. Luther, sermon on John 16 (1525), WA 17^1.255.11.

52. Luther, sermon on Exodus 12 (1525), WA 16.217.32.

53. See the classic study by [Johann] Wilhelm Herrmann (1846–1922), *The Communion of the Christian with God, Described on the Basis of Luther's Statements*, trans. J. Sandys Stanyon, 2d English ed., revised in accordance with the 4th German ed. (1903) by R. W. Stewart (1906; reprint in the Lives of Jesus Series, Philadelphia: Fortress Press, 1971).

54. Gerrish, *A Prince of the Church: Schleiermacher and the Beginnings of Modern Theology* (Philadelphia: Fortress Press, 1984), 49.

55. *CG* §94.2 (my trans.).

56. See chap. 1, conclusion.

57. See chap 2, at n. 4, above.

58. Calvin, *Inst.*, 1.6.1 (cited previously in chap. 2, n. 48, and chap. 5, n. 4).

59. Some sources lack the saying "Father, forgive them."

60. See chap. 1, at n. 42, above.

61. Calvin, Comm. on Matt. 27:46, *CO* 45:779.

62. Notice that *fides* in the passage cited refers to the faith *of* Christ: "fixam tamen stetisse fidem in eius corde." See chap. 1, n. 6, above.

63. Luther, "Preface to the New Testament" (1522), *WADB* 6.10.20; *LW* 35:362.

64. See C[harles] H. Dodd, *The Apostolic Preaching and Its Developments: Three Lectures* (London: Hodder & Stoughton, 1936).

65. See C. E. B. Cranfield, *A Critical and Exegetical Commentary on the Epistle to the Romans*, 2 vols., International Critical Commentary (Edinburgh: T. & T. Clark, 1975–79), 2:534, 537. NSRV gives "word *about* Christ" as an alternative translation.

66. My first epigraph to the present chapter comes from Troeltsch, *Glaubenslehre*, 356 (my trans.; cf. Garrett Paul's trans., 283).

67. This certainly is how Bultmann understood the New Testament itself, which, he says, "claims that faith only became possible at a definite point in history in consequence of an *event*—viz., the event of Christ" ("New Testament and Mythology" [1941], in Hans Werner Bartsch, ed., *Kerygma and Myth: A Theological Debate*, trans. Reginald H. Fuller [London: SPCK, 1954], 22).

68. I should perhaps repeat the disclaimer made already: I do not come to the dialogue with a ready-made theory of what constitutes the essence of religion or of being human, although, naturally, I would not rule out the possibility of mounting an argument for such a theory either.

69. Sarah Coakley, *Christ without Absolutes: A Study of the Christology of Ernst Troeltsch* (Oxford: Clarendon Press, 1988), 155–63. For my article, see n.37 above.

70. *JR* 71 (1991); 270–72.

71. *Christ without Absolutes*, 158–59.

72. Ibid., 136.

73. The reason is well stated by Schubert Ogden: "Bultmann distinguishes our situation today from that of the first proclaimers insofar as our faith arises in response to the *kerygma* rather than the historical Jesus." Schubert M. Ogden, "Rudolf Bultmann and the Future of Revisonary Christology," in Bernd Jaspert, ed., *Rudolf Bultmanns Werk und Wirkung* (Darmstadt: Wissenschaftliche Buchgesellschaft, 1984), 155–73; quotation on 169.

74. *Christ without Absolutes*, 160.

75. *OPN* 242.

76. *Christ without Absolutes*, 160, n.66.

77. Cf. David L. Bartlett, "The Historical Jesus and the Life of Faith," *Christian Century* 109 (1992): 489–93.

78. For a resolute defense of this view, see Leander E. Keck, *A Future for the Historical Jesus: The Place of Jesus in Preaching and Theology* (Nashville, Tenn.: Abingdon Press, 1971).

79. Sometimes the demand-and-supply mechanism is unconscious, but at other times it has been recommended as a serious theological procedure, as, for instance, when Gerald Birney Smith (1868–1929) wrote that we need to portray Jesus as having "power to stimulate and to develop moral idealism" ("The Religious Significance of the Humanity of Jesus," *American Journal of Theology* 24 [1920]:191–208; quotation on 206).

80. George Tyrrell, *Christianity at the Crossroads* (1909; reprint, London: George Allen & Unwin, 1963), 44.

81. Troeltsch, "Die alte Kirche" (1916/17), *Gesammelte Schriften*, 4 vols. (1912–25; reprint, Aalen: Scientia Verlag, 1961–66), 4:71. Cf. "On the Possibility of a Liberal Christianity" (German, 1910), in Troeltsch, *Religion in History*, trans. James Luther Adams and Walter F. Bense, Fortress Texts in Modern Theology (Minneapolis: Fortress Press, 1991), 348.

82. Calvin, *Catechism*, q. 94, *OS* 2:89 (my trans.); cf. *TT* 2:50.

83. Alfred Loisy, *The Gospel and the Church* (French, 1902), trans. Christopher Home (1903; reprint in the Lives of Jesus series, Phildelphia: Fortress Press, 1976), 166.

BIBLIOGRAPHY

An exhaustive list of books and articles on faith in general would be enormous and quickly dated, and full coverage of any of the individual themes explored in the chapters of this volume would require a bibliography to itself. Listed below are only works and authors that I have had occasion to cite, together a few additional items that I think might prove helpful as guides for further reading.

Anchor Bible Dictionary (abbreviated *ABD*). Ed. David Noel Freedman et al. 6 vols. New York: Doubleday, 1992.

Anselm, *Cur Deus Homo* (1098). Translated as *Why God Became Man* in LCC 10:100–83.

Armstrong, Maurice W., Lefferts A. Loetscher, and Charles A. Anderson, eds. *The Presbyterian Enterprise: Sources of American Presbyterian History*. Presbyterian Historical Society Publications. Philadelphia: Westminster Press, 1956; reprint 1963.

Ashmore, Harry S. *Unseasonable Truths: The Life of Robert Maynard Hutchins*. Boston: Little, Brown & Co., 1989.

Astley, Jeff, and Leslie J. Francis, eds. *Christian Perspectives on Faith Development: A Reader.* Grand Rapids, Mich.: William B. Eerdmans Publishing Co., 1992.

Athanasius. *On the Incarnation of the Word* (ca. 318). Eng. trans. LCC 3:55–110.

Augustine. *Confessions* (397–98). LCC 7:31–333.

Baillie, D[onald] M. *Faith in God and Its Christian Consummation*. Edinburgh: T. & T. Clark, 1927.

Bainton, Roland H. *Hunted Heretic: The Life and Death of Michael Servetus, 1511–1553*. Boston: Beacon Press, 1953.

———. *The Travail of Religious Liberty: Nine Biographical Studies*. Philadelphia: Westminster Press, 1951.

Balfour, Arthur James. *Theism and Humanism*. New York: George H. Doran Company, 1915.

———. *Theism and Thought: A Study in Familiar Beliefs*. New York: George H. Doran Company, 1924.

Ballou, Robert O., ed. *The Bible of the World*. New York: Viking Press, 1939.

Barbour, Ian G. *Myths, Models, and Paradigms: A Comparative Study in Science and Religion*. New York: Harper & Row, Publishers, 1974; paperback ed., 1976.

Barr, James. *The Semantics of Biblical Language*. Oxford: Oxford University Press, 1961.

Barth, Karl. *Church Dogmatics*, vol. 1, pt. 1. Trans. G. W. Bromiley. Edinburgh: T. & T. Clark, 1975.

———. "The Desirability and Possibility of a Universal Reformed Creed" (1925), in Barth, *Theology and Church*, 112–35.

———. "The Doctrinal Task of the Reformed Churches" (1923), in Barth, *The Word of God and the Word of Man*, 218–71.

———. *The Göttingen Dogmatics: Instruction in the Christian Religion*, vol. 1 (German 1990). Ed. Hannelotte Reiffen. Trans. Geoffrey W. Bromiley. Grand Rapids, Mich.: William B. Eerdmans Publishing Company, 1991.

———. *Theology and Church: Shorter Writings 1920–1928*. Trans. Louise Pettibone Smith. London: SCM Press, 1962.

———. *The Word of God and the Word of Man* [German: *Das Wort Gottes und die Theologie*, 1925]. Trans. Douglas Horton. London: Hodder & Stoughton, 1928.

Bartlett, David L. "The Historical Jesus and the Life of Faith." *Christian Century* 109 (1992): 489–91.

Bellah, Robert N., et al. *Habits of the Heart: Individualism and Commitment in American Life*. Berkeley: University of California Press, 1985.

Berger, Peter L. *A Far Glory: The Quest for Faith in an Age of Credulity*. New York: Free Press, 1992.

———. *The Sacred Canopy: Elements of a Sociological Theory of Religion*. Garden City, N.Y.: Doubleday & Co., 1967.

Berger, Peter L., and Thomas Luckmann. *The Social Construction of Reality: A Treatise in the Sociology of Knowledge*. Garden City, N.Y.: Doubleday & Co., 1966.

Book of Concord, The: The Confessions of the Evangelical Lutheran Church (abbreviated *CELC*). Trans. and ed. Theodore G. Tappert et al. Philadelphia: Fortress Press, 1959.

Book of Confessions (abbreviated *BC*). *The Constitution of the Presbyterian Church (U.S.A.), Part I: Book of Confessions*. Louisville, Ky.: Office of the General Assembly, 1994.

Borg, Marcus J. *Jesus, A New Vision: Spirit, Culture, and the Life of Discipleship*. San Francisco: Harper & Row, 1987.

Brandon, S[amuel] G. F. *Jesus and the Zealots: A Study of the Political Factor in Primitive Christianity*. Manchester: Manchester University Press, 1967.

Bready, J. Wesley. *England, Before and after Wesley: The Evangelical Revival and Social Reform*. London: Hodder & Stoughton, 1938.

Brooke, Stopford A., ed. *Life and Letters of Frederick W. Robertson, M.A., Incumbent of Trinity Chapel, Brighton, 1847–53*. London: Smith, Elder & Co., 1865.

Brown, Raymond E. "Does the New Testament Call Jesus God?" *Theological Studies* 26 (1965): 545–73.

Brunner, [Heinrich] Emil. *Dogmatics*. Trans. Olive Wyon, David Cairns, and T.H.L. Parker. 3 vols. London: Lutterworth Press, 1949–62.

Buber, Martin. *Two Types of Faith*. Trans. Norman P. Goldhawk. 1951. Reprint, New York: Collier Books, 1986.

Bultmann, Rudolf. "The Christological Confession of the World Council of Churches" (1951). *Essays Philosophical and Theological* [German: *Glauben und Verstehen, Gesammelte Aufsätze*, II, 1952]. Trans. James C. G. Greig. London: SCM Press, 1955, 273–90.

———. "New Testament and Mythology" (1941). In: Hans Werner Bartsch, ed., *Kerygma and Myth: A Theological Debate*. Trans. Reginald H. Fuller. London: SPCK, 1954, 1–44.

Bultmann, Rudolf, and Artur Weiser, *Faith*. Bible Key Words from Gerhard Kittel's *Theologisches Wörterbuch zum Neuen Testament*, no. 10. Trans. Dorothea M. Barton: London: Adam & Charles Black, 1961.

Bunyan, John. *Grace Abounding to the Chief of Sinners and the Pilgrim's Progress from This World to That Which Is to Come*. Ed. Roger Sharrock. London: Oxford University Press, 1966.

Burnet, John. *Early Greek Philosophy*. 4th ed. London: Adam & Charles Black, 1948.

Byrne, Peter. *Natural Religion and the Nature of Religion: The Legacy of Deism*. London: Routledge, 1989.

Calvin, John [Jean]. *Calvin's Ecclesiastical Advice*. Trans. Mary Beaty and Benjamin W. Farley. Louisville, Ky.: Westminster/John Knox Press, 1991.

———. *Catechism of the Church of Geneva* (Latin 1545). *OS* 2:59–157. *TT* 2:33–94.

———. *Commentaries*. Edinburgh: Calvin Translation Society, 1844–56. Reprinted in 22 vols. Grand Rapids, MI: Baker Book House, 1981. Listed below, with their location in the *Opera*, are the commentaries cited.

———. *Commentary on Acts* (1552–54). *CO* 48:1–574.

———. *Commentary on Isaiah* (1551). *CO* 36–37:455.

———. *Commentary on John* (1553). *CO* 47:1–458.

———. *Commentary on Matthew* (*Harmony of the Gospels*, 1555). *CO* 45.

———. *Defensio contra Pighium* (1543). *CO* 6: 225–404.

———. *The Form of Prayers* (1542). *OS* 2:1–58. *TT* 2:100–28. The "Essay on the Lord's Supper," not translated in *TT,* will be found as an appendix in *Calvin's Ecclesiastical Advice*.

———. *Institutio Christianae religionis* (abbreviated *Inst.*). Cited in the 1559 Latin ed. by book, chapter, and section. *OS* 3–5. LCC 20–21.

———. Letter to Heinrich Bullinger (25 February 1547). *CO* 12:480–89.

Cameron, James K. "Scottish Calvinism and the Principle of Intolerance." In: B. A. Gerrish, ed., *Reformatio Perennis*, 113–28.

Castellio [Châteillon, Castellion], Sebastian [Sébastien]. *Concerning Heretics, Whether They Are to be Persecuted, and How They Are to be Treated: A Collection of the Opinions of Learned Men Both Ancient and Modern, An Anonymous Work [1554] Attributed to Sebastian Castellio, Now First Done into English, Together with Excerpts from Other Works of Sebastian Castellio and David Joris on Religious Liberty* Trans. Roland H. Bainton. New York: Columbia University Press, 1935.

———. *De arte dubitandi et confidendi, ignorandi et sciendi*. Ed. Elisabeth Feist Hirsch. Leiden: E. J. Brill, 1981.

Cave, Sydney. *The Doctrine of the Person of Christ*. London: Duckworth, 1925.

Chillingworth, William. *The Religion of Protestants: A Safe Way to Salvation* (1638). *The Works of W. Chillingworth*. 12th ed. London: B. Blake, 1806.

Coakley, Sarah. *Christ without Absolutes: A Study of the Christology of Ernst Troeltsch*. Oxford: Clarendon Press, 1988.

Coalter, Milton J., John M. Mulder, and Louis B. Weeks. *The Re-forming Tradition: Presbyterians and Mainstream Protestantism*. The Presbyterian Presence. Louisville, Ky.: Westminster/John Knox Press, 1992.

Coalter, Milton J., John M. Mulder, and Louis B. Weeks, eds. *The Confessional Mosaic: Presbyterians and Twentieth-Century Theology*. The Presbyterian Presence. Louisville, Ky.: Westminster/John Knox Press, 1990.

———, eds. *The Presbyterian Predicament: Six Perspectives*. The Presbyterian Presence. Louisville, Ky.: Westminster/John Knox Press, 1990.

Cochrane, Arthur C., ed. *Reformed Confessions of the Sixteenth Century*. Philadelphia: Westminster Press, 1966.

Come, Arnold B. "The Occasion and Contribution of the Confession of 1967." *Journal of Presbyterian History* 61 (1983): 13–32.

"Confessional Nature of the Church: Report and Recommendations." *Minutes* of the 198th General Assembly of the Presbyterian Church (U.S.A.), part 1, *Journal.* New York and Atlanta, GA: Office of the General Assembly, 1986, 516–27.

The Constitution of the Presbyterian Church (U.S.A.), Part II: Book of Order. Louisville, Ky.: Office of the General Assembly, 1997.

Cranfield, C.E.B. *A Critical and Exegetical Commentary on the Epistle to the Romans.* The International Critical Commentary, vol. 36. 6th ed. in 2 vols. Edinburgh: T. & T. Clark, 1975.

Crossan, John Dominic. *The Historical Jesus: The Life of a Mediterranean Jewish Peasant.* San Francisco: HarperSanFrancisco, 1991.

———. *Jesus: A Revolutionary Biography.* San Francisco: HarperSanFrancisco, 1994.

———. "A Tale of Two Gods." *Christian Century* 110 (1993): 1270–78.

Culbertson, Diana. *The Poetics of Revelation: Recognition and the Narrative Tradition.* Studies in American Biblical Hermeneutics, no. 4. Macon, Ga.: Mercer University Press, 1989.

Defoe, Daniel. *Robinson Crusoe.* Everyman's Library, no. 59. London: J. M. Dent & Sons, 1906; reprinted 1929.

Dodd, C[harles] H. *The Apostolic Preaching and Its Developments: Three Lectures.* London: Hodder & Stoughton, 1936.

Dowey, Edward A., Jr. *A Commentary on the Confession of 1967 and an Introduction to "The Book of Confessions."* Philadelphia: Westminster Press, 1968.

Dulles, Avery. *The Assurance of Things Hoped For: A Theology of Christian Faith.* New York: Oxford University Press, 1994.

Dykstra, Craig. "What Is Faith? An Experiment in the Hypothetical Mode." In: Craig Dykstra and Sharon Parks (see next entry), 45–64.

Dykstra, Craig, and Sharon Parks, eds. *Faith Development and Fowler.* Birmingham, Ala.: Religious Education Press, 1986.

Engel, Mary Potter, and Walter E. Wyman Jr., eds. *Revisioning the Past: Prospects in Historical Theology.* Minneapolis, Minn.: Fortress Press, 1992.

Fernhout, J. Harry. "Where Is Faith? Searching for the Core of the Cube." In: Dykstra and Parks (see above), 65–89.

Forberg, Friedrich Karl [Carl]. "Entwickelung des Begriffs der Religion" (1798). Reprinted in both Medicus (pp. 17–32) and Lindau (pp. 37–58). See below.

———. *Friedrich Karl Forbergs der Philosophie Doctors und des Lyceums zu Saalfeld Rectors Apologie seines angeblichen Atheismus.* Gotha: Justus Perthes, 1799.

———. [Fred. Chas. Forberg]. *Manual of Classical Erotology (De figuris Veneris).* Latin text and Eng. trans. by Julian Smithson (1884). Facsimile ed. 2 vols. in 1. New York: Grove, 1966.

Fowler, James W. "Faith and the Structuring of Meaning," 15-42. In: Dykstra and Parks (see above).

———. *Faith Development and Pastoral Care.* Theology and Pastoral Care Series. Philadelphia: Fortress Press, 1987.

———. *Stages of Faith: The Psychology of Human Development and the Quest for Meaning.* San Francisco: Harper & Row, 1981.

Frankl, Viktor E[mil]. *The Doctor and the Soul* (German 1952). Trans. Richard and Clara Winston (1955). Expanded ed., with the subtitle *From Psychology to Logotherapy.* New York: Alfred A. Knopf, 1965.

———. *Man's Search for Meaning: An Introduction to Logotherapy* (German, 1946; first English version, 1959). Part I trans. Ilse Lasch. 3d ed. New York: Simon & Schuster, 1984.

———. *Psychotherapy and Existentialism: Selected Papers on Logotherapy*. New York: Washington Square Press, 1967.

———. *The Unconscious God: Psychotherapy and Theology* (German 1948). Eng. trans. New York: Simon & Schuster, 1975.

———. *The Will to Meaning: Foundations and Applications of Logotherapy* (1969). Expanded ed. New York: New American Library, 1988.

Funk, Robert W., and the Jesus Seminar, eds. *The Acts of Jesus: The Search for the Authentic Deeds of Jesus*. San Francisco: HarperSanFrancisco, 1998.

Funk, Robert W., Roy W. Hoover, and the Jesus Seminar. *The Five Gospels: The Search for the Authentic Words of Jesus—New Translation and Commentary*. New York: Macmillan Publishing Company, 1993.

Gerrish, B[rian] A. "Christian Creeds." *The Encyclopedia of Religion*. Ed. Mircea Eliade et al. 16 vols. New York: Macmillan Publishing Company, 1987, 4:140–50.

———. "The Confessional Heritage of the Reformed Church." *McCormick Quarterly* 19 (1966): 120–34.

———. *Continuing the Reformation: Essays on Modern Religious Thought* (abbreviated *CR*). Chicago: University of Chicago Press, 1993.

———. "Errors and Insights in the Understanding of Revelation: A Provisional Response." *JR* 78 (1998):64–88.

———, ed. *The Faith of Christendom: A Source Book of Creeds and Confessions*. Cleveland, Ohio: World Publishing Company, 1963.

———. *Grace and Gratitude: The Eucharistic Theology of John Calvin*. Minneapolis, Minn.: Fortress Press, Edinburgh: T. & T. Clark, 1993.

———. "The Nature of Doctrine." *JR* 68 (1988):87–92. (Review article on George Lindbeck's *Nature of Doctrine*.)

———. "The New Presbyterian Confession." *Christian Century* 83 (1966):582–85.

———. *The Old Protestantism and the New: Essays on the Reformation Heritage* (abbreviated *OPN*). Chicago: University of Chicago Press, Edinburgh: T. & T. Clark, 1982.

———. *A Prince of the Church: Schleiermacher and the Beginnings of Modern Theology*. Philadelphia: Fortress Press, 1984.

———, ed., in collaboration with Robert Benedetto. *Reformatio Perennis: Essays on Calvin and the Reformation in Honor of Ford Lewis Battles*. Pittsburgh Theological Monograph Series, no. 32. Pittsburgh: Pickwick Press, 1981.

———. Review of Sarah Coakley, *Christ without Absolutes*. *JR* 71 (1991):270–72.

———. *Tradition and the Modern World: Reformed Theology in the Nineteenth Centuiry*. Chicago: University of Chicago Press, 1978.

———. "Tradition in the Modern World: The Reformed Habit of Mind." In: Willis and Welker (see below), 3–20.

Gilkey, Langdon B. *Creationism on Trial: Evolution and God at Little Rock*. Minneapolis, Minn.: Winston Press, 1985.

———. "A Theological Voyage with Wilfred Cantwell Smith." *RSR* 7 (1981):298–306.

Goethe, Johann Wolfgang. *Gedenkausgabe der Werke: Briefe und Gespräche*, vol. 23. Zurich: Artemis, 1950.

Green, Garrett. *Imagining God: Theology and the Religious Imagination*. San Francisco: Harper & Row, 1989.

Grisar, Hartmann. *Martin Luther: His Life and Work*. Trans. ("adapted") from the 2d German ed. by Frank J. Eble. Ed. Arthur Preuss. Westminster, Md.: Newman Press, 1950.

Hacker, Paul. "Martin Luther's Notion of Faith." In: Jared Wicks, ed, *Catholic Scholars Dialogue with Luther*. Chicago: Loyola University Press, 1970, 85–105.

Hare, R[ichard] M. "The Simple Believer." In: Gene Outka and John P. Reeder, Jr., eds., *Religion and Morality: A Collection of Essays*. Garden City, N.Y.: Anchor Press/Doubleday, 1973, 393–427.

Harnack, Adolph [Adolf von]. *History of Dogma*. Trans. from the 3d German ed. by Neil Buchanan et al. 7 vols. London: Williams & Norgate, 1894–99.

Harris, Murray J. *Jesus as "God": The New Testament Use of Theos as a Christological Term*. Grand Rapids, Mich.: Baker Book House, 1992.

Harrison, Peter. *"Religion" and the Religions in the English Enlightenment*. Cambridge: Cambridge University Press, 1990.

Harvey, Van A. *Feuerbach and the Interpretation of Religion*. Cambridge: Cambridge University Press, 1995.

Hays, Richard B. *The Faith of Jesus Christ: An Investigation of the Narrative Substructure of Galatians 3:1–4:11*. Society of Biblical Literature Dissertation Series, no. 56. Chico, Calif.: Scholars Press, 1983.

Herrmann, [Johann] Wilhelm. *The Communion of the Christian with God, Described on the Basis of Luther's Statements*. Trans. J. Sandys Stanyon. 2d English ed. (1906), revised in accordance with the 4th German ed. (1903) by R. W. Stewart. Reprinted in the Lives of Jesus Series. Philadelphia: Fortress Press, 1971.

Heyer, C. J. den. *Jesus Matters: 150 Years of Research*. London: SCM Press, 1996; Valley Forge, Pa.: Trinity Press International, 1997.

Hick, John. *Faith and Knowledge: A Modern Introduction to the Problem of Religious Knowledge*. Ithaca, N.Y.: Cornell University Press, 1957.

———, ed. *The Myth of God Incarnate*. London: SCM Press, 1977.

———. "Seeing-as and Religious Experience." In: Terence Penelhum, ed., *Faith*, 183–92.

Hudson, Winthrop S. *American Protestantism*. Chicago: University of Chicago Press, 1961.

Hutchins, Robert Maynard. *The Higher Learning in America*. New Haven: Yale University Press, 1936.

———. Preface to William Adams Brown, *The Case for Theology in the University*. Chicago: University of Chicago Press, 1938.

Interpreter's Dictionary of the Bible, The: An Illustrated Encyclopedia (abbreviated IDB). Ed. George Buttrick et al. 4 vols. Nashville, Tenn.: Abingdon Press, 1962. Supplementary volume. Ed. Keith Crim et al. Ibid., 1976.

Jacob, James R. *Henry Stubbe, Radical Protestantism and the Early Enlightenment*. Cambridge: Cambridge University Press, 1983.

Jacobi, Friedrich Heinrich. *David Hume über den Glauben, oder Idealismus und Realismus: Ein Gespräch*. 2d ed. (1815). JW 2:3-123 (introduction), 125–288 (text).

———. *Über die Lehre des Spinozas, in Briefen an Herrn Moses Mendelssohn* (1785). JW 4, 1.

Jaki, Stanley L. *The Road of Science and the Ways to God*. Chicago: University of Chicago Press, 1978.

Johnson, Luke Timothy. *The Real Jesus: The Misguided Quest for the Historical Jesus and the Truth of the Traditional Gospels*. San Francisco: HarperSanFrancisco, 1996.

Kant, Immanuel. *Vorlesungen über die philosophische Religionslehre*. Ed. Karl Heinrich Pölitz. 2d ed. (1830). Reprint, Darmstadt: Wissenschaftliche Buchgesellschaft, 1982.

———. "What Is Enlightenment?" (1784). Trans. Lewis White Beck in Kant, *On History*. Ed. Beck. Indianapolis: Bobbs-Merrill Company, 1963, 3–10.

Kaufman, Gordon D. *God the Problem*. Cambridge, Mass.: Harvard University Press, 1972.

———. *In Face of Mystery: A Constructive Theology*. Cambridge, Mass.: Harvard University Press, 1993.

———. *The Theological Imagination: Constructing the Concept of God*. Philadelphia: Westminster Press, 1981.

Keck, Leander E. *A Future for the Historical Jesus: The Place of Jesus in Preaching and Theology*. Nashville, Tenn.: Abingdon Press, 1971.

Kenny, Anthony. *What Is Faith? Essays in the Philosophy of Religion*. Oxford: Oxford University Press, 1992.

Larson, Roy. "Psychiatrist Has Words of Hope." *Chicago Sun-Times*, 15 April 1984.

Lee, James Michael, ed. *Handbook of Faith*. Birmingham, Ala.: Religious Education Press, 1990.

Lerner, Michael. *The Politics of Meaning: Restoring Hope and Possibility in an Age of Cynicism*. Reading, Mass.: Addison-Wesley, 1996.

Lindau, Hans, ed. *Die Schriften zu J. G. Fichte's Atheismus-Streit*. Munich: Georg Müller, 1912.

Lindbeck, George. *The Nature of Doctrine: Religion and Theology in a Postliberal Age*. Philadelphia: Westminster Press, 1984.

Locke, John. *An Essay Concerning Human Understanding* (1690). Ed. Peter H. Nidditch. Oxford: Clarendon Press, 1975.

Loetscher, Lefferts A. *The Broadening Church: A Study of Theological Issues in the Presbyterian Church Since 1869*. Philadelphia: University of Pennsylvania Press, 1954.

Loisy, Alfred. *The Gospel and the Church* (French 1902). Trans. Christopher Home (1903). Reprinted in the Lives of Jesus Series. Philadelphia: Fortress Press, 1976.

Longfield, Bradley J. *The Presbyterian Controversy: Fundamentalists, Modernists, and Moderates*. New York: Oxford University Press, 1991.

Luther, Martin. *The Blessed Sacrament of the Holy and True Body of Christ, and the Brotherhoods* (1519). WA 2:742–58. *LW* 35:49–73.

———. *A Brief Explanation of the Ten Commandments, the Creed, and the Lord's Prayer* (1520). WA 7.204–29. PE 2:354–84.

———. *Eight Wittenberg Sermons* (1522). WA 10^3.1–64. *LW* 51:69–100.

———. *Heerpredigt wider den Türken* (1529). WA 30^2.160–97.

———. *The Large Catechism* (1529). *CELC* 357–461.

———. *Lectures on Galatians* (1535). WA 40^1–40^2.184. *LW* 26–27:149.

———. *Lectures on Romans* (1515–16). WA 56–57 (first division). *LW* 25.

———. *Ninety–Five Theses* (*Disputation on the Power and Efficacy of Indulgences*, 1517). WA 1:233–38. *LW* 31:25–33.

———. "Preface to the New Testament" (1522). WADB 6.2–11. *LW* 35:357–62.

———. "Preface to the Epistle of St. Paul to the Romans" (1546). *WADB* 7.3–27. *LW* 35:365–80.

———. *Proceedings at Augsburg* (1518). WA 2:6–26. *LW* 31:259–92.

———. Sermon on Exodus 12 (1525). WA 16.213–26.

———. Sermon on John 16 (1525). WA 17^1.248–55.

———. *Sermons on the Gospel of St. John Chapters 6–8* (1530–32). WA 33. *LW* 23.

———. *Table Talk* (see *WATR*). Selections only in *LW* 54.

McCarthy, Gerald D., ed. *The Ethics of Belief Debate*. American Academy of Religion Academy Series, no. 41. Atlanta, Ga.: Scholars Press, 1986.

Mack, Burton L. *The Lost Gospel: The Book of Q and Christian Origins*. San Francisco: HarperSanFrancisco, 1993.

———. *A Myth of Innocence: Mark and Christian Origins*. Philadelphia: Fortress Press, 1988.

Marshall, Molly Truman. *No Salvation outside the Church? A Critical Inquiry*. NABPR Dissertation Series, no. 9. Lewiston, N.Y.: Edwin Mellen Press, 1993.

Medicus, Fritz, ed. *Johann Gottlieb Fichte: Die philosophischen Schriften zum Atheismusstreit, mit Forbergs Aufsatze "Entwickelung des Begriffs der Religion."* Leipzig: Felix Meiner, 1910.

Meier, John P. *A Marginal Jew: Rethinking the Historical Jesus*, vol. 1: *The Roots of the Problem and the Person*. New York: Doubleday, 1991. Vol. 2: *Mentor, Message, and Miracles*. Ibid., 1994.

Moorhead, James H. "Redefining Confessionalism: American Presbyterians in the Twentieth Century." In: Coalter, Mulder, and Weeks, eds., *The Confessional Mosaic*, 59–83.

Moule, C[harles] F. D. Review of Wright, *Who Was Jesus? Theology* 96 (1993):409.

Niebuhr, H[elmut] Richard. *Faith on Earth: An Inquiry into the Structure of Human Faith*. Ed. Richard R. Niebuhr. New Haven, Conn.: Yale University Press, 1989.

———. *Radical Monotheism and Western Culture*. New York: Harper & Row, 1960.

Ogden, Schubert M. *On Theology*. San Francisco: Harper & Row, 1986.

———. *The Reality of God, and Other Essays* (1966). Paperback ed. (with a new preface). New York: Harper & Row, 1977.

———. "Rudolf Bultmann and the Future of Revisionary Christology." In: Bernd Jaspert, ed. *Rudolf Bultmanns Werk und Wirkung*. Darmstadt: Wissenschaftliche Buchgesellschaft, 1984, 155–73.

Oman, John. *The Natural and the Supernatural*. Cambridge: Cambridge University Press, 1931.

———. "The Sphere of Religion." In: Joseph Needham, ed. *Science, Religion, and Reality*. New York: The Macmillan Company, 1925, 259–99.

Osmer, Richard R. "James W. Fowler and the Reformed Tradition: An Exercise in Theological Reflection in Religious Education." In: Astley and Francis, eds. (see above), 135–50.

Pailin, David A., ed. *Attitudes to Other Religions: Comparative Religion in Seventeenth- and Eighteenth-Century Britain*. Manchester: Manchester University Press, 1984.

Penelhum, Terence. "The Analysis of Faith in St. Thomas Aquinas." In: Penelhum, ed., *Faith,* 113–33.

———, ed. *Faith*. New York: Macmillan Publishing Company, 1989.

Pfleiderer, Otto. *The Development of Theology in Germany Since Kant, and Its Progress in Great Britain Since 1825*. Trans. J. Frederick Smith. London: Swan Sonnenschein & Co., 1890.

Placher, William C., and David Willis-Watkins. *Belonging to God: A Commentary on A Brief Statement of Faith*. Louisville, Ky.: Westminster/ John Knox Press, 1992.

Plantinga, Alvin. "Reason and Belief in God." In Alvin Plantinga and Nicholas Wolterstorff, eds., *Faith and Rationality: Reason and Belief in God*. Notre Dame: University of Notre Dame Press, 1983, 16–93.

Reimarus, Hermann Samuel. *Reimarus: Fragments*. Ed. Charles H. Talbert. Trans. Ralph S. Fraser. Lives of Jesus Series. Philadelphia: Fortress Press, 1970. Reprinted in the Scholars Press Reprints and Translations Series. Chico, Calif.: Scholars Press, 1985.

Robertson, Frederick W. *Sermons by the Rev. Frederick W. Robertson Preached at Brighton*. 2d series. People's Ed. London: Kegan Paul, Trench, Trübner & Co., 1904.

Rogers, Jack. *Presbyterian Creeds: A Guide to the Book of Confessions*. Philadelphia: Westminster Press, 1985.

Rohls, Jan. *Reformed Confessions: Theology from Zurich to Barmen* (German, 1987). Trans. John Hoffmeyer. Columbia Series in Reformed Theology. Louisville, Ky.: Westminster/ John Knox Press, 1998.

Sanders, E. P. *The Historical Figure of Jesus*. London: Allen Lane/Penguin Press, 1993.

Schafer, Thomas A. "The Beginnings of Confessional Subscription in the Presbyterian Church." *McCormick Quarterly* 19 (1966):102–19.

Schaff, Philip. *Bibliotheca Symbolica Ecclesiae Universalis: The Creeds of Christendom With a History and Critical Notes* (abbreviated *CC*). 4th ed. 3 vols. New York: Harper & Brothers, 1919.

Schleiermacher, F[riedrich] D. E. *The Christian Faith* (abbreviated *CF*). Eng. trans. of the 2d German ed. (1830–31). Ed. H. R. Mackintosh and J. S. Stewart. Edinburgh: T. & T. Clark, 1928.

———. *Der christliche Glaube nach den Grundsätzen der evangelischen Kirche im Zusammenhange dargestellt*. 1st ed. (1821–22, abbreviated *CG*[1]). *Kritische Gesamtausgabe*, division 1, vol. 7 (in three parts). Ed. Hermann Peiter and Ulrich Barth. Berlin: Walter de Gruyter, 1980–84.

———. Ibid. 7th ed. based on the 2d ed. (1830–31, abbreviated *CG*). Ed. Martin Redeker. 2 vols. Berlin: Walter de Gruyter, 1960.

———. *Friedrich Schleiermacher's Reden über die Religion*. Ed. G. Ch. Bernhard Pünjer. Brunswick: C. A. Schwetschke and Son [M. Bruhn], 1879.

———. *On Religion: Speeches to Its Cultured Despisers*. Trans. John Oman from the 3d German ed. (1821). 1894. Reprint, Louisville, Ky.: Westminster/John Knox Press, 1994.

———. *On the Glaubenslehre: Two Letters to Dr. Lücke* (German 1829). Trans. James Duke and Francis Fiorenza. American Academy of Religion Texts and Translations Series, no. 3. Chico, Calif.: Scholars Press, 1981.

Schopenhauer, Arthur. *The World as Will and Idea* (German, 1819). Trans. R. B. Haldane and J. Kemp. 3 vols. New York: Charles Scribner's Sons, 1883.

Schwarz, Walter. "Man and Myth—More Bad News for Believers." *Guardian Weekly*. 18 October 1992.

Schweitzer, Albert. *The Quest of the Historical Jesus: A Critical Study of Its Progress from Reimarus to Wrede*. Trans. W. Montgomery from the 1st German ed. (*Von Reimarus zu Wrede*, 1906). 1910. 2d ed. London: Adam & Charles Black, 1911.

Sessions, William Lad. *The Concept of Faith: A Philosophical Investigation*. Cornell Studies in the Philosophy of Religion. Ithaca, N.Y.: Cornell University Press, 1994.

Smith, Gerald Birney. "The Religious Significance of the Humanity of Jesus." *American Journal of Theology* 24 (1920):191–208.

Smith, Huston. "Faith and Its Study: What Wilfred Smith's Against, and For." *RSR* 7 (1981):306–10.

Smith, Ronald Gregor. *J. G. Hamann: 1730–1788: A Study in Christian Existence*. London: Collins, 1960.

Smith, Wilfred Cantwell. *Belief and History*. Charlottesville: University Press of Virginia, 1977.

———. *Faith and Belief*. Princeton, N.J.: Princeton University Press, 1979.

———. *The Meaning and End of Religion: A New Approach to the Religious Traditions of Mankind*. New York: The Macmillan Company, 1963. Paperbound reprint. San Francisco: Harper & Row, 1978.

———. *Towards a World Theology: Faith and the Comparative History of Religion*. Maryknoll, N.Y.: Orbis Books, 1981.

Streeter, B[urnett] H. *The Buddha and the Christ*. London: Macmillan, 1932. American ed. New York: The Macmillan Company, 1933.

Sullivan, Francis A. *Salvation outside the Church? Tracing the History of the Catholic Response*. New York: Paulist Press, 1992.

Talon, Henri A. *John Bunyan: The Man and His Works*. Trans. Barbara Wall. London: Rockliff Publishing Corporation, 1951.

Tatum, W. Barnes. *In Quest of Jesus: A Guidebook*. Atlantat, Ga.: John Knox Press, 1982.

Taylor, Charles. *Sources of the Self: The Making of the Modern Identity*. Cambridge, Mass.: Harvard University Press, 1989.

Taylor, Vincent. "Does the New Testament Call Jesus God?" *Expository Times* 73 (1961–62): 116–18.

Thiering, B[arbara] E. *Jesus the Man: A New Interpretation From the Dead Sea Scrolls*. Sydney, Australia: Doubleday, 1992. American ed., *Jesus and the Riddle of the Dead Sea Scrolls: Unlocking the Secrets of His Life Story*. San Francisco: HarperSanFrancisco, 1992.

Thomas Aquinas. *Summa contra Gentiles* (abbreviated *ScG*). Eng. trans., *On the Truth of the Catholic Faith: Summa contra Gentiles*. Trans. and ed. Anton C. Pegis. 4 vols. in 5. Garden City, N.Y.: Image Books (Doubleday & Company), 1955–57.

———. *Summa theologiae* (abbreviated *ST*). Trans. Fathers of the Dominican Province. 3 vols. New York: Benziger Brothers, 1947–48.

Thompson, Craig R., ed. *Inquisitio de fide: A Colloquy by Desiderius Erasmus Roterodamus, 1524* (1950). 2d ed. Hamden, Conn.: Archon Books, 1975.

Tillich, Paul. *Dynamics of Faith*. World Perspectives Series, no. 10. New York: Harper & Row, 1957.

Trinterud, Leonard J. *The Forming of an American Tradition: A Re-examination of Colonial Presbyterianism*. Philadelphia: Westminster Press, 1949.

Troeltsch, Ernst. "Die alte Kirche" (1916/17). *Gesammelte Schriften*. 4 vols. (1912–25). Reprint. Aalen: Scientia Verlag, 1961–66. 4:65–121.

———. *The Christian Faith: Based on Lectures Delievered at the University of Heidelberg in 1912 and 1913*. Trans. Garrett E. Paul. Fortress Texts in

Modern Theology. Minneapolis, Minn.: Fortress Press, 1991. (See Troeltsch, *Glaubenslehre*.)

———. *Christian Thought: Its History and Application*. Ed. Baron F. von Hügel. 1923. Reprint. New York: Meridian Books, 1957.

———. *Ernst Troeltsch: Writings on Theology and Religion*. Trans. and ed. Robert Morgan and Michael Pye. 1977. Paperback ed. Louisville, Ky.: Westminster/John Knox Press, 1990.

———. *Glaubenslehre: Nach Heidelberger Vorlesungen aus den Jahren 1911 und 1912* Ed. Gertrud von le Fort . 1925. Reprint. Aalen: Scientia Verlag, 1981. (See Troeltsch, *The Christian Faith.*)

———. "On the Possibility of a Liberal Christianity" (German, 1910). In: Troeltsch, *Religion in History*, 343–59.

———. *Protestantism and Progress: The Significance of Protestantism for the Rise of the Modern World* (German 1906; 2d ed., 1911). Trans. W. Montgomery. 1912. (The first printing of the Eng. trans. had the subtitle *A Historical Study of the Relation of Protestantism to the Modern World*.) Reprinted in the Fortress Texts in Modern Theology series. Philadelphia: Fortress Press, 1986.

———. *Religion in History*. Essays trans. James Luther Adams and Walter F. Bense. Fortress Texts in Modern Theology. Minneapolis, Minn.: Fortress Press, 1991.

———. "Schleiermacher und die Kirche." In: Troeltsch et al., *Schleiermacher der Philosoph des Glaubens*. Moderne Philosophie, no. 6. Berlin-Schöneberg: Buchverlag der "Hilfe," 1910.

Tweedie, Donald F., Jr. *Logotherapy and the Christian Faith: An Evaluation of Frankl's Existential Approach to Psychotherapy*. Grand Rapids, Mich.: Baker Book House, 1961.

Tyrrell, George. *Christianity at the Cross-Roads* (1909). Reprint. London: George Allen & Unwin, 1963.

Vermes, Geza. *Jesus the Jew: A Historian's Reading of the Gospels*. London: Collins, 1973.

Vischer, Lukas, ed. *Reformed Witness Today: A Collection of Confessions and Statements of Faith Issued by Reformed Churches*. Bern: Evangelische Arbeitsstelle, Oekumene Schweiz, 1982.

Wainwright, A. W. "The Confession 'Jesus Is God' in the New Testament." *Scottish Journal of Theology* 10 (1957):274–99.

Wainwright, Geoffrey. *Doxology—The Praise of God in Worship, Doctrine and Life: A Systematic Theology*. New York: Oxford University Press, 1980.

Williams, George Huntston. "Erasmus and the Reformers on Non-Christian Religions and *Salus extra ecclesiam*." In: Theodore K. Rabb and Jerrold E. Siegel, eds. *Action and Conviction in Early Modern Europe: Essays in Memory of E. H. Harbison*. Princeton: Princeton University Press, 1969.

Willis, David, and Michael Welker, eds. *Toward the Future of Reformed Theology: Tasks, Topics, Traditions*. Grand Rapids, Mich.: William B. Eerdmans Publishing Company, 1999.

Wilson, A[ndrew] N. *Jesus*. New York: W. W. Norton, 1992.

Wolterstorff, Nicholas. *John Locke and the Ethics of Belief*. Cambridge Studies in Religion and Critical Thought, no. 2. Cambridge: Cambrige University Press, 1996.

Wright, N[icholas] T. ("Tom"). *Who Was Jesus?* London: SPCK, 1992. Grand Rapids, Mich.: William B. Eerdmans Publishing Company, 1993.

Wuthnow, Robert. "The Restructuring of American Presbyterianism: Turmoil in One Denomination." In: Coalter, Mulder, and Weeks, eds., *The Presbyterian Predicament*, 27–48.

———. *The Restructuring of American Religion: Society and Faith since World War II*. Princeton, NJ: Princeton University Press, 1988.

Wyman, Walter E., Jr. "Revelation and the Doctrine of Faith: Historical Revelation Within the Limits of Historical Consciousness." *JR* 78 (1998):38–63.

Yearbook of American and Canadian Churches. Nashville, Tenn.: Abingdon Press (annually).

INDEX